PEACE AGREE

To Emma and Sebastian

PEACE AGREEMENTS

FINDING SOLUTIONS TO INTRA-STATE CONFLICTS

NINA CASPERSEN

polity

First published in 2017 by Polity Press

Polity Press
65 Bridge Street
Cambridge CB2 1UR, UK

Polity Press
350 Main Street
Malden, MA 02148, USA

ISBN-13: 978-0-7456-8026-2
ISBN-13: 978-0-7456-8027-9(pb)

A catalogue record for this book is available from the British Library.

Library of Congress Cataloging-in-Publication Data

Names: Caspersen, Nina, 1976- author.
Title: Peace agreements : finding solutions to intra-state conflicts / Nina Caspersen.
Description: Malden, MA : Polity Press, 2016. | Includes bibliographical
    references and index.
Identifiers: LCCN 2016020511| ISBN 9780745680262 (hardback : alk. paper) |
    ISBN 9780745680279 (pbk. : alk. paper) | ISBN 9781509515691 (epub) | ISBN
    9781509515684 (Mobi)
Subjects: LCSH: Peace-building. | Self-determination, National. | Autonomy
    and independence movements. | Partition, Territorial. | Regionalism. |
    World politics--1989-
Classification: LCC JZ5538 .C375 2016 | DDC 303.6/9--dc23 LC record available at
https://lccn.loc.gov/2016020511

Typeset in 10.5 on 12pt Sabon by
Servis Filmsetting Ltd, Stockport, Cheshire
Printed and bound in the UK by Clays Ltd, St Ives, PLC

For further information on Polity, visit our website:
politybooks.com

CONTENTS

ACKNOWLEDGEMENTS

While working on this book I have become indebted to a large number of people. Particular thanks are owed to my colleagues and students in the Department of Politics at the University of York, who provided a stimulating intellectual environment that allowed me to try out some of my initial ideas. The British Academy awarded me a Mid-Career Fellowship which gave me much-needed time for research and writing. I am immensely grateful for this. Polity has been a supportive and patient publisher throughout, and I thank Louise Knight, Nekane Tanaka Galdos and the two anonymous reviewers for their constructive comments which helped me clarify, improve and shorten my arguments. Finally, I thank my beloved partner Keith for enabling me to finish a book with two small children in the house; this is undoubtedly the biggest debt of them all.

ABBREVIATIONS

ABC: Abyei Boundaries Commission (Sudan)
AEC: Assistance and Evaluation Commission (Sudan)
AMM: Aceh Monitoring Mission (Indonesia)
ASEAN: Association of Southeast Asian Nations
CHT: Chittagong Hill Tracts (Bangladesh)
DDR: Disarmament, demobilization and reintegration
DUP: Democratic Unionist Party (Northern Ireland)
ECHR: European Convention of Human Rights
ECtHR: European Court of Human Rights
EU: European Union
GAM: Free Aceh Movement (Indonesia)
HDZ: Croatian Democratic Union (Bosnia)
ICC: International Criminal Court
ICTFY: International Criminal Tribunal for the Former
               Yugoslavia
IDPs: Internally displaced people
IFOR: The Implementation Force (Bosnia)
IGAD: Intergovernmental Authority on Development
INTERFET: International Force for East Timor
IRA: Irish Republican Army
LRA: The Lord's Resistance Army (Sudan)
LTTE: Tamil Tigers (Sri Lanka)
MDFC: Movement of Democratic Forces of Casamance
               (Senegal)
MILF: Moro Islamic Liberation Front (the Philippines)
MNLF: Moro National Liberation Front (the Philippines)
NCP: National Congress Party (Sudan)
OIC: Organization of the Islamic Conference

OHR:	Office of the High Representative (Bosnia)
ORA:	Organization of the Armed Resistance (Niger)
OSCE:	Organization for Security and Co-operation in Europe
PA:	Palestinian Authority (Israel–Palestine)
PJCSS:	United People's Party of the Chittagong Hill Tracts (Bangladesh)
PLO:	Palestine Liberation Organization (Israel–Palestine)
PNG:	Papua New Guinea
RS:	Republika Srpska (Bosnia)
SDLP:	Social Democratic and Labour Party (Northern Ireland)
SPLM/A:	Sudanese People's Liberation Movement/Army
SSDF:	South Sudan Defence Force
SSR:	Security sector reform
STV:	Single-Transferable Vote (Northern Ireland)
UN:	United Nations
UNITA:	National Union for the Total Independence of Angola
UNMIS:	United Nations Mission in Sudan
UNOMB:	United Nations Observer Mission in Bougainville
UUP:	Ulster Unionist Party (Northern Ireland)

INTRODUCTION

The announcement of a peace agreement is, with good reason, marked as an important breakthrough: former enemies have managed to put their difference aside and agreed to a negotiated settlement. The popular image of such events is of dark-suited men – and it is almost always men – emerging bleary-eyed from marathon negotiations. The mediators pat them on the back, urging a handshake for the cameras. The public may have been aware that talks were ongoing, but rarely will they have knowledge of what was being discussed. This is only discovered once the agreement is announced. However, interpretations of what has been agreed to often vary wildly, with both sides claiming a victory for their position and hardliners typically denouncing the agreement as a betrayal.

Since the end of the Cold War a significant number of such peace agreements have been reached, including in bloody intra-state conflicts that were previously thought beyond resolution, such as in Bosnia, Northern Ireland, Aceh (Indonesia) and Sudan. Some of these peace agreements have displayed a great deal of ingenuity when it comes to engineering compromises and crafting institutions that address both individual aspirations and collective grievances and fears. Territory has been divided, power has been shared, rights have been guaranteed, and these arrangements have in a number of cases crossed state-borders thus addressing the trans-border nature of many of these conflicts. However, as many – if not more – peace processes have failed in the same period. Peace talks have been ongoing but compromise solutions are still eluding the mediators. Decades of negotiations have for example failed to bring a solution to the conflicts in Cyprus, Georgia–Abkhazia and Azerbaijan–Nagorno Karabakh. The solutions proposed in these cases were often similar

1

to the successful agreements, yet either the specific package of mechanisms put forward did not fully address the dynamics of the conflict, or the timing was just not right.

Reaching an agreement is often a formidable challenge, but the challenges involved in making it work are equally daunting, and many agreements do not last. The Oslo Accords for Israel–Palestine quickly ran into problems and were never fully implemented; the General Peace Agreement for Casamance (Senegal) barely got off the ground; while war broke out again in Mindanao (the Philippines) a few years after the signing of the 1996 peace agreement, and it took until 2014 before a new comprehensive agreement was signed. The settlements for Mali and Crimea (Ukraine) both survived for more than a decade. However, war reignited in Mali in 2012 when rebels proclaimed an Islamic state in the northern part of the country. Russian-backed separatists took control over Crimea in 2014 and Russia subsequently annexed the peninsula.

This book explores how post-Cold War peace agreements have addressed issues of territory, security, power and justice. It identifies common trends and common problems: Do these agreements reveal a blueprint for peace, and what can we learn from both their successes and their failures? The analysis focuses on how these different solutions interact with the conflict context and with the specifics of the peace process. Are some solutions for example only feasible in case of moderate divisions or in case of third party involvement? It emphasizes that peace agreements should be analysed as 'packages', with a focus on the interaction of their different elements. The content of these agreements matters; for the prospect of reaching a negotiated solution in the first place, for post-settlement stability, and for the quality of the peace that ensues.

A Post-Cold War Package for Peace

Kaldor (2007a) argues that the end of the Cold War saw the increased importance of what she calls 'new wars'. These are intrastate wars centred on identity politics, they involve non-state actors, are financed through transnational networks, and civilians are the primary targets. While I am unconvinced of the newness of such wars (see Berdal, 2003), we clearly did see an upsurge after the end of the Cold War and the international responses also changed. Firstly, there was a greater international willingness to intervene and an expansion of the remit of peacekeepers. Peacekeeping was no longer just about separating armies; the 1990s and 2000s saw the creation of international missions that aimed to rebuild war-torn states and in a number of cases took over the running of these states until stability was ensured (or this was at least the idea) (see e.g. Bellamy & Williams, 2010; Gutteri & Piombo, 2007). Secondly, the solution proposed by these international interveners came to be described as the 'liberal peace'. The emphasis was on introducing political and economic reforms and thereby creating (multi-ethnic) democracy and market economy, which was seen as the key to stability. However, this approach has been heavily criticized by the critical peace-building literature for reflecting global power inequalities and for being insensitive to local culture, identity and history (see e.g. Mac Ginty & Richmond, 2013).

This debate has generally focused on the post-settlement period and has largely ignored the agreement that preceded it. Peace agreements tend to be seen simply as 'contextual or permissive conditions for post-conflict activity' (Selby, 2013, p. 64). However, other authors have shown greater interest in peace agreements and argue that the tool kit available to mediators has expanded since the end of the Cold War, and more creative and dynamic approaches are now available. Weller (2008, p. 156) argues that we have escaped the 'self-determination trap' and that the range of possible solutions to separatist conflicts has been significantly enhanced, while Bell (2008) identifies a rapidly evolving new Law of Peace, which includes both a 'new law of hybrid self-determination' and a 'new law of transitional justice'. But the question is to what extent these solutions are widespread or remain the exception: are we predominantly dealing with creative, liberal agreements? Moreover, we still lack knowledge of the way in which the different elements of an agreement interact and the conditions under which they are likely to succeed.

In the existing conflict resolution literature we find a rich debate on the relative merit of different institutional designs, including autonomy and federalism, and forms of power-sharing (see e.g. Lapidoth, 1996; Reilly, 2001; Roeder & Rothchild, 2005). But these mechanisms tend to be treated separately not analysed as a package (Cordell & Wolff, 2009, p. 138) and the focus is primarily on their impact on long-term stability rather than how they affect the prospect for getting the conflict parties to agree to a settlement in the first place. These questions are addressed in some quantitative studies but, although very valuable, these studies do not provide a detailed analysis of the content of peace agreements. On the issue of territorial autonomy, we are for example often left with a dichotomy: decentralization or no decentralization,[1] but this does not fully capture the differences between these agreements and the importance of, sometimes rather subtle, details.

When it comes to peace talks, the tendency in the literature is to focus on the process and the context rather than the content. Zartman's (2001a) concept of a 'ripe moment' for peace has proved hugely influential, and the emphasis when explaining the success or failure of peace talks tends to be on the relative military strength of the two sides, the availability of external support, or the existence of spoilers (see Stedman, 1997). In empirical cases of failed peace talks, the typical argument is similarly that what is needed is a change in the conflict context. The agreement did not fail because of its content; no amount of institutional creativity will resolve the situation. The content of peace agreements is therefore under-analysed – at least if we look at the agreement as a package – and the crucial interaction between content, context and process is rarely subjected to in-depth scrutiny.

This book fills a gap in the literature by providing a comprehensive and systematic analysis of the content of peace agreements *and* the ways in which this content interacts with the conflict context,[2] and the process of the peace talks. In other words, the content of the peace agreement matters: peace is not simply a question of 'ripeness', nor can crucial decisions be left to the post-settlement phase, even in case of significant third party involvement. The agreement, the institutions it creates and the actors it empowers, significantly constrains what is possible at a later stage. This book stresses that peace agreements must be viewed as a whole: the different elements interact and this affects both the extent to which different arrangements are acceptable to the conflict parties and the sustainability of the agreement. A full analysis of the effects of different institutional designs, moreover, necessitates an understanding of intra-communal dynamics, including the political contestation and governance capacity found within the separatist movement. This is not usually afforded much attention in existing literature on peace agreements.

The following chapters find that autonomy – usually territorially- and ethnically-defined – is an overwhelming trend in peace agreements signed in separatist conflicts, while human rights are surprisingly marginal. The illiberal nature of many settlements can in part be explained by the 'core deal', and its prioritization of collective rights, but also owes something to the narrowness of the typical peace process and an assumption that such 'soft concerns' can be left for later. The agreements demonstrate some ingenuity when it comes to trans-border

4

dimensions, but the dominant, binary, conception of sovereignty and statehood still poses significant constraints and the examples of 'simple autonomy' are more numerous. The analysis warns against 'destructive ambiguity', exclusive agreements and a lack of sub-state capacity. It suggests that a greater emphasis on intra-communal dynamics and political contestation within conflict parties could help temper the tendency of peace agreements to reflect unduly the narrow interests and perspectives of the negotiating elites. A broadening of the peace process and of the resulting institutional design could result in a more legitimate and therefore more sustainable peace.

Bridging the Gap: Peace Agreements and Case Studies

The book combines a systematic analysis of peace agreements signed in self-determination conflicts after the end of the Cold War with more in-depth case studies and examples. It thereby endeavours to bridge the current gap between quantitative and qualitative studies of peace agreements. The peace agreements have been selected according to two criteria. Firstly, they attempted to find a solution to intra-state conflicts that involved a confrontation between a sovereign independent state and a rebel movement that sought self-rule or outright independence. The self-determination movement is in most cases ethno-nationalist, but there are exceptions, such as the Sudanese People's Liberation Movement/Army in South Sudan. Secondly, they are comprehensive agreements that were signed by major parties in the conflict and aimed to address the underlying causes of the conflict.

The focus is limited to self-determination, or separatist, conflicts in order to make an in-depth analysis manageable and since these conflicts are more directly comparable than other types of intra-state conflicts. It has moreover been argued that although separatist wars are often 'unending' and violence tends to reoccur, they more commonly end in negotiated settlements than other types of civil wars (Heraclides, 1997). Finally, by only focusing on self-determination conflicts that all involve a territorial element, it is possible to analyse the interaction between all four types of mechanisms – relating to territory, security, power and justice. Some of the findings will however also have implications for other types of intra-state conflicts, especially since solutions proposed in these conflicts sometimes also include a territorial element, such as a federal model for Syria (Reuters, 2016).

5

The second criterion, a comprehensive peace agreement, is commonly used in peace agreement datasets.[3] My interpretation is however less strict than what is used by, for example, the Peace Accords Matrix. Firstly it allows for some substantive issues to be left for later, as this can be an important negotiation technique that for example proved successful in the case of the Belfast Agreement for Northern Ireland. It also allows for a peace agreement to take the form of an agreed change to the constitution, such as in the case of Ukraine–Crimea. Secondly, all potential 'spoilers' are not necessarily included in the agreement: spoilers do not always succeed in undermining an agreement and I am specifically interested in how spoiler activity, and its effectiveness, is influenced by the content of the agreed settlement. But I do require both sides to have accepted the agreement – even if under considerable pressure. The Comprehensive Proposal for the Kosovo Status Settlement, also known as Ahtisaari's Plan, is therefore not included, even though it was later implemented by the Kosovo Government. Determining what is, and what is not, a comprehensive agreement is of course not always straightforward. I chose for example to include the very brief Khasavyurt Accord for Chechnya, although it contains very few institutional mechanisms and is deliberately vague on the issue of status. Including this agreement helps me examine possible solutions at the extreme end of the spectrum – in cases where the separatist movement has achieved de facto independence – and the problem of postponing crucial issues.

Finally, unlike most datasets on peace agreements, I also include settlements signed in non-armed conflicts, including Serbia & Montenegro, Moldova–Gagauzia, Ukraine–Crimea and Russia–Tatarstan.[4] These conflicts all posed significant challenges to the state and there was a clear potential for violence, as evidenced by later developments or by other separatist conflicts facing the state. Including these agreements allows me to examine the effect of violence, or its absence, on possible solutions.

This results in a list of twenty agreements signed between 1990 and 2010 (see table 0.1). In addition to an in-depth analysis of these main settlements, I also examine any subsequent agreements which added details to the original agreement or included new actors. Such as the Interim Agreement on the West Bank and the Gaza Strip (Oslo II, 1995), in the case of Israel–Palestine, and the Comprehensive Agreement on the Bangsamoro (2014), in the case of Mindanao–Philippines. Later developments, in particular implementation difficulties, also form a core part of the analysis.

Table 0.1. Twenty Agreements Signed between 1990 and 2010

Case	Main settlement
Bangladesh–Chittagong Hill Tracts	Chittagong Hill Tracts Peace Accords, 1997
Bosnia	General Framework for Peace/ Dayton Peace Agreement, 1995
Croatia–Eastern Slavonia	Basic Agreement on the Region of Eastern Slavonia, Baranja and Western Sirmium/ Erdut Agreement, 1995
India–Bodoland	Memorandum of Settlement/ Bodo Accord, 1993
Indonesia–East Timor	Agreement on the Question of East Timor, 1999
Indonesia–Aceh	Memorandum of Understanding, 2005
Israel–Palestine	Declaration of Principles/ Oslo Accords, 1993
Macedonia	Framework Agreement/ Ohrid Agreement, 2001
Mali	National Pact, 1992
Moldova–Gagauzia	Law on the Special Legal Status of Gagauzia, 1994
Niger	Agreement Establishing Permanent Peace, 1995
Papua New Guinea–Bougainville	Bougainville Peace Agreement, 2001
Philippines–Mindanao	Final Peace Agreement, 1996
Russia–Tatarstan	Treaty on Delimitation of Jurisdictional Subjects and Mutual Delegation of Authority, 1994
Russia–Chechnya	Khasavyurt Accord, 1996
Senegal–Casamance	General Peace Agreement, 2004
Serbia–Montenegro	Agreement on Principles/ Belgrade Agreement, 2002
Sudan–South Sudan	Comprehensive Peace Agreement, 2005
Ukraine–Crimea	Ukraine's Constitution, 1996
UK–Northern Ireland	Good Friday Agreement/ Belfast Agreement, 1998

This list of agreements tells us two things about separatist conflicts. First of all it points to the surge in these conflicts in the early 1990s, which explains why most of the settlements were concluded in this decade. Secondly, although the list covers a range of different conflict contexts and a wide geographic domain – including cases from Europe, Africa, Asia and Australasia – the lack of cases from Latin America is noticeable. This does not reflect an absence of intra-state conflicts or settlements on this continent, but it does reflect an absence of separatist conflicts. I will briefly analyse agreements signed in non-territorial conflicts, including in Latin America, when examining the effect of territorial provisions on issues relating to security, power and human rights, but the focus of this book is on territorial conflicts. The list is intended to be complete, but it is possible that I have left out agreements that others would characterize as comprehensive or that I am missing certain conflicts with a separatist element.[5] Intra-state conflicts are fluid: conflicts that were initially about who should govern can acquire a territorial dimension and come to involve the continued existence of the state. However, even if a couple of cases are missing, the list should be comprehensive enough to identify key trends and common problems, and analyse the interaction between different parts of the agreements and the effects of different conflict contexts.

Tabulation is used to provide an overview of these agreements, but this is combined with detailed analysis of their content. This makes the analysis different from existing datasets. For example, I examine the specific form of territorial autonomy (extent, along what lines, how guaranteed?) and the interaction between the different mechanisms. In addition to the analysis of the content of these agreements, a number of failed peace proposals are also scrutinized. These add to the analysis of the effects of the conflict context: what are the limits to different institutional approaches, when do they provide a possible solution? Comprehensive proposals put forward in six cases of self-determination conflicts are examined: Georgia–Abkhazia, Cyprus, Serbia–Kosovo, Azerbaijan–Nagorno Karabakh, Sri Lanka, Morocco–Western Sahara.

The analysis of the content of peace agreements and proposals is combined with more in-depth analysis of specific cases. The purpose of this is to analyse more closely the interaction of the different elements of an agreement and between the peace agreement, the peace process and the conflict context. It will, in other words, allow for a fuller analysis of what explains the failure and success of peace agreements. The case studies draw on extensive research that I have conducted over the years in the Balkans and the Caucasus, but additional examples from other regions will also be included. These examples draw on secondary sources and I have, as far as possible, triangulated any information obtained from these. This did present a challenge with some of the conflicts that have only received limited media and scholarly attention, and a few errors and misapprehensions can therefore likely be found by area specialists. However, I base none of my conclusions on one case only, let alone just one source, so this should not undermine the main thrust of my argument.

Evaluating Success and Failure

Any attempt to evaluate peace agreements should ideally make use of fairly well-defined success criteria. All the twenty agreements are successful in the short-term in the sense that it was possible to get major parties to agree to them. An additional success criterion commonly used is that they have lasted for five or ten years. Both of these will be referred to in the analysis. However, it is not always clear what it means for an agreement to have lasted. It may be fairly clear that an agreement has collapsed if full-scale war breaks out anew, but what if significant provisions were not implemented, or if only some factions continued their violent campaign? Hartzell and Hoddie (2007, p. 137) describe the 1996 peace agreement for Mindanao as a success, since hostilities between the Philippine Government and the Moro National Liberation Front (MNLF) did not reignite. I would however characterize it as a failure since the strongest armed faction, the Moro Islamic Liberation Front (MILF), was not included, several provisions were left unimplemented, and war broke out again in 2000 (see e.g. International Crisis Group, 2013a). The 1997 Chittagong Hill Tracts Peace Accords is even more difficult to classify; most observers agree that significant parts of the agreement have never been implemented, but although tensions remain and violence occasionally flares up, the separatist conflict has not reignited (see e.g. Fortna, 2008). Another problem is deciding at what point an agreement fails. It is for example hard to find anyone who would argue that the Oslo Accords for Israel–Palestine were successful, but at what point did they fail: was it when key provisions were left unimplemented, when Rabin was assassinated and Netanyahu was elected new Israeli prime minister, when Hamas launched a series of suicide bombings in Israel, or was it not until the collapse of the Camp David talks in 2000 and the outbreak of the Second Intifada? Did it therefore pass the five-year threshold, or not? It is consequently difficult to decide on clear-cut criteria for success, and for failure. This is made even more difficult by the post-settlement violence that characterizes many cases but does not necessarily spell the end of an agreement.

The benefit of not doing a large-N study is that it allows for a more nuanced analysis. The specific threshold is not crucial, nor are binary understandings of success and failure. I am interested in institutional provisions that lead to tension, and sometimes violence, and also in the quality of the peace that results; not simply in whether an agreement makes it past an arbitrary threshold. An agreement may survive despite significant tensions, but these tensions still hold important lessons for the effects of different provisions. Moreover, some agreements that did make it past the ten-year mark eventually broke down, which suggests that they did not succeed in addressing the underlying causes of the conflict. The kind of regime that results from the agreement is another important concern: have they ensured 'good enough governance', which some authors argue we should settle for, or have they managed to achieve a 'legitimate peace' which is supported both horizontally and vertically (Themner & Ohlson, 2014)? This matters for the longer-term sustainability of the agreement and it matters for the conditions faced by the civilian population. Finally, it should be noted that secession will not be considered a failure if the agreement allows for the break-up of the state and the separation does not result in the outbreak of widespread violence. The purpose of a peace agreement is to ensure peace, not the continued existence of the state.

A Word on Terminology

In the analysis I tend to refer to either 'self-determination conflict' or 'separatist conflict' and I use 'separatist forces' and 'rebel forces' interchangeably. The term separatist does come with negative connotations; it is used by central governments to suggest a lack of legitimacy and even illegality. It is therefore unsurprising that the self-proclaimed authorities (another value-laden term) in Donetsk in Eastern Ukraine declared: 'we are not separatists' (Walker, 2014) and prefer to be known as rebels. I therefore agonized over whether or not to use this term and use it without any value judgement implied. Linguistically, 'separatist' often works better as an adjective than 'self-determination' and 'rebel' can suggest that what is at stake in the conflict is the nature of the government. And these forces are of course separatist in the sense that they are trying to separate from the central government and achieve at least extensive self-rule.

Plan of the Book

The first part of the book examines the content of the agreements. It analyses how they have addressed contentious issues relating to territory, security, power and justice; discusses advantages and disadvantages of these approaches; examines how these mechanisms are affected by the conflict context, such as the degree of violence experienced; and finally analyses how the different mechanisms inter-act. Chapter 1 focuses on territory and finds that autonomy is clearly the dominant solution, even if this is sometimes an interim solu-tion and may include attempts to fudge sovereignty. Such attempts are constrained however by dominant conceptions of sovereignty. Chapter 2 examines security provisions found in the agreements; it argues that rather than a centralized monopoly of force, which is typi-cally recommended in the literature, we find complex compromises and frequent creation of autonomous coercive forces. Legitimacy as well as effectiveness matters and this helps address the commit-ment problem often emphasized in the literature, and helps explain why a robust third party guarantee is not always needed. Chapter 3 focuses on power and finds that (political) power-sharing is much less frequent than we might expect; instead what we see is territorial and military power-sharing. It discusses the limitations of the dominant power-sharing approaches and suggests that a hybrid model may provide a way forward, although this does necessitate third party involvement. Chapter 4 examines if the 'core deal' found in these agreements, with its emphasis on territorial autonomy and rights for the dominant groups, leaves any space for justice and rights for individuals and non-dominant groups. It finds that human rights are much less emphasized than what the 'liberal peace' literature would lead us to believe; these agreements may be written in the language of human rights but are lacking in substance. Chapter 5 sums up this analysis and asks if we can identify a post-Cold War blueprint for peace. It argues that there are commonalities but the agreements also respond to the conflict context and we are therefore at most dealing with blueprints, in plural. The chapter emphasizes the importance of viewing agreements as a package, when examining the effect of spe-cific provisions; the sometimes destructive impact of ambiguity; the importance of intra-communal dynamics and sub-state capacity; and the difficulty of moving beyond the initial agreement.

The second part of the book focuses on the interaction between the conflict context, the peace process and the content of the peace agreement. Chapter 6 addresses the internal dynamics of the conflict: the balance of power between the two sides and the intra-communal balance between hardliners and moderates. It stresses that both ripe-ness and the existence of (effective) spoilers are, at least in part, a product of the peace process and the content of the agreement, and proposes an enriched concept of ripeness, which takes into account intra-communal dynamics and is focused on the sustainability of a negotiated settlement. Chapter 7 examines the external side of the equation and discusses the effect of third party involvement. It emphasizes the positive contribution that third parties can make, even if the involvement is not 'robust'. But there are clear limitations and one of the main constraints is the content of the settlement. The conclusion summarizes the findings and discusses policy implications.

Part 1

Content

— 1 —

TERRITORY

Self-determination conflicts are above all about territory. Even if they do not involve an outright demand for independence, but simply for internal self-rule, the demands made and the rights they invoke are either directly or indirectly linked to territory. Questions such as 'Whose homeland is it?' and 'Who has the right to govern this territory?' fuel these conflicts and are used to mobilize popular support. In the case of Crimea, Sasse (2002, p. 3) points out that the territory 'had multiple ethnic claims to it, all of which were plausibly historically grounded'. Even conflicts that are not initially about territory, but rather about the nature of the regime, can take on a territorial dimension. Rebels may abandon the idea of reforming the joint state and may indeed see the potential, for their community and for themselves, in having a separate state. The Sudanese People's Liberation Movement (SPLM) for decades fought for the creation of a reformed 'New Sudan' and only later came to demand an independent South Sudan (see e.g. Rolandsen, 2011).

The importance of a territory does not depend simply on its material value. Territory is symbolically important as the home of the imagined community. As Toft puts it, 'no matter how barren, no territory is worthless if it is a homeland' (2003, p. 1) and even barren territories can become the object of intense, violent struggles. For the central government, one of the main concerns is to maintain the (de jure) territorial integrity of the state and ensure that no territory is beyond their control. Territory goes to the heart of statehood; it matters both for legitimacy and identity, and for security and political power. If a group controls its own territory it is much more likely to feel secure, especially following a bloody intra-state war, and control of territory comes with power; this provides guarantees for the group as a whole

15

and significant privileges for its leaders. It is therefore unsurprising that territory is one of the most contentious issues in peace talks, and the territorial solution agreed on significantly impacts on other parts of the peace agreement.

The International Community has generally promoted solutions that maintain the existing state, and although there have been some movements towards negotiated secessions in particularly protracted conflicts, the preferred option remains for self-determination to be realized through various forms of autonomy arrangements. The merits of autonomy are however contested. Proponents argue that autonomy offers a viable compromise between demands for separate statehood and for a unitary state (Ghai, 2008, p. 245). Critics however see it as an unstable solution which empowers separatist forces and risks causing the break-up of the state (see e.g. Roeder, 2009).

This chapter analyses post-Cold War trends in territorial solutions and identifies common problems encountered in the twenty cases. The analysis focuses on how these territorial solutions interact with the external and internal context, including dynamics and competition *within* the communities. It focuses particularly on the position of the separatist movement, which is often under-analysed in the existing literature. It finds that autonomy is at the core of almost all the peace agreements, either as a permanent or an interim solution. Somewhat surprisingly, these agreements typically do not include power-sharing provisions and the dominant model can be described as 'simple autonomy'. The overall track record is better than argued by the critics of autonomy, but the specific form of autonomy is crucial and the chapter points to two under-analysed factors that have led to serious tensions and even the collapse of settlements: the capacity of the autonomous territories and the ambiguity of autonomy provisions, especially in relation to the delineation of internal borders and the extent of autonomy. When it comes to the survival of autonomy arrangements, the devil is in the detail. The chapter finds only limited support for Bell's (2008) argument that we are witnessing the emergence of a 'new law of hybrid self-determination'. Although we do find some attempts to blur sovereignty, including trans-border dimensions and postponed independence referenda, the fudging of sovereignty is extremely difficult to sell to the parties and to implement. It will be interpreted in terms of centralization or secession. This is compounded by the prevailing dichotomous view of sovereignty: you are either sovereign or you are not; sovereignty cannot be divided, it cannot be shared. 'Simple autonomy' does not require the state to be fundamentally redefined and the fudging of sovereignty is limited, but it does address many of the demands made by separatist leaders. This helps explain its popularity, but also points to its limitations.

The Popularity of 'Ethnic Autonomy'

Wolff observes that 'territorial self-governance has been included in a very significant number of actual and proposed settlements' (2009, p. 28). Roeder agrees that 'ethnofederalism', in which the constituent units are homelands for ethnic minorities, is now embraced with enthusiasm as a solution to intra-state conflicts (2009, p. 204). He points to calls for a federation of autonomous ethnic regions in Iraq; the Boden plan for Abkhazia, which suggested making Abkhazia 'a sovereign entity ... within the State of Georgia'; and the 'Dual federation' once suggested for Nagorno Karabakh, which would have linked the disputed entity to both its de jure parent state, Azerbaijan, and its kin-state, Armenia (ibid., pp. 203–4). More recently, a federal solution has been mooted for Syria (Reuters, 2016) and extended autonomy for Eastern Ukraine is also envisaged in the vague, and as yet unimplemented, Minsk II Accord (Sasse, 2016).

Why is territorial self-governance, in its various forms, such a popular response to separatist conflicts? As Wolff points out, the rationale is that it allows 'the different segments of diverse societies to realize their aspirations for self-determination while simultaneously preserving the overall social and territorial integrity of existing states' (2009, p. 28). Ghai (2008, p. 245) similarly argues that autonomy constitutes a mid-point of competing claims; that of separate statehood and a unitary state. It therefore presents a possible compromise in a situation where compromises are hard to come by and where zero-sum rhetoric dominates. For the separatist movement it offers self-rule and a degree of protection against the central government. For the central government it ensures the survival of the state within its existing border. This is particularly important in states with more than one potential separatist region. Autonomy may reduce the level of control exercised by the leaders of the central government, but it does not significantly undermine their power and privileges.

Autonomy, moreover, covers a variety of solutions. At one extreme, we find cultural autonomy which affords minorities self-rule over education, media and cultural affairs. Cultural autonomy does not have to be territorial and it does not come with wider legislative, executive and judicial powers. At the other extreme, we find solutions that maintain only on paper the sovereignty of the central government over the disputed territory. For all intents and purposes the autonomous region acts as an independent state with its own parliament, government, courts and security forces. In between these extremes we find various degrees of territorial self-rule; the extent of exclusive powers varies and the degree to which the arrangement is guaranteed for the future also varies. In some cases self-rule is combined with shared rule, for example in a federal system, whereas in other cases the ties to the centre are minimal. It is therefore not a blueprint as such, and as a solution it is clearly adaptable to the conflict situation (Hannum, 2004, p. 275).[6]

Its proponents may concede that autonomy, especially in the form of ethnic federalism, has a 'terrible track record' (Snyder, 2000, p. 327), but they counter that the major federal failures, such as the Soviet Union and Yugoslavia, were largely 'sham or pseudo-federations' which therefore provide limited lessons for today's mediators (McGarry & O'Leary, 2009, p. 9). The very idea of solving intra-state conflicts by giving autonomy to separatist groups has however been strongly criticized as a misguided and dangerous strategy. Roeder (2009, p. 206) argues that ethnic federalism or autonomy is 'particularly imprudent after civil wars' and Lake and Rothchild (2005, p. 112) find that 'warring factions have never realized full political decentralization along territorial lines as part of a civil war settlement' between 1945 and 1999. Ethnically-defined autonomy is criticized for reifying divisions; instead of addressing the divides that caused the conflict, it actually exacerbates them. As Erk and Anderson (2009, p. 192) point out, the paradox of group recognition is that it 'perpetuates the very divisions that it aims to manage'. But not only that, it also creates proto-states which reduces the cost of secession, thereby making it a realistic option (ibid.). Roeder (2009, pp. 212–13) similarly argues that the 'balance of coercive and defensive capabilities is likely to shift to the advantage of the secessionists' and they can therefore force deadlock. Ethnic autonomy traps politics 'between two perils – centralization and dissolution – with no stable equilibrium between these two extremes' (ibid., p. 208). The resulting system will therefore be unstable with constant attempts to move it either closer to secession or closer to recentralization, with the accompanying creation of mistrust and risk of renewed violence.

But autonomy can mean different things and be more suited to some situations than others. The question is if it is possible to construct successful autonomy arrangements that respond to and address the dynamics of specific conflicts. According to Roeder, the problem is with the ethnic basis of the system, not with the specific institutional design. However, a number of authors suggest that we have to look at different *types* of autonomy and the *conditions* under which they risk exacerbating the conflict (see e.g. Bakke, 2015; Brown, 2009; Cederman et al., 2015; McGarry & O'Leary, 2009; Wolff, 2011).

Autonomy Trends

The preference for autonomy arrangements is clearly pronounced; the large majority of the peace agreements analysed in this book include some form of autonomy and this is in most cases territorially defined (see table 1.1): of the twenty agreements, nineteen offer some form of autonomy. Even agreements that include provisions for an independence referendum, have autonomy arrangements in the interim period (Bougainville, Montenegro, South Sudan) or autonomy is one of the choices available to voters in the referendum (East Timor). The only exception is Senegal's 2004 General Peace Agreement, which does not include any form of territorial self-government for the region of Casamance, or any non-territorial autonomy. This agreement however failed to ensure peace. Two agreements only include non-territorial autonomy. The 1995 Erdut Agreement which reintegrated Eastern Slavonia into Croatia offered only cultural autonomy to the Croatian Serbs.[7] But this was essentially a capitulation: the Serb state-let Republika Srpska Krajina had collapsed and the local Serb leaders had very limited bargaining power. The more moderate faction which had become dominant consequently insisted that they were not asking for political autonomy, 'that is in the past, a finished matter' (Hedl, 1997, p. 18). The 1998 Belfast Agreement for Northern Ireland also provides only cultural autonomy within Northern Ireland, which can be explained by the lack of territorial concentration of the two communities. But Northern Ireland itself enjoys a significant level of autonomy within the United Kingdom.

Non-Federal Autonomy

While the popularity of autonomy seems unabated, what we may be witnessing is the death of federalism as a solution to intra-state conflicts (see also Weller, 2008, p. 145). If a federation is understood to include a bicameral legislature, with the second chamber representing the regional units, and a constitutionally guaranteed distribution of power between the two (or more) levels of government (Keil, 2013, pp. 14–15), then there are only two examples of new federations and one of these even departs from the federal model in important ways. The Dayton Agreement for Bosnia created a federation of two entities, while Sudan's Comprehensive Peace Agreement created a complex asymmetric federation with southern Sudan as a 'federal type entity' with ten states, its own constitution, institutions and legislation (Weller, 2005a, p. 169).[8] However the arrangements for southern Sudan were expressly designated as an 'autonomy' arrangement, thereby maintaining – at least on paper – Sudan as a unitary state, and the southern Sudan entity was not matched by a second unit (the North) (ibid.). In addition two agreements were based on existing federal systems: Serbia & Montenegro's Belgrade Agreement and the Treaty between Russia and Tatarstan.[9]

The recognition of federal republics from the former Yugoslavia and the Soviet Union as independent states has set a precedent in international law that appears to have made central governments wary of this solution. In the ongoing conflict in Eastern Ukraine, the separatist forces along with their backers in Moscow are demanding federalization (Goncharenko, 2014), but some clearly view this as a step towards independence, or indeed unification with Russia. The Government in Kiev on its part has strongly opposed a federal solution, with President Poroschenko describing it as 'tantamount to breaking apart the country' (Herszenhorn, 2015). Kiev instead prefers to talk about autonomy and decentralization (Goncharenko, 2014), although even this is severely contested (Sasse, 2016). In the cases of Sudan and Serbia & Montenegro, the threat of secession made little difference as the right to independence had already been recognized, while the continued territorial integrity of Bosnia was guaranteed by the international presence. The landlocked position of Tatarstan made secession an unlikely prospect, the federal system was already in place, and the Russian Government had in any case demonstrated in Chechnya how it would respond to renewed separatist threats. This helps explain why federations were still adopted in these cases. The Annan Plan for Cyprus, with its proposed federation of two constituent states, would therefore appear to be going against the grain, but this structure has so far not proved acceptable to the Greek Cypriot side who complain that too many Turkish demands are conceded, for too little in return (International Crisis Group, 2005a, p. 6).

An additional problem with (new) federal solutions is that they entail the reorganization of the entire state and the central government may therefore fear further fragmentation. This was one of the reasons for the Indonesian Government's insistence in the Aceh peace talks on maintaining a unitary state (Stepan, 2013, p. 241). A compromise solution was modelled on the Åland Islands in Finland and offered the Free Aceh Movement (GAM) extensive autonomy that could not be altered unilaterally,[10] but allowed the unitary Indonesian state to be maintained (Stepan, 2013). As will be further discussed below, the problem with autonomy arrangements, however, is that implementation often falls short and the asymmetrical structure offers little recourse.

Simple, Ethnic Autonomy

Another trend that stands out is the definition of autonomy in non-ethnic or less ethnic terms, including in conflicts that were clearly identity conflicts. For example, in the case of Macedonia, the Ohrid Agreement does not refer to the Albanian minority that is meant to benefit from the autonomy arrangements; instead it refers to 'communities not in the majority in the population of Macedonia' and grants autonomy to those constituting more than 20 per cent of the population. But even if not explicitly named, these agreements still guarantee rights for a specific group and power for their leaders. The demographic balance in the autonomous territory makes clear who will be the holders of the autonomous powers. In other agreements, the lack of an explicit ethnic definition reflects the diversity of the separatist region. This is for example the case in Northern Mali, Mindanao, Montenegro and South Sudan, which all encompass a number of different ethnicities or communities and where an ethnic demand for separation is not made. However, this does not entail an attempt to create an overarching identity and reduce the divide with the centre. What tends to happen is that the dominant community within the autonomous region, such as the Dinka in South Sudan, become the effective 'holder' of the autonomous powers. In effect, we are therefore looking at 'ethnic autonomy' in all the agreements analysed; the fundamental workings of these systems do not differ from the type of autonomy that Roeder and others warn against.

A number of theorists argue that political power-sharing is needed in order to make an autonomy agreement sustainable (see e.g. Cederman et al., 2015; McGarry & O'Leary, 2009, pp. 15, 17; Wolff, 2011). The argument is that it ties the separatist region to the centre, protects the minority group against domination (and the abolishment of their autonomy) and, if implemented at the local level, protects minorities within the self-rule areas. Power-sharing and its link with territorial autonomy will be more fully addressed in chapter 3, but it is noticeable how few of the agreements actually include it. Substantial power-sharing at either the central or the local level is only included in the case of Bosnia, Serbia & Montenegro, Sudan, Northern Ireland and Macedonia.[11]

Levels of Autonomy

While most of the agreements institute ethnic autonomy without a federal structure, they vary significantly when it comes to the extent of autonomy provided: from Serbia and Montenegro's 'Union of States' which foresees minimal integration of two essentially separate political and economic systems, to the low level of autonomy, primarily related to cultural and administrative matters, found in India's Bodo Accord.

The level of autonomy included in an agreement appears to depend on two factors in particular: the strength of the separatist position, including the degree of international support, and the

Table 1.1. Levels of Autonomy

Level of autonomy[12]	High	Bosnia
		Indonesia–Aceh
		Indonesia–East Timor[13]
		Papua New Guinea–Bougainville
		Russia–Chechnya[14]
		Serbia–Montenegro
		Sudan–South Sudan
	Medium	Israel–Palestine
		Mali
		Moldova–Gagauzia
		Philippines–Mindanao
		Russia–Tatarstan
	Low	Bangladesh–Chittagong Hill Tracts
		Croatia–Eastern Slavonia
		India–Bodoland
		Macedonia
		Niger
		Ukraine–Crimea
		UK–Northern Ireland[15]
	No autonomy	Senegal–Casamance

intensity of the conflict. In five of the seven cases of high levels of autonomy, the separatist movement was already in de facto control of the territory; the autonomy agreement simply recognized this control. In the case of Bosnia this could be done while preserving the state, but in Bougainville, Montenegro and South Sudan the autonomy was an interim solution before a referendum on (de jure) independence. Chechnya's final status was postponed for future talks but the Chechen leaders clearly expected to be moving towards (de jure) independence, and de facto independence would be maintained in the interim (Hughes, 2007). In the two remaining cases, Aceh and East Timor, the high levels of autonomy owe a lot to international pressure. East Timor's right to self-determination was recognized by the UN Security Council (Fabry, 2010, p. 172, n. 48) and high levels of autonomy provided the only possible, but ultimately unsuccessful, option for maintaining Indonesia's territorial integrity. Aceh's autonomy was reduced during the process of implementation (Stepan, 2013, p. 249), but the agreement does provide autonomous powers over both coercive forces and monetary policy.

High levels of autonomy do not depend on support from a powerful neighbouring state, but the absence of third party support helps explain the limited strength of the separatist movements in a number of cases and the consequent low levels of autonomy. Third party support was for example largely absent in the case of Bodoland, the Albanian insurgency in Macedonia and the Tuareg rebellion in Niger. In the case of Crimea, Russia decided not to support the demands for secession in the early 1990s, and third party support for the tribes in the Chittagong Hill Tracts and the Serbs in Eastern Slavonia was much reduced by the time the settlements were signed.[16] The lack of an international border can also temper separatist demands (McGarry & O'Leary, 2009, p. 15) and this may account for the willingness of Tatarstan's leaders to accept a relatively low, or at least ambiguous, level of autonomy (Hughes, 2001).

The cases also appear to show that the greater the violence, the stronger the demand for extensive autonomy. Five of the six cases of high levels of autonomy experienced very violent and prolonged wars. Extensive autonomy is in these cases combined with additional measures to address the level of mistrust between the parties: including external guarantees (e.g. Bosnia), or the holding of independence referenda following an interim period (e.g. Sudan and Bougainville), or at least the expectation of such an exit option (Chechnya). Among the cases of low levels of autonomy, we find more cases of minor armed conflicts (Bodoland, Macedonia, Niger) or non-violent conflicts (Crimea).

More Successful than Expected

The tendency is therefore for simple autonomy arrangements, in the sense that most of the agreements do not combine territorial autonomy with provisions for power-sharing. The autonomy is moreover ethnically-defined, either explicitly or in effect, and the degree of autonomy varies significantly. Some agreements can be said to require a redefinition of the state, and certainly entail a significant dislocation of power by essentially creating states-within-states (see Bell, 2008), but many others only entail limited institutional reforms, and hardly any at the central level. But has it worked: do the data from 1990 to 2010 tell a different story about autonomy than Lake and Rothchild's data from 1945 to 1999?

To a large extent they do. Of the thirteen agreements that instituted autonomy as a permanent solution, all but three were implemented and have lasted over ten years. The only exceptions are the agreements for the Chittagong Hill Tracts, Bodoland and Mindanao, and only in the latter two cases did the violent conflict return. The early post-settlement period in Mali and Niger was characterized by violence, but the agreements were eventually implemented (or partly implemented in the case of Niger), and made it past the ten-year mark before violence resumed. The autonomy arrangement for Crimea lasted nearly two decades, but collapsed following Russian covert intervention in 2014. Five interim agreements were also based on autonomy. In Sudan and Serbia & Montenegro this eventually gave way to secession, but this did not represent a collapse of the agreement and was not opposed by the central state. Bougainville is heading towards an independence referendum, which may well cause tensions, but the autonomy arrangement has so far ensured stability for over a decade. The interim autonomy arrangement in the case of Israel–Palestine must be seen as a failure, even if the Oslo Accord did haltingly and imperfectly make it past the five-year threshold before fully collapsing, and the Chechen agreement only provided a highly unstable break in the fighting before war broke out again three years later. The failure of these two agreements is however more indicative of the problems of postponing final status talks (more on this in chapter 5).

Autonomy is clearly no panacea but its track record in post-conflict settings is better than what has been argued by its critics.

Lapidoth asserts that, 'so far, no arrangements of autonomy have succeeded in a hostile atmosphere. ... If there is hatred and frustration, it is too late' (quoted in Roeder, 2009, p. 206; see also Cederman et al., 2015). But the good news is that it has been possible to reach lasting agreements even after very bloody and lengthy wars, for example in Eastern Slavonia, Bosnia and Aceh. In other words, it appears that the risks associated with autonomy arrangements can be managed. But how? This has been discussed in existing literature, but most factors highlighted have only been hypothesized not analysed in detail (see e.g. McGarry & O'Leary, 2009). The autonomy arrangement has to fit the conflict context – including depth of divisions, demographic balance and distribution, significance of the breakaway region – otherwise it will not prove sustainable (Wolff, 2011). However a peace agreement will also be affected by other factors, including international pressures, intra-communal dynamics and elite motivations. Moreover, the need for an agreement may necessitate significant ambiguities and the rushed nature of many settlements could result in significant design flaws. Some autonomy agreements will therefore be better able to ensure sustainability than others. The following section analyses how the type of autonomy affects both attempts to reach an agreement in the first place and its long-term stability.

Types of Autonomy and Sustainability

The specifics of the autonomy arrangement matter but not necessarily in the ways expected. The literature often points to the degree of autonomy, the number of units, the way in which the autonomy is guaranteed, and whether or not power-sharing is included. While agreeing that these may be important factors, the following analysis highlights the importance of two, usually under-analysed factors: ambiguity in the agreements – especially regarding the extent of autonomous powers and the delineation of internal borders – and the capacity of the autonomous region.

Level of Autonomous Powers

The risk of secession would be expected to be highest in the case of agreements that offer extensive autonomy. Such arrangements empower separatist forces, allowing them to create the kind of proto-state – with its own government, courts, police force and other

25

state-like attributes – that the critics warn against (see e.g. Roeder, 2007). Moreover, it has been argued that in order to be successful, institutions must 'reinforce those specific interests that groups have in the undivided state' (Horowitz, 1985, p. 628), for example by providing security and other state-supplied services. Such benefits would be largely absent in the case of high levels of autonomy. But the problem is of course that policies originating in the centre, in particular security, are not necessarily seen as benefits; they will frequently be seen as threats. The cases where we find high levels of autonomy are also arguably the cases where an alternative would be hardest to imagine and the conflict potential is highest. Autonomy may not be enough, and secession may result. In that case the peace agreement has not managed to solve the conflict, but the agreement is not the *cause* of the further separation.

If we look at the cases, a significant number of agreements with no or low levels of autonomy have also failed: out of eight agreements, two failed within five years (Casamance and Bodoland), one has never been fully implemented (Chittagong Hill Tracts), while one (Crimea) eventually collapsed and resulted in the de facto break-up of the state. If we look at the agreements with medium levels of autonomy, we also find a number of failures or high levels of instability, such as in the Philippines–Mindanao, Israel–Palestine, Mali and Niger. These agreements are often characterized by a great deal of ambiguity regarding the division of powers which, as I will argue below, has been a recurring source of instability. Of the seven cases of high levels of autonomy, the autonomy arrangement still exists in three of them. In Bosnia, the degree of autonomy has gradually been reduced as the central government has been strengthened (Bieber, 2006b), but without this resulting in the dissolution of autonomy or in a secessionist backlash, even if threats have been made on more than one occasion. Disagreements remain in Aceh over the degree of autonomy enjoyed by the region (International Crisis Group, 2013b), but the agreement has held and separatist violence has not broken out anew. Bougainville is getting closer to an independence referendum, but the situation is stable; violence has not re-erupted (see e.g. Woodbury, 2015). Autonomy was in the remaining four cases an interim arrangement (Sudan and Serbia & Montenegro), the rejected option in an independence referendum (East Timor), or the effective outcome of a highly ambiguous agreement (Chechnya). As will be discussed in chapter 3, high levels of autonomy can cause problems for effective governance when combined with power-sharing at the central level. But the degree of autonomy is not on its own a good predictor for the likelihood of success. Renewed secessionist attempts are rare; recentralization is the dominant trend (see also McGarry & O'Leary, 2009, p. 11). In fact, too little autonomy is at least as big a problem as too much autonomy, and ambiguity regarding the extent of self-rule enjoyed, or the lack of transfer of promised powers, is particularly associated with instability.

Ambiguity

Ghai (2008, p. 245) argues that one of the benefits of autonomy is that it allows for flexibility in negotiations and permits a gradual transfer of power, but that can also cause problems. The ambiguity of the Oslo Declaration resulted in much less autonomy for the Palestinian Authority (PA) than what was expected, which contributed to the agreement's lack of popular legitimacy and eventual collapse (see e.g. Roy, 2002). Likewise, the failure of the highly ambiguous Mindanao agreement to provide stability has, at least in part, been attributed to the lack of transfer of autonomous powers. This undermined popular support for the agreement and strengthened hardline challengers (see e.g. International Crisis Group, 2013a; Tuminez, 2007). Ambiguity has caused tensions in a number of other cases: the implementation of Niger's 1995 agreement proved very difficult and although some decentralization programmes and laws were eventually passed, the promised autonomy was never implemented in full.[17] The often conflicting legal basis of Gagauzia's autonomy within the Moldovan state has also similarly caused repeated deadlock and clashes over who has the authority over different issues (Wolff, 2008). Ambiguity often makes it easier to reach an agreement, but it is likely to cause problems in the post-settlement period, especially in a context of deep mistrust and persisting fears of domination.

Delineation of Internal Borders

Another source of tension is the process by which internal borders are delineated. This varies considerably between the cases. In the majority of the cases – such as the Chittagong Hill Tracts, Niger, Tatarstan and Montenegro – existing administrative borders were used with no possibility of redrawing these, but there were also a number of cases that did not clarify the exact borders of the regions that would enjoy autonomy. In these cases, referenda were to be held (e.g. Mindanao and Gagauzia), or it depended on a future census (e.g. Macedonia), or the agreement allowed for the autonomous region to propose a change to its borders (e.g. Mali).

Maintaining existing administrative borders has the benefit of simplicity and it avoids postponing potentially explosive issues for the implementation phase when it could derail the agreement. However, existing borders do not necessarily correspond with ethnic groups and this could lead to new minority problems. Deferring a decision on the exact borders is however likely to cause problems in the short- and medium-term and could even deter separatist groups from agreeing to a settlement in the first place. If there is uncertainty over the precise territory they will control, separatist forces may fear that they will be short-changed and that the resulting territory will not be sustainable as a self-governing unit. They could also potentially lose control over territory of great strategic or symbolic importance.

The extent of the autonomous region has been a huge source of controversy in Mindanao. The 1996 agreement raised the prospect of an expanded region through the holding of referenda in adjoining provinces and cities. This had been crucial in the negotiations (Hartzell & Hoddie, 2007, pp. 131, 134), but it took five years before it was finally implemented, and out of fourteen provinces and nine cities, only one additional province and one city voted for inclusion in the expanded region.[18] This limited, and delayed, expansion strengthened the hardline Moro Islamic Liberation Front and its demand for a considerably larger 'ancestral domain' (Tuminez, 2007, p. 83). Borders are such a contentious issue in Israel–Palestine that the Declaration of Principles (Oslo I) postponed it for the final settlement talks. In the interim period, the Palestinian Authority was to cover the West Bank and Gaza Strip territory, 'as a single territorial unit' (art. IV), but when implemented by Oslo II this contiguous territory was converted into a multitude of small enclaves. The reduction in the territory controlled by the PA clearly disappointed the Palestinian community and contributed to popular resistance against the settlement (Newman, 1995–6). In the case of Bodoland, villages were to be scrutinized in terms of population mix and the border would also be drawn in a way that made the autonomous area contiguous (art. 3a). However, the final demarcation of the territory did not meet these promises: contested villages were not included in the autonomous territory, which was also not contiguous. The Bodo signatories to the agreement rejected the outcome and large-scale violence resulted (George, 1994).

Even in cases where most of the territory is clearly delineated, ambiguity can still cause problems. In the case of Bosnia, the territorial division between the two entities was carefully negotiated at Dayton, apart from one territory, the district of Brčko. Following intense negotiations, it was finally decided to put it to international arbitration. It took four years for the International Arbitral Tribunal to rule that the district was to be shared by the two entities, thereby creating overlapping territories. State-level institutions were to protect the interests of the District[19] but, given the weakness of these institutions, Brčko was put under international administration for a transitional period (Jeffrey, 2006, p. 214). The ruling caused an outcry in Bosnia's Serb entity (Republika Srpska) and led to the resignation of the entity's prime minister. Without the international presence such tension could have proved fatal. In the case of Abyei, Sudan's contested oil-rich territory, no such intensified international supervision was foreseen. The demarcation of the disputed border was to be decided by an Abyei Boundaries Commission (ABC). The decision was to be 'final and binding', but the ABC report was seen as more favourable to southern Sudan, and the National Congress Party (NCP) refused to accept the conclusion (Brosché, 2008, pp. 239–40). In 2008, fighting again broke out in the area (Tendai, 2011). The delineation of borders goes to the heart of separatist conflicts where territorial control is of both strategic and symbolic importance. Ambiguity is therefore often a significant source of conflict and even breakdown.

Lack of Capacity

Some authors have mentioned the division of resources as a possible source of tension for autonomy arrangements (see e.g. McGarry & O'Leary, 2009, p. 19) and the need for proper financing of autonomy arrangements (Wolff, 2011, p. 181). A perceived failure by the central government to supply resources to the autonomous region has fuelled tensions in several cases, including Bougainville and Mindanao (Tuminez, 2007; Woodbury, 2015).

But lack of resources also affects the ability of the autonomous authorities to provide public services, which in turn impacts on the legitimacy of the arrangement in the community and in the state as a whole. For example, in the case of Mindanao, the autonomous government was 'neither autonomous nor capable of governing' (Lara Jr & Champain, 2009, p. 11). It lacked fiscal autonomy and did not wield effective control over the local police and armed forces. This had been part of the original deal, but the implementation was blocked by the Philippine Congress. As a result, basic public services, including law and order, could not be provided and this undermined the legitimacy of the agreement (ibid.) Similarly, the Palestinian Authority did not manage to ensure internal order and terrorist attacks continued which eroded Israeli support for the agreement (Perlmutter, 1995, pp. 59–60). Part of the problem for the PA was that the territory under their control consisted of a 'large number of disconnected territorial nodes and exclaves'. This lack of territorial contiguity hindered effective governance (Newman, 1995–6, p. 76). Moreover, the Israeli 'closure policy' led to serious economic decline in the West Bank and Gaza (Roy, 2002). Similarly, Russia failed to deliver the economic and reconstruction aid to Chechnya that it had promised and instead imposed a blockade on the entity. The resulting international isolation and lack of resources contributed to the increasingly chaotic situation in Chechnya, which became known as a 'hotbed of crime and terror', and to the outbreak of internal violence that ultimately spread across the republic's borders (Hughes, 2007, p. 93; see also Hughes, 2001, p. 34).

Increasing the capacity of the autonomous territories is however likely to be resisted by central governments, who fear that by devolving powers and supplying resources to the regions – even if these have already been agreed to in the settlement – they increase the risk of future secessionist attempts. It is also important to note however that the starting point for the autonomous territories varies; some rebel forces will have created fairly well-developed governance structures during the war and can build on these in the post-settlement period, while others have to start from a much lower starting point (see e.g. Arjona et al., 2015; Mampilly, 2011). The issue of sub-state capacity, and its effect on security, will be discussed further in the following chapters.

Power-Sharing, Guarantees and Number of Units

The argument that territorial autonomy must be complemented by power-sharing is gaining ground (see Cederman et al., 2015). However, it is actually only found in a minority of the cases analysed. The lack of power-sharing provisions in case of heterogeneous units (Wolff, 2009) has caused problems and lead to renewed tensions. For example the popular backlash against the Chittagong Hill Tracts Peace Accord was caused to a large degree by the discrimination against Bengalis that it was seen to institute in the autonomous region (see e.g. Zaman, 2009). The agreement reserved seats for the non-tribal population but they were still under-represented in the region.

The use of power-sharing at the local level is arguably important to avoid abuse within the autonomous territory (Wolff, 2011), but it will also restrict the self-government and could be manipulated by the state's dominant group.

The lack of power-sharing at the centre can in some cases be explained by the relatively small size of the separatist communities, which makes central power-sharing inappropriate, but simple autonomy is also found in cases with larger groups, such as the Russian-speaking minority in Ukraine (29.6 per cent according to the 2001 census).[20] Although power-sharing would tie a region to the centre, the central government may be reluctant to accept the reforms, and restrictions on majoritarian power, that this would entail. The separatist movement may similarly prefer autonomy on its own; precisely because it does not require them to cooperate with the central authorities, and recognize their legitimacy. The links, and trade-offs, between territorial autonomy, power-sharing and human rights will be further discussed in chapters 3 and 4. For now it suffices to say that although the lack of power-sharing provisions has led to tensions, cases such as Aceh demonstrate that it is not a *necessary* condition for successful autonomy arrangements, even following a violent conflict.

Following a bloody intra-state war, rebel forces will in many cases demand additional guarantees for their autonomy arrangements (Cederman et al., 2015). An agreement embedded in the constitution provides additional reassurance to the separatist forces; it would make it harder for the central government to abolish the autonomous powers once the separatist forces have laid down their arms. It has been suggested that such a constitutional guarantee is a condition for success (Wolff, 2011). This does not however appear to have been a stumbling block in any of the negotiations. In the case of Aceh, the autonomy arrangement ended up being passed as an ordinary law, rather than protected by the Constitution as stated in the agreement. But although this caused some tensions it did not result in the collapse of the agreement (Stepan, 2013). Overall, about half of the peace agreements are constitutionally guaranteed and about half by an ordinary law, with no clear correlation between the extent of autonomy and the way in which it is guaranteed, and no correlation with success or failure. The strength of such guarantees will in any case often be questioned by the weaker side. Separatist forces in the Caucasus frequently point out that constitutions can be amended and autonomy abolished, as happened during the dissolution of the former Soviet Union (see e.g. Natella, 2011, p. 15).

Such guarantees are further weakened by the significant ambiguities found in peace agreements, which allow for conflicting interpretations of the extent of autonomous powers and the precise delineation of the autonomous territory. Relatively powerful separatist groups will therefore be inclined to demand more tangible guarantees in the form of separate coercive forces. This will be discussed in the next chapter. In addition, they may demand international guarantees, and international oversight was indeed included in a number of these agreements, ranging from over twenty years of international administration in the case of Bosnia, to relatively short-term EU-ASEAN monitoring in Aceh. Such international presence cannot guarantee that autonomy will never be abolished, but it helps ensure that it is in fact implemented. Finally, there is one case that presents a novel way of guaranteeing autonomy: the Belfast Agreement for Northern Ireland is in fact an international treaty, and therefore legally binding, between the United Kingdom and the Republic of Ireland. The promise, as well as limitations, of international guarantees will be further discussed in chapters 2 and 7.

An additional factor pointed to in the literature is the number of constituent units in a federation. The more units, the more stable the federation, and McGarry and O'Leary (2009, p. 19) argue that there are no successful two-unit federations. There are, as mentioned above, few federations among the analysed cases and only one is clearly dyadic. Both northern and southern Sudan were divided into states, and only the former was constituted as a federal unit, but this did not moderate the dyadic dynamic of the system. Bosnia's federation technically contains three units but the third unit, Brčko, is not part of the federal structure. Nevertheless the dominant post-war dynamic has not been dyadic: it is not so much driven by antagonisms between the two entities, but rather by competition and sometimes alliances between nationalist parties from the three constituent nations. Serbia & Montenegro's Union of States was dyadic, but the course towards separation was already set. This suggests that the number of units has a limited effect on conflict dynamics.

The specific content of the peace agreement, the way in which the autonomous institutions are designed, is therefore highly significant. It matters for the ability of the parties to reach a compromise in the first place *and* it matters for future stability. But there will often be a tension between what is needed to get the parties to sign an agreement and what is needed for future stability. The dominant model of 'simple' but ambiguous autonomy arrangements comes with significant problems, but not all of these are inherent; the design of autonomy arrangements can be improved upon. However, sometimes autonomy is just not enough, at least not as a permanent solution, and we have to look to alternative solutions: secession and different ways of blurring sovereignty. These will be discussed in turn.

Secession

Hannum (1998) and Fearon (2004) both oppose secession because there are alternatives that maintain the existing states. However, maintaining a common state seems a near impossibility in some conflicts. This is especially the case in conflicts where the separatist territories are already de facto independent and their leaders therefore have little incentive to compromise (see Caspersen, 2012). As King asks, 'why be a mayor of a small city if you can be president of a country?', 'why be a lieutenant in someone else's army if you can be a general in your own?' (2001, p. 551). These de facto states often emerged from bloody conflicts and the resulting mistrust between the conflict parties has only been heightened by years of separation and propaganda. According to an anecdote from the Nagorno Karabakh peace process, the Karabakh leaders were once presented with the Åland Islands as a possible model for a solution, and responded that they would consider such an autonomy arrangement, 'but only within Finland' (Tavitian, 2000, p. 12). This clearly not being feasible, they insist that (de jure) sovereignty is non-negotiable.

The International Community has however been very reluctant to accept the creation of new states outside the colonial context, viewing it as a source of instability, both locally and internationally. The fear is that violence within states would simply be replaced by violence between states, that new minority problems would be created, that unviable entities would result, and that the granting of independence would embolden other secessionist movements. But since the end of the Cold War there has been a gradual relaxation of this view. The former Yugoslavia was deemed to be in a process of dissolution when Slovenia and Croatia were recognized in 1991, but recognition was also seen as a means to dissuade Serbian aggression. This strategy failed, but the idea that the creation of new states can sometimes be the only way to achieve peace has become more widely accepted. One of the arguments used for the recognition of Kosovo was that all other attempts to reach a solution had failed and independence was the only way to ensure stability, and it thereby provided an exit strategy for the International Community (Merikallio & Ruokanen, 2015).

In these cases, the central government did not accept the break-up of the state and such unilateral creations of new states are still framed as 'unique' solutions that do not set a precedent (Fabry, 2010). However, the International Community has been prepared to accept secession when it is part of a peace agreement, and thereby (reluctantly) accepted by the parent state, and when it follows administrative borders rather than redrawn borders along ethnic lines. Three of the agreements provided for independence referenda following an interim period: Sudan, Papua New Guinea–Bougainville and Serbia & Montenegro.[21] The interim period is a way of 'giving unity a chance' (Weller, 2005a), and in the case of Serbia & Montenegro, the EU strongly pushed for an interim period, instead of an immediate independence referendum (Van Meurs, 2003). Such agreements have also been suggested in other conflicts. The Nagorno Karabakh peace talks have, for example, since 2005 been based on a set of principles that include an interim period and a popular vote on the future status of the territory.[22] Weller (2008) argues that new strategies for solving separatist conflicts have become available and our understanding of the legal right to self-determination has consequently been significantly extended.

However, opening up for the possibility of secession is also associated with risks. It could for example make it harder to find a compromise solution in other cases, as separatist forces will hold out for independence. There is also the risk that non-viable states will be created. Such fears will only have been heightened by the outbreak of civil war in South Sudan. Interim periods could help in this regard, as it would allow time for capacity-building, although South Sudan also shows that this is not guaranteed to happen. Interim agreements and their associated problems will be further discussed in chapter 5, but one of the main problems with such postponed independence referenda is that they are unlikely to be acceptable to the central government. No central government has, as yet, convinced a separatist territory to stay following an interim peace agreement, and they are likely to insist on their territorial integrity.

Blurring Sovereignty

Some of the more creative parts of recent peace agreements and proposals are attempts to blur or fudge sovereignty, in ways that do not necessarily maintain full sovereignty on paper as autonomy does. This typically involves shared sovereignty – or less drastically special links with neighbouring states – or international administrations, but could also include making sovereignty conditional or other ways of reconceptualizing traditional views of sovereignty and statehood. Such blurring of sovereignty can be a way of finding a compromise where autonomy is not enough for the separatist movement and the central government will not accept secession. Bell (2008, p. 220) argues that post-Cold War peace agreements link continued territorial integrity to 'new requirements for the internal configuration of the state'. This is done through a redefinition of the state (e.g. constitutional recognition of excluded groups), a disaggregation of power (e.g. autonomy) and a dislocation of power (e.g. postponed independence referendum) (ibid., pp. 108ff). Bell acknowledges that such settlements contain tensions (ibid., pp. 231ff), and I find that there are significant constraints, in particular when it comes to permanent compromises between territorial integrity and *external* self-determination. Although there are some examples of this, it is akin to squaring the proverbial circle.

The Belfast Agreement contains a crucial trans-border dimension which enabled it to address the legacies of partition and the self-determination dispute at the heart of the Northern Irish conflict (McGarry & O'Leary, 2006a). Strand 2 of the agreement provides for a number of institutions that join together Northern Ireland and the Republic of Ireland, while Strand 3 creates institutions between the UK and the Republic of Ireland. The inhabitants of Northern Ireland also have citizenship rights in both states (Annex: Agreement between the Government of the United Kingdom of Great Britain and Northern Ireland and the Government of Ireland). Another example of a trans-border dimension is found in the case of Bosnia where both entities are allowed to establish 'special parallel relationships' with neighbouring states (Annex 4, art. III.2). The implementation of the agreement is moreover left to an international administration, thereby further blurring issues of sovereignty. Sovereignty can also be made conditional, as in the case of Gagauzia where the autonomous region gains the right to external self-determination if the status of Moldova were to change (art. 1.4). This was to address Gaugaz fears in the early 1990s that Moldova might join neighbouring Romania. Finally, the interim agreements mentioned above can also be seen as ways of fudging the issue of sovereignty, as long as the outcome of the independence referendum is not a given.

Even more creative solutions can be found in some of the proposals (official and unofficial) put forward in other intractable conflicts. For example the Annan Plan for Cyprus maintained the 1960 Treaties of Alliance and Guarantee, which means that a maximum of 6,000 Turkish and Greek troops would provide a security guarantee for the two communities, until Turkey's accession to the EU (art. 8.1). Continued Turkish military presence on the island however proved an anathema to many Greek Cypriots (International Crisis Group, 2005a, p. 7). In the case of Nagorno Karabakh we have seen a whole host of attempts to blur sovereignty. In 1997 it was suggested that Azerbaijan should lease the strategic Lachin corridor to the Organization for Security and Co-operation in Europe (OSCE) and the OSCE would then lease it to the Armenian side, thereby maintaining de jure Azerbaijani sovereignty (Ziyadov, 2010). In 1998 it was suggested that Azerbaijan and Armenia would share sovereignty over Nagorno Karabakh (Libaridian, 2005; Tavitian, 2000). Now the discussions centre on an interim solution, possibly with some international status for Karabakh in the transitional period.[23]

A more ambitious rethink of sovereignty and statehood is found in the 'two-state condominialism' that some observers have suggested as an alternative solution in Israel–Palestine. This approach is an attempt to find a compromise between the one-state and two-state solution, as both are currently unfeasible. What is suggested is to have two states sharing the same territory. Although each would have a 'heartland', reflecting existing population concentrations, it is essentially a form of non-territorial or deterritorialized statehood: the state to which you belong would not depend on where you live but solely on whether you are Palestinian or Jewish (Spears, 2014). The problem is if this is at all feasible. Non-territorial autonomy has been tried successfully elsewhere, but the question is if core state-functions could also be fulfilled on a non-territorial basis. For example, if you get mugged, will you need to know the citizenship of the perpetrator before you decide which police force to call? Territory is not just symbolic; it is also closely related to security. These are not just technical issues; it is doubtful if such an approach would in fact address the key demands of the conflict parties. One of the suggestions argues that in order to address Israeli security concerns, there would be some restrictions on the Palestinian state, especially when it came to the size of its armed forces and outside alliances (Spears, 2014, p. 205). This indicates that in order to make it work, and in order to address Israeli fears, there would still have to be a hierarchical relationship between the two states. This implies that we are not really talking about a Palestinian state, but rather extensive autonomy over a non-contiguous territory, with 'heartlands' under Palestinian control. Similarly, all suggestions appear to be transitional with a common state being the endpoint (ibid., p. 205). Dalsheim (2014) argues that Palestinians may be willing to accept less than popular sovereignty, if they are able to live in their homeland. But although I agree with the need to 'think beyond the camp fire', I fail to see how such a solution would satisfy Palestinian demands and address their grievances.

The more general problem with these attempts to blur sovereignty is that although traditional views of sovereignty and statehood have been widely, and rightly, criticized (see e.g. Sørensen, 1999), they are so engrained that they are hard to escape in practice. A territory will tend to be viewed as either sovereign or non-sovereign (see e.g. Bartelson, 2001), and various attempts at creative compromises will be perceived as a springboard to secession or to recentralization. It is hard to find a lasting compromise between the two claims. This is a problem because, as Spears (2014, p. 202) argues, such a solution 'must be *believed* if it is to be seen'. In order for it to work there is moreover a need for trust, which is usually in very short supply in these conflicts. One solution could be to provide international guarantees, or possibly even provide for sovereignty to be shared with an international organization (see Krasner, 2004). But such involvement comes with its own set of problems, as will be discussed in chapter 7. Similarly, even if we know that identity groups are constructed, it is very difficult to move beyond them. This is how people perceive themselves, especially after a violent conflict waged in the name of such groups, and powerfully vested interests will continue to essentialize them.

Conclusion: Optimism, with Caveats

The territorial solution that clearly predominates in post-Cold War separatist conflicts is autonomy, possibly as an interim solution. In most cases, this could be termed as 'simple' autonomy in the sense that power-sharing is rarely included. Power is disaggregated and dislocated (Bell, 2008), but central governments will seldom view autonomy as signifying a change in the basis of state sovereignty. As Roeder has argued, autonomy was historically associated with 'attempts by dynastic or communist autocracies to forestall the process of national liberation' (2009, p. 204) and it continues to be largely a pragmatic response to the need for a settlement.

External sovereignty was blurred in a few cases but although such creativity is most welcome, and very much needed in some intractable conflicts, these approaches are largely untested. Zartman (2004,

p. 153) argues that 'creativity has responded positively' to the challenge of stark invisibility, but also warns that sovereignty presents a particular challenge. It remains difficult to completely escape the binary view of sovereignty: a territory is either independent or not independent, sovereign or non-sovereign. This makes it hard to solve conflicts where (extensive) autonomy is not enough for the separatist movement, but the central government refuses to accept secession.

Nevertheless, the chapter found some reason for optimism. Lake and Rothchild's (2005) pessimistic findings regarding pre-1999 territorial decentralization leave out some cases of successful autonomy agreements, and there are also several post-1999 examples. Autonomy *can* provide a solution to separatist conflicts, even in cases of prolonged wars. Roeder (2009) argues that the problem with ethnic autonomy is that it always tends towards secession and recentralization. This often is a problem, and this chapter has pointed in particular to the dangers of recentralization, but such dynamics are not always signs of instability. Rather it could indicate that divisions were becoming less deep or that an agreement had been reached to solve the conflict through political means. For example, recentralization is what was hoped for by the international mediators in Bosnia, while in the case of Serbia & Montenegro the fact that it ended in secession cannot be seen as a failure of the agreement.

However, autonomy does not always work and the specific design of the autonomy arrangement plays an important role. Four features, in particular, were found to cause tensions and instability: insufficient autonomous powers; highly ambiguous provisions, especially as regards the extent of autonomy and the delineation of internal borders; lack of capacity in the autonomous regions; and a lack of power-sharing or even recognition of diversity in autonomous regions. Ambiguity can, as will be discussed in chapter 5, play a useful role both before and after an agreement is reached, but it can also lead to instability. Moreover, the failure to recognize intra-communal or regional diversity means that the representativeness of the separatist leaders is accepted at face value and the agreement thereby empowers actors who may not be best suited to ensure sustainable peace.

— 2 —

SECURITY

The destruction of weapons following a successful process of disarmament is an important symbolic event in a peace process and is frequently marked by solemn ceremonies. The 'Flame of Peace' bonfire in Mali destroyed close to 3,000 arms (Lode, 2002), while they relied on a steel saw in Aceh when former fighters from the Free Aceh Movement ceremoniously handed over, what were deemed to be, the last remaining weapons (Merikallio & Ruokanen, 2015, p. 312). The disposal of weapons is however not merely symbolic. Putting an end to the fighting is often seen as the main purpose of a settlement, but it does not stop there. In order for peace to be sustainable, new security institutions will often have to be created and former rebels will in most cases have to be demobilized, disarmed and reintegrated into civilian society. Law and order must be (re)established.

Security is often a significant stumbling block during negotiations. Peace processes are periods of transition that are associated with great uncertainty and potential vulnerability. Giving up on, or reducing, one's military might requires a level of trust in the opponent and in the peace agreement, and such trust is usually lacking. Controversies typically arise over the timing and verification of military withdrawals and disarmament and over the type of armed forces that will ensure post-settlement security. These questions are also crucial for the sustainability of the agreement. Longer- and even shorter-term stability may be undermined if separate armies are maintained or if the process of disarmament, demobilization and reintegration (DDR) has been incomplete, leaving secret weapons stocks and unemployed former combatants. In the case of Northern Ireland, the issue of IRA decommissioning has for example refused to go away. It proved to be a stumbling block both before and during the negotiations that led to the Belfast Agreement (see e.g. Powell, 2008). The agreement ended up postponing the issue for later and it took more than three years before it was settled. Even so, the possible continued existence of the IRA still periodically threatens to unravel the peace process (BBC News, 2015c).

Despite the importance of security issues, both for reaching an agreement and for making it last, security was until fairly recently seen predominantly as a technical issue. Once the parties had agreed to a political solution, security issues were simply a question of working out the details. However, the literature has made a complete about-turn and 'security first' has become the new mantra, both among scholars and policymakers: political and economic reforms must wait until security has been addressed, or peace will not be sustainable (Paris, 2004). This literature is very much focused on the problem of commitment: how can the other side be trusted to meet its obligations, and not just wait for an opportune moment to re-launch the war? In order to overcome this, defectors must be punished, either by 'robust' international intervention (Walter, 2002) or by effective domestic security institutions that enjoy a monopoly of force within the state (Toft, 2009).

This chapter again analyses the interaction between the wider conflict context, including intra-communal dynamics, and the content of peace settlements, and it emphasizes how agreements on security issues are significantly affected by the territorial provisions discussed in the previous chapter. I argue that peace agreements are not doomed to collapse even if effective central security institutions are often not realistic, and third party willingness to provide a credible security guarantee is the exception rather than the rule. Security holds a dominant place in most peace agreements, but it is addressed in a number of different ways. While some form of third party guarantee is often included, the nature of this varies considerably; it is not always necessary and need not take the form of a *military* guarantee. The legitimacy of security institutions is as important as their effectiveness, and commitment problems are not solely about the risk of the other side secretly stockpiling weapons. Lack of implementation of political provisions is as much of a risk and the overall agreement therefore matters for the severity of the commitment problem. The chapter questions the priority given to (narrow) security in much recent literature and emphasizes that it cannot be analysed in isolation from political institutions. It points to the need for both capacity and legitimacy, and the former should not be limited to the building of effective, central security institutions: decentralized capacity is

40

highly significant but usually overlooked. Finally, the chapter argues that the emphasis on macro-security, whether centralized or decentralized, often involves a trade-off with micro- or human security (Collier, 1994; Kaldor, 2007b). This could undermine an agreement's long-term sustainability.

Commitment Problems: Reducing the Risk of Cheating

Compared to territorial issues, the theorizing on security issues in peace agreements is rather more limited. However, there is one dominant argument found in the literature: the need for third party guarantees. Walter (2002) argues that security guarantees in intra-state wars cannot be provided by the parties themselves; they have to be backed by an external power that is willing to use force, if necessary. The problem is one of credible commitment: the parties can never feel sure that the other side will not cheat and return to violence once conditions are more favourable. A third party guarantee allows the parties to make the necessary leap of faith and agree to reduce, and eventually demobilize, their military capabilities. This argument focuses on the risk of one side reneging on its promises, but the primary risk of post-settlement violence often comes from *within* the group: from hardliners targeting pro-settlement forces (Nilsson, 2008; see also Stedman, 1997). Such spoiler violence, or even its potential, will however also impact on the commitment problem: fears of being cheated would be even more pronounced if significant factions are calling for a military 'solution' (see also Kydd & Walter, 2002). As Jakobsen argues, 'more often than not a force capable of defeating *any armed attempts* to derail a peace process will be required to keep a peace process on track' (2000, p. 41, my emphasis). The argument does not, therefore, depend on viewing each side as a unitary actor.

Walter (2002) argues that the *degree* of third party guarantee needed depends on the political part of the agreement, but the most likely form of third party guarantee is an international peacekeeping force. Such a force can provide a physical constraint against attack and otherwise play a monitoring function (Hoffman & Bercovitch, 2011, p. 408). A security guarantee could however also conceivably be provided by a neighbouring state, or even by a more distant great power or regional power, although the time-delay involved in deploying troops would risk undermining the credibility or effectiveness of the guarantee. Most authors emphasize that in order to ensure stability, the third party guarantee must be 'robust' (see e.g.

Doyle & Sambanis, 2000; Jakobsen, 2000). Toft argues that third parties must make a credible threat to harm one or both sides if the provisions of the settlements are undermined, but finds that most peace agreements do not contain enough 'harm' and they therefore fail: 'third parties are rarely accorded the right to impose the terms of settlement through the use of force' (2009, p. 46). In most cases external actors will simply not have sufficient strategic interests in the conflict to be willing to make a credible commitment (Toft, 2009). It would therefore significantly constrain the options for lasting peace, if robust third party guarantees were indeed a necessary condition.

Third Party Guarantees, Phased Approaches and Autonomy

My findings appear to qualify the need for third party guarantees. Of the twenty agreements, only five included third party security guarantees in the form of an *armed* peacekeeping mission. This was the case in Bosnia, Croatia, East Timor, Macedonia and Sudan.[24] It can even be questioned if these missions all represented a credible threat of 'harm' in case either of the conflict parties reneged on their promises. The NATO Implementation Force (IFOR) in Bosnia with its 60,000 soldiers constituted the kind of robust peacekeeping that is discussed above. IFOR was mandated to 'take all necessary measures to effect the implementation' of the security aspects of the agreement and was to work closely with the international High Representative who was in charge of the civilian aspects.[25] The 5,000-strong UN peacekeeping force deployed in Eastern Slavonia was also a Chapter VII Operation but it was less robust and its mandate not as strong as in the Bosnian case: it was primarily to 'supervise and facilitate the demilitarization as undertaken by the parties'. However Resolution 1037 also established a transitional UN administration for an initial period of twelve months.[26] The mandate for Macedonia was not as far-reaching: the 3,500-strong NATO force was to monitor the disarmament of the rebel forces and was otherwise to provide protection for other third parties assisting with the implementation of the agreement (see also Bieber, 2013, p. 315).[27] Similarly, the UN Mission in Sudan, although a sizeable (10,000 troops) Chapter VII Operation, was not mandated to enforce the peace. Its mandate was to support the implementation of the agreement, in particular with regard to disarmament and demobilization; facilitate the delivery of humanitarian assistance and the return of refugees/internally displaced people (IDPs); assist in demining efforts; and contribute towards the protection of human rights and civilians.[28] Finally, in the case of East Timor, the intention was initially for the Indonesian Government to provide security during the independence referendum and the UN peacekeepers were only deployed to oversee the implementation of the result. It was only after the outbreak of violence that the 7,000-strong multinational International Force for East Timor (INTERFET) was established to restore peace and security in the territory, facilitate humanitarian assistance and protect the UN mission. Resolution 1264 also invited the Secretary General to plan and prepare for a UN transitional administration, incorporating a peacekeeping operation.[29]

Several of the agreements that did not include 'guaranteed harm' have nevertheless proved stable (see also Fortna, 2008). This suggests that a third party security guarantee is not a *necessary* condition for a successful peace agreement, although it may well be a facilitating one. Some of the agreements have instead tried to address the commitment problem through a phased approach. The Bougainville negotiating team insisted on linking weapons disposal to progress in the implementation of the political agreement and the holding of the independence referendum (Smith, 2002). Weapons disposal was a precondition for the holding of both elections and the referendum, and the process of disposal was staged with each stage conditional on progress in the passing of the promised constitutional amendments (art. 6–8). A phased approach is also found in the case of Niger where disarmament is similarly linked to progress in the implementation of territorial autonomy; development programmes; the creation of special, integrated, military units; and the reintegration of former combatants (art. 13). In Sudan, the limited mandate of the peacekeeping force was made up for by building in targets and conditions for redeployment. The redeployment of both armies was to take place in stages, thereby making it easier to reverse if the other side did not reciprocate, and full redeployment from the still-disputed border areas was conditional on the creation of joint army units (Ch. 6 and Annex 1, part II). Moreover, the agreement only foresees 'proportional downsizing' of the two armies, 'at a suitable time' (art. 6.1). In other cases, deadlines are used which provides an element of a phased approach, even if the consequences of failure to meet the deadline are not always specified. For example in the case of Mali, a programme for integrating former combatants into the armed forces will be put into effect within sixty days following the signing of the Pact. This is conditional upon weapons being handed over (art. 7).

Walter (2002) rejects that such phased approaches or built-in targets can help overcome the commitment problem as cheating would still be possible. Fortna agrees that there is a limit to what self-monitoring can achieve and a neutral arbiter in the form of a peacekeeping force is often needed, although she stresses that it does not have to be 'robust' (2008, p. 94). It would however appear that, at least in some cases, the international mission does not even have to be armed. The Bougainville negotiation team insisted on the involvement of the UN (Smith, 2002), but the United Nations Observer Mission in Bougainville (UNOMB) was unarmed and comprised of only a Head of Mission, a political adviser and two support staff.[30] The main international presence was the equally unarmed Australian-led Peace Monitoring Group (Reddy, 2008). A similar international observer mission was deployed in Aceh, where 222 unarmed observers from the EU and the Association of Southeast Asian Nations (ASEAN) oversaw the implementation of the agreement, including the process of disarmament and demobilization (Merikallio & Ruokanen, 2015, p. 316). The international monitors in both cases declared that weapons disposal had been a success (Merikallio & Ruokanen, 2015, p. 316; Woodbury, 2015, p. 9). Third parties were also involved in the implementation of other agreements, including the Belfast Agreement for Northern Ireland where an independent international commission was to deal with issues related to decommissioning (Strand 3, Decommissioning). The implementation process for Niger was intended to be monitored by a Special Committee, which was to include international representatives, and by a group of military observers (art. 12). However this international mission was apparently never deployed. This may explain why demobilization and disarmament were not fully implemented,[31] although lack of implementation of the political part of the agreement would also be a factor.

As will be further discussed in chapter 7, non-coercive third party involvement can have a positive impact on both the negotiation phase and the post-settlement phase (see also Hoddie & Hartzell, 2010). However such involvement does not provide a robust guarantee to parties worried that the other side will launch a military attack. Moreover third party involvement was in a number of cases absent from the post-settlement phase – the international mediators left as soon as the agreement was signed – and a couple of the conflicts were never internationalized. What can explain why some negotiated settlements appear to be sustainable without robust third party guarantees?

For the rebel movements, the process of demobilizing and disarming is particularly sensitive. It means that they give up their main, and in some cases only, leverage against the central government, whereas the central government, even if it has to withdraw or scale down its military capacity, can much more easily rearm (Regan, 2002). It could therefore seem surprising that not all agreements include robust third party guarantees or at least some form of phased approach. In the case of the Chittagong Hill Tracts, Fortna (2008, p. 63) argues that political inexperience explains why the United People's Party of the Chittagong Hill Tracts (PCJSS) did not insist on enforcement mechanisms. However another reason is likely to be the 'core deal' of territorial autonomy, which in many cases includes control of coercive forces. Although this does not eliminate the risk of being cheated by the central government – and lack of implementation is a frequent source of instability – it does reduce the vulnerability of the rebel forces. Such a solution does however also present its own set of security problems, as will be further discussed below.

This is not to suggest that the use of built-in targets or the promise of autonomy is always enough to reduce the risk of cheating. Sometimes the level of mistrust is just too high. In the case of the Nagorno Karabakh peace processes the sequencing of the different parts of the proposed framework has for example proved extremely contentious. The current proposal envisages the withdrawal of Armenian forces from the districts surrounding Nagorno Karabakh in return for an interim status of autonomy for Nagorno Karabakh and a future vote on the status of the region. However, the Armenian side is unwilling to accept this, fearing that withdrawal from these strategic areas would be followed by a renewed military offensive by Azerbaijan, and the promised benefits would never be realized.[32] After a full-scale war, it is even more difficult to trust the other side not to return to violence, and Doyle and Sambanis (2000) find that the higher the intensity of the conflict, the more 'robust' the international presence needs to be. If we only look at the seven cases that are coded as wars in the UCDP/ PRIO Armed Conflict Dataset (2013) then it is noticeable that the agreements collapsed in the three cases without third party presence: Israel–Palestine, Mindanao and Chechnya, whereas they lumbered on in the others: Bosnia, Croatia, East Timor, Sudan.

However we should not necessarily jump to the conclusion that third party security guarantees are necessary following full-blown wars. One problem is that the distinction between a minor armed conflict and a full-scale war is somewhat arbitrary, and it is impossible to determine at what point the need for security guarantees kicks in. None of the conflict years in Aceh and Bougainville are for example classed as a war,[33] but this does not take into account the systematic violations of human rights (Amnesty International, 2013b), or the people who died as an indirect result of the conflict. The latter was particularly significant in Bougainville where a year-long blockade resulted in a desperate lack of medical supplies and food (see e.g. Braithwaite et al., 2010). It is unclear that mistrust will be less of an issue in such a conflict than in a conflict with many battle deaths. There is also a potential problem of causality. The reluctance of the parties to ask for international guarantees in the three failed cases could be based on a lack of genuine commitment to the peace agreement. Fortna (2008, p. 95) argues that peacekeepers can act as an important signalling device: by accepting their presence, the conflict parties signal their commitment to the agreement. But she also finds that central governments are generally reluctant to accept peacekeeping forces as they see this as an indictment of their capacity, or indeed as an admission of culpability. Both the failure of the agreement and the lack of third party guarantees may therefore reflect insufficient support for the agreement. Finally, it is hard to argue that the lack of third party guarantees provides the main explanation for the failed agreements in Israel–Palestine, Mindanao and Chechnya. As has already been argued in the previous chapter – and will be further argued in the following – ambiguities in the agreements, lack of capacity in the autonomous territories and a failure to address key grievances provide a more convincing explanation. These characteristics of the agreements empowered spoilers who were set on undermining the settlement. I argued above that commitment-based arguments do not have to view groups as unitary actors, however the commitment problem only covers one of the possible motivations that can lead to a return to violence (Hoddie & Hartzell, 2010). Fears for the community's safety may be one factor, but individual motivations and the perceived fairness of the agreement will be equally important (Caspersen, 2008a).

In conclusion, although some third party presence is likely to be needed in severe conflicts, this can take different forms and will not necessarily constitute 'robust' peacekeeping. Moreover, the overall agreement matters; it matters for the risk of spoiler violence and for the severity of the commitment problem. If we go back to the Nagorno Karabakh example, then underlying the refusal of the Armenian side to withdraw troops is a fundamental disagreement over the final status of the territory. The Armenian side insists on independence, while Azerbaijan refuses to consider a popular vote that includes this as an option. Any compromise that departs from these positions would almost inevitably result in spoiler activity. The importance of the overall agreement for security issues has also been emphasized by

Knight and Özerdem, who point out that DDR 'depends predominantly upon the political context in which it is carried out, and the political will among the belligerent parties will remain the chief criterion for determining success' (2004, p. 500). Spear (2002) similarly emphasizes the interconnectedness of the political agreement, third party involvement and DDR, and argues that the implementation challenges posed by the latter depend on the two former factors.

The rest of the agreement also matters because it affects the ability of the third party to leave. As Toft (2009) points out, a third party security guarantee does not solve the commitment problem; it merely postpones it, as the third party must eventually withdraw. The hope is that the passing of time will gradually (re)build trust: memories of violence fade, the conflict parties may have shown themselves willing and able to cooperate, and a degree of normalization returns. However, this again highlights the importance of the rest of the agreement. The 'security first' literature stresses the importance of building effective domestic security institutions. This reflects a Weberian concept of the state which we also encounter in much of the state-building literature: once territory is controlled, the monopoly on the use of force must be ensured. Conflict resolution has, in fact, become almost inseparable from state-building. However three important issues often get lost in this discussion. Firstly, the importance of legitimacy: the need to address minority fears may necessitate compromising on institutional effectiveness. Secondly, the significance of intra-communal security and therefore of decentralized state-building. And thirdly, the possible tension between stability and human security; between security in the narrow and the wide sense.

Conflict Resolution as State-Building

In order for peace to be durable, the state has to be put back together (Zartman, 1995a). Toft (2009) argues that security institutions must be reformed and strengthened so that defectors can be punished effectively. A negotiated settlement will thereby come to resemble an outright victory and Toft suggests that this is possible, 'if SSR [security sector reform] is done well' (ibid., p. 50). The need to find a solution that is acceptable to both sides of the conflict would however appear to undermine such efforts. Peace agreements often involve complicated compromises such as integrated security forces, with separate command structures, ethnic quotas, etc. They also often link security issues to progress in implementing other parts of the peace agreement.

Strong security institutions may address the central government's fear of being cheated by the rebel forces, but they will not generally address the fears of minority communities. Although the withdrawal of the army from the contested territory is often part of a peace agreement, the main fear of minority communities tends not to be renewed warfare but rather the return to business as usual, and even reformed security institutions could serve as an instrument of majority dominance. We can therefore expect resistance to a strong centralized force – precisely because it can guarantee 'harm' – and other security arrangements will therefore often be needed.

Hartzell and Hoddie (2007) find that rather than being a recipe for disaster, peace agreements that include military power-sharing actually have a greater chance of survival than agreements that do not. Their definition of military power-sharing is however very broad and includes any incorporation of rebel forces, ranging from a more representative army to separate forces (ibid., p. 32), and the impact on the fears and motivations of both leaders and communities is therefore far from uniform.

The following analysis examines three different strategies for addressing security issues; three variations of SSR, or indeed three forms of state-building: (1) no reform of the armed forces and only limited reform of other coercive forces, (2) creating a more representative army, (3) maintaining separate coercive forces. These strategies respond to the commitment problem in different ways, and have different effects on wider security issues. They may all ensure a de jure monopoly of force, but without necessarily relying on the strengthening of central institutions and central control. Options 2 and 3 respond to the need for legitimacy, and the often predatory nature of the armed forces, and they also address the need for intra-communal capacity for managing spoilers. However, such security strategies could risk undermining the peace agreement or impact negatively on the quality of peace.

No Reform of the Armed Forces

As table 2.1 shows, several agreements include no or only very limited reforms of the armed forces. This is the case in the Chittagong Hill Tracts, Eastern Slavonia, Bodoland, Macedonia, Gagauzia, Tatarstan, Casamance, Crimea and Northern Ireland. These cases however share certain similarities, which suggest the limited circumstances under which such an approach is possible: they were either not violent (Gagauzia, Tatarstan and Crimea), the separatist forces

Table 2.1. Security Reforms

No reform of armed forces	Bangladesh–Chittagong Hill Tracts
	Croatia–Eastern Slavonia
	India–Bodoland
	Macedonia
	Moldova–Gagauzia
	Russia–Tatarstan
	Senegal–Casamance
	Ukraine–Crimea
	UK–Northern Ireland
More representative army	*Rebel forces integrated:*
	Mali
	Niger
	Philippines–Mindanao
	Joint forces, shared command:
	Serbia & Montenegro
	Sudan
Separate coercive forces	Bosnia
	Israel–Palestine
	Indonesia–Aceh
	PNG–Bougainville
	Indonesia–East Timor[34]
	Russia–Chechnya[35]

were facing defeat (Eastern Slavonia), or the separatist violence posed a limited threat to the centre of the state (Chittagong Hill Tracts, Bodoland, Casamance, Northern Ireland). Crucially in the latter cases, some security reforms appear to have been necessary for success.

In the case of Northern Ireland, the Belfast Agreement includes the withdrawal of the British army and a full-scale reform of the police service is announced (Strand 3, Policing and Justice, art. 3). In the case of Macedonia, only limited police reforms are included in the agreement (Annex B, art. 4), but the agreement does provide for improved minority rights, and the presence of NATO forces moreover reduces the need for agreement on security issues. Where security sector reforms have been more limited, problems have tended to arise. In the case of the Chittagong Hill Tracts, the agreements granted the autonomous institutions some powers over the local police and the Bangladeshi army was meant to withdraw. This helped make the agreement acceptable to the PJCSS, but the local police force has still not been created and the army remains in the region. This lack of implementation of security provisions, and the resulting continuation of human rights violations and lack of law and order, has added to dissatisfaction with the agreement and caused tensions in the region (Fortna, 2008, p. 134; Mikkelsen, 2009, p. 380; 2015, pp. 315–16). The relative weakness of the PJCSS has however so far avoided a return to violence (Fortna, 2008, p. 134; Mohsin, 2003, p. 41). Renewed outbreak of violence could not be avoided in Bodoland, however, where the autonomous institutions were meant to have had some monitoring functions over the police and a degree of influence over which officers were posted to the region. Additional recruitment from the region to the army, paramilitary forces and police units was also promised (art. 16). But the agreement collapsed over the demarcation of the autonomous region and these limited reforms were never implemented (George, 1994).[36] The lack of reform is even more glaring in the case of Senegal, where no autonomous institutions were created and rebel combatants could only under exceptional circumstances be integrated into the state's armed forces (art. 3.1). Perhaps unsurprisingly, the agreement failed.

Rebel forces cannot simply be expected to disarm and demobilize unless key grievances are being addressed, even if the armed conflict is relatively minor: DDR, and the extent to which it is achievable, will always depend on the rest of the agreement. Given the lack of legitimacy of the state's armed forces and the need for managing spoilers, it will in most cases be necessary to grant the former rebels some autonomous powers over coercive forces. It is indeed noteworthy that some autonomy over security issues was even included in three non-violent conflicts: in the cases of Tatarstan, Gagauzia and, much more extensively, Montenegro (to which I will return shortly). The precise powers in the former two cases are ambiguous, but security is not simply the prerogative of the central state. In these cases it is significant that we are dealing with territories that were already, de facto, in control of these coercive powers. Legitimacy matters and security sector reform cannot simply be reduced to a question of institutional effectiveness. This is even clearer when we look at the second option: the creation of a more representative army.

More Representative Army

There are also five cases in which an integrated army was envisaged. Three in which demobilized rebel forces were to be integrated into existing armed forces (Mali, Niger and the Philippines) and two in which joint forces, with a shared command, were to be created (Serbia & Montenegro and Sudan). In the case of Mali the agreement refers to 'all combatants' being integrated on an 'individual and voluntary basis' (art. 7A). The agreement also provides for autonomous powers over the police force (art. 15). In Niger the army and the police were similarly to integrate 'demobilized elements' from the Organization of the Armed Resistance (ORA) and generally increase recruitment from the conflict region (art. 17). In the Philippines, the agreement specified that 5,750 combatants from the Moro National Liberation Front (MNLF) were to be integrated into the army and 1,750 into the police force (art. 2.19). All of these agreements thereby ensure more representative coercive forces, at least as far as the forces deployed in the conflict regions are concerned. Initially the former rebel combatants are to serve in separate units, but these units are subsequently to be fully integrated.

Here we are dealing with much more severe conflicts that have posed a significant military threat. In order to address the grievances of the separatist movement, convince them to back an agreement, and address the problem of reintegrating sizeable rebel forces, it is therefore necessary to undertake a reform of the armed forces. An integrated army follows Toft's idea of security sector reforms ensuring a monopoly of force, but it will take time before this is achieved and these three agreements illustrate the problems associated with such a strategy.

In the case of the Philippines, the agreement failed to include the most powerful armed group, the Moro Islamic Liberation Front (MILF), a large number of MNLF combatants changed sides, and violence soon broke out again. One key factor was the ambiguity surrounding the regional security force. The MNLF anticipated that its former combatants would be integrated into the armed forces as a unit and that the autonomous government would control this Special Regional Security Force. The central government and the army however insisted that the former combatants were integrated as individuals and could be deployed anywhere in the country (Martin, 2011, pp. 184–5). The regional security force was never established (International Crisis Group, 2013a, p. 4) and the army and the police continued to be accused of human rights violations in the region (see e.g. Amnesty International, 1997). The lack of autonomous powers over security undermined the legitimacy of the agreement and it also meant that the local leaders were unable to prevent the internal violence; they did not have the capacity to defeat more extreme challengers (Lara Jr & Champain, 2009, p. 11). The reforms in Niger and Mali also faced difficulties and delays. There was still a high level of tension and suspicion, which became clear when a group of integrated rebel combatants in Mali in 1994 murdered their new comrades (Keita, 1998, p. 18). Two years later, however, a significant number of rebel forces had been successfully integrated into the army, national guard and gendarmerie (ibid., pp. 33–4). In the case of Niger, the promised special units of the army were created, but the integration of rebel combatants took a long time, and several factions in the meantime returned to violence. Another problem was that the armed forces were otherwise left unreformed. Mutinies were frequent, as were abuses of power; the army is argued to be ineffective and, despite integration efforts, it still harbours a deep mistrust of the Tuareg people (Jellow, 2013).[37]

Iraq provides an additional example of the importance and problems of creating a representative army, and also underscores the crucial importance of intra-communal dynamics and capacity. The Iraqi army, trained and built by the US, did have a sectarian balance in 2005, but an 'accelerated Shiite-ification of the force began in 2006' and effective Sunni and Kurdish commanders were purged. The emergence of a Shiite-dominated army has undermined the legitimacy of the Iraqi state in the eyes of the Sunni population, and has also affected the willingness and ability of the army to ensure security within the Sunni community: the army was unable and unwilling to fight Islamic State in Sunni-dominated territories (see e.g. Al-Khatteeb, 2015; Simcox & Pregent, 2015).

More generally, the problem with the integration of rebel forces into the army is that unless reforms are also introduced at the command level, then the risk of cheating and of human rights violations and other abuses remains. Such top-level reforms are typically resisted by the centre, whose leaders fear that their powerbase will be undermined. Rebel leaders may therefore be tempted to make any separate military units a permanent feature, which is likely one of the reasons why we have seen the central government hesitant to implement such provisions.

An alternative solution would be to forego integration of rebel forces and instead focus on creating a joint command; thereby still addressing the argued need for a monopoly of force but better responding to rebel fears of being cheated and the need for intra-communal stability. In the case of joint forces, i.e. separate forces with a joint command, rebel forces do not have to fear being 'tricked', that the integration does not fundamentally alter the nature of the military forces and that domination will continue. It could also easily be undone, thereby providing assurance against renewed violence from the other side (see also Walter, 2002). In terms of more selfish motives, it would allow rebel commanders to retain much of their status.

This solution is however only found in two cases: in Serbia & Montenegro and Sudan. These agreements are interim agreements and both sides wanted to retain control of coercive forces until the issue of status was resolved. The objective was therefore not necessarily to ensure a functioning state, but rather to ensure stability until the independence referendum was held. In the case of Sudan, Joint Integrated Units were also to be created. These were to form the core of a fully integrated army, in case southern Sudan voted against independence. However, implementation proved difficult: the joint units existed mostly on paper and their personnel in reality remained under separate commands. As a result of the lack of full deployment of these units, the Sudanese army refused to withdraw from contested territories (Small Arms Survey, 2008; Toft, 2009, p. 146) and the promised 'proportional downsizing' of the two armies never occurred (Verheul, 2011). The joint command was implemented in Serbia & Montenegro and the Supreme Defence Council was one of the only central institutions in which Montenegro cooperated. This cooperation was to ensure that the army was placed under civilian control and nationalist forces inside the military reined in. These were suspected of wanting to influence Montenegrin politics, protect war criminals, and perhaps even support a coup (International Crisis Group, 2005b, p. 5). However, the Montenegrin police, which effectively functioned as a separate army, was also maintained and a monopoly of force was therefore in practice not ensured in either of the two cases.

Separate Coercive Forces

One way of dealing with the commitment problem is, as mentioned above, to maintain separate forces. Such solutions exist to varying degrees in many autonomy arrangements – and can also be the unintended consequence of attempts to create an integrated army. With separate forces both sides retain the ability to defend themselves and are therefore less vulnerable to a resumption of violence, and minorities will be less fearful of a return to majority dominance. This solution can coexist with a monopoly of force, even if the armed movement is essentially allowed to continue to exist. The central government can argue that it formally delegates authority to the now legalized movement. However, retaining separate coercive forces also means retaining the ability to restart the war, and the fear would be that although this may seem necessary in the short run, in order to get the parties to sign an agreement, the situation never becomes stable and the risk of renewed violence always looms. One of the important implications of such an arrangement is that without an effective (central) army presence in the autonomous region, the autonomous forces have to ensure intra-communal security and be able to defeat potential spoilers. This may be an advantage, since it could cause a backlash if the army attempted to police the region, but the risk is that the local forces do not have the necessary capacity.

Separate coercive forces were either maintained or created in the case of Bosnia, Israel–Palestine, Indonesia–Aceh and Papua New Guinea–Bougainville. It was also promised for East Timor if autonomy had been accepted in the referendum, and was the de facto outcome of the Khasavyurt Accord for Chechnya. A clear distinction between separate armies and autonomous powers over the regional security forces will often be difficult to make, although in the latter case a hierarchy between the armed forces will exist, at least on paper. However, the agreements do illustrate that separate armed forces can mean different things, and they do not necessarily spell the end of a unified state.

In the case of Bosnia, no integration of armies was included in the agreement, but a joint command was in fact achieved during its implementation when a defence ministry was created. This was strongly pushed by the international administration, but was ultimately accepted by the local parties and not imposed (Bieber, 2006b). In the other cases, autonomous powers extend to the coercive forces, but the separation is not complete. The agreement for Aceh promises extensive autonomous powers over the territory's coercive forces but there are limitations. For example, the agreement allows for former rebel combatants to seek employment in the 'organic' military forces of Aceh, but they have to do so 'in conformity with national standards' (art. 3.2.7). Moreover, the Indonesian army remains responsible for upholding external defence, and redeployment in Aceh is held out as an option: it is in '*normal* peacetime circumstances' that '*only* organic military forces will be present in Aceh' (art. 4.11, my emphasis). A hierarchy between the armed forces therefore exists in this case and we are not dealing with a complete continuation of the rebel army.

Similar arrangements are found in the interim agreements for Israel–Palestine and Bougainville. A hierarchy of armed forces also exists here, but the emphasis is more clearly than in Aceh on local coercive forces which are to ensure security in the autonomous territories. In the case of Israel–Palestine, both Oslo I and II include the gradual withdrawal of the Israeli military from the West Bank and Gaza and the transfer of responsibility for internal security and public order to a Palestinian police force. Despite, or indeed because of, the interim nature of this agreement there are however restrictions on this autonomy. Firstly, it only applies to Palestinians; the Israeli military remains responsible for the security of Israelis (see e.g. Oslo I, art 8). Secondly, the withdrawal of Israeli military is gradual and it is also incomplete. A number of crucial aspects of the security arrangements are postponed for future talks and Israeli forces are redeployed to specified military locations, not completely withdrawn from Palestinian territory (Oslo II, art. 10.2). Thirdly, Israel military law remained the legal framework for governing the Palestinian territories (Roy, 2002) and a clear hierarchy of coercive forces is therefore maintained. One of the primary objectives of the Oslo Declaration was to ensure internal order (ibid.), but the Palestinian Authority lacked both the capacity and the legitimacy to do so effectively. As Usher (1999, p. 24) argues, each successive crackdown on Hamas, 'chipped away' at Yasser Arafat's support in the territories, and it also showed to the Israeli side that negotiating with, and empowering, the Palestine Liberation Organization (PLO) was not enough. The agreement for Bougainville is another interim agreement, but the interim status in this case points more clearly towards future independence (with a timetable for the independence referendum). This is reflected in the security arrangements. The agreement is brief when it comes to security, but it does contain three important elements: the decommissioning of weapons, under UN supervision; the withdrawal of the Papua New Guinean (PNG) army and mobile police units; and the creation of an autonomous police force in Bougainville (art. 6–8). Bougainville had been plagued by violent factional infighting, but a local police force, completely under the control of the autonomous government, was now to ensure internal security (art. 210–11). The establishment of this police force was to be funded by the national government (art. 229–332), which gave the centre a degree of control, but these powers were not (mis)used and an autonomous coercive force was created. Unusually for a post-conflict situation, the local police force is unarmed! But although some parts of Bougainville remain beyond its control it has, in conjunction with the political processes, managed to ensure a measure of internal stability (Woodbury, 2015, pp. 9–10). The agreement makes no mention of the creation of integrated armed forces, even if the PNG army continues to be responsible for defence and formally recruits throughout the entire territory (art. 60–1). The objective of these security provisions is to separate the forces, stop the fighting and ensure the internal security of Bougainville.

Legitimacy and Intra-Communal Security

In order to provide stability, peace agreements will need to enjoy a level of legitimacy, in the sense of support from key actors and groups. This can be narrow at first, limited to the signatories of the agreement, but will need to be broadened if the agreement is to prove sustainable.[38] However, following violent conflicts which often include widespread human rights violations, such legitimacy may require a degree of separation and can therefore only be achieved at the expense of effectiveness. In many cases, the state's coercive forces must, as Hartzell and Hoddie argue (2007, p. 32), be neutralized or balanced. The compromises needed to reach an agreement will therefore often be at odds with the much-cited need for strong security institutions and a monopoly of force.

Such solutions are arguably better able to address the fears and grievances of the weaker party. They can help diminish the commitment problem faced by the separatist forces and the risk of a deliberate return to violence should therefore be reduced. For the central government and army the attraction would be that it does not require a root-and-branch reform of the armed forces. Such solutions, if properly implemented, are moreover better able to address the risk of spoiler violence.[39] Stability does not simply depend on maintaining peace between the agreement signatories, but the effect of a peace agreement on security *within* communities is often overlooked in the literature. If there is a lack of intra-communal security, the whole agreement is under threat. The leaders who signed the agreement risk being replaced by more extreme rivals and instability in the autonomous region signals to the opposing side that peace is not working; it is not bringing security. The failure of the PA to control Hamas and the continued attacks on Israel, for example, led to a marked reluctance to implement the rest of the peace agreement (Perlmutter, 1995, pp. 59–60).

Strengthening the armed forces and relying on them to ensure stability in the autonomous region will in many conflicts not be a realistic option. The rebel forces will not accept a security framework that provides them with no reassurances, the army will not be seen as legitimate, and any attempt to defeat spoilers in the region would risk provoking a backlash. Coercive forces under the control of the autonomous region may be in a better position to ensure intra-communal stability, but this requires them to have enough resources – which will often be anathema to the central government – and their success also depends on the overall legitimacy of the agreement. The inability of the Mindanao autonomous government and the PA to defeat more extreme challengers owed a lot, respectively, to a lack of resources and devolution of powers, and the lack of a contiguous territory. But the failure of the agreements to address key grievances and the resulting lack of popular legitimacy also mattered. These issues also impact on the process of DDR – the extent to which it is needed and its success – and it affects the degree to which *human* security can be prioritized. While the granting of autonomous coercive powers to rebel forces may solve some problems, it risks creating others.

Disarmament, Demobilization and Reintegration (DDR)

The extent to which DDR is needed depends significantly on the security strategy adopted: are separate armies maintained, will former rebels be integrated into the army, etc.? DDR and SSR are consequently closely linked. Other authors have argued that they serve the same overall objective and should consequently be coordinated (Civic & Miklaucic, 2011, p. xxii), but the interaction goes further than that. The strategy for SSR creates a framework for the DDR programme and the success of this programme significantly affects the implementation of the SSR strategy. In the case of Sudan, separate armies were maintained and the DDR process was consequently very limited and only covered 'other armed groups' that were to be incorporated or reintegrated into either side's 'armed forces, other organized forces, the civil service and civil societal institutions' (Annex 1, art. 11.1). The SPLA was legalized by the agreement and therefore not covered by DDR, which typically refers to illegal forces. The agreement did include the voluntary demobilization of child soldiers as well as elderly and disabled combatants, but these were described as 'nonessentials' (Verheul, 2011, p. 194). A lack of DDR does therefore not necessarily result in the collapse of an agreement; it may in fact be a precondition for its implementation, depending on the type of security forces agreed upon.

Implementing any DDR programmes will be associated with significant challenges including lack of details in the peace agreement, unrealistic timetables, local mistrust and fears and weak institutions

(Spear, 2002). But just like other security issues, the severity of such depends on the rest of the agreement: does it address key grievances and include ways of minimizing fears and vulnerabilities? The success is moreover affected by the involvement of third parties who can supply resources and provide much-needed monitoring and verification. Bosnia demonstrates the effect of both. The Dayton Agreement only includes disarmament of civilians and the withdrawal of foreign forces. Soldiers and heavy weapons are to withdraw to barracks but will only be demobilized if they 'cannot be accommodated in cantonment/barracks areas' (Annex 1-A, art. 5b). The presence of NATO forces however effectively neutralized the armed forces (Walter, 2002), and it is indeed remarkable that a degree of DDR happened spontaneously (Knight & Özerdem, 2004) and a joint command of the armed forces was created in the implementation phase. However to the international presence must be added the power-sharing institutions, which enabled the conflict parties, in particular the Bosnian Serbs, to retain control. The Ohrid Agreement for Macedonia is, as a number of other agreements, very brief when it comes to the details of the DDR process (or DD process in this case). It merely refers to the 'complete voluntary disarmament of the ethnic Albanian armed groups and their complete voluntary disbandment' (art. 2). However, the presence of NATO forces and the general low level of violence meant that security issues were less pressing, and although separate coercive forces are not intended, police reform is included and the whole agreement is based on a framework of (informal) power-sharing institutions, which at least provides a political guarantee against cheating. In the case of Northern Ireland, the Belfast Agreement set up an Independent International Commission on Decommissioning (Strand 3, Decommissioning) but all the crucial decisions were left for later. However, there was acceptance on both sides that decommissioning had to happen; the disagreement related to the timing and verification. The deferral of these issues appears to have been made possible by the existence of strong power-sharing institutions and the willingness of both sides to leave the decision to an independent international commission. To this must be added the role of the British Government: Tony Blair managed to avoid a last-minute Unionist walkout with the help of a hastily written letter that guaranteed that Sinn Fein would be excluded from the power-sharing government should the IRA not decommission (Powell, 2008). Much more recently, the involvement of Westminster allowed the Unionist parties to effect a 'controlled collapse' of the power-sharing institutions when decommissioning once again became an issue.[40]

A failure to include DDR or a lack of detail can, on the other hand, prove detrimental if the overall agreement is weak, and no third party is involved in its implementation. The agreement for Mindanao included the integration of a specified number of former MNLF combatants into the Philippine armed forces (art. 2.19), but there were otherwise no provisions for DDR. The text is moreover ambiguous and does not for example specify that the 'MNLF elements' had to be active combatants. The MNLF refused to dismantle its 'revolutionary organization' and become a political movement: it did not trust the Philippine Government and wanted to wait and see how, and if, the agreement was implemented. As a result, the integrated MNLF individuals tended to be either older combatants or relatives of fighters (Martin, 2011, pp. 184–5). The lack of DDR proved detrimental as it meant that the combatants who defected and joined the anti-agreement MILF still had their weapons, which strengthened the spoiler (International Crisis Group, 2013a). Importantly, their decision to oppose the agreement appears to have been caused in large part by dissatisfaction with its very ambiguous, and largely unimplemented, autonomy provisions (International Crisis Group, 2013a).

The risk presented by 'cheating' – for example by rebel forces keeping hold of some weapons – is similarly contingent on the strength of the political agreement. Spear (2002, pp. 156–7) describes how in the case of Mozambique, which had a strong agreement, the UN special representative was quoted as saying: 'I know very well that they will give us old and obsolete material … I don't care. What I do is create the political situation in which the use of guns is not the question. So they stay where they are.' However, in the case of Angola, which did not have a strong agreement, such 'cheating' by UNITA had disastrous consequences and was one of the factors in the collapse of the agreement and the renewed outbreak of war (ibid.). Similarly, in the case of Bougainville, the weapons disposal is argued to have been incomplete, but international observers verified the process thereby allowing for the next stage of the implementation process to proceed (Woodbury, 2015, p. 10). This was accepted by the central governments. As Knight and Özerdem (2004, p. 503) point out, a total collection and disposal of weapons is rarely ensured by the process and its real importance lies at the symbolic level. A recent report into paramilitary activities in Northern Ireland found that the Provisional IRA still exists and still has access to some weapons, but it also concluded that the 'army council' now has a 'wholly political focus'. This was enough to convince members of the Democratic Unionist Party (DUP), who had resigned from the power-sharing executive over the continued activities of the IRA, to return to office (BBC News, 2015c; McDonald, 2015a). A solid agreement can build trust and reduce the severity of the commitment problem, even if the other side still retains (non-legal) coercive capacity.

Finally, there is the effect of DDR on intra-communal security. DDR is clearly needed if more than one (significant) rebel group exists and not all are to form the core of the, now legalized, autonomous forces, Otherwise, the autonomous government and its coercive forces risk facing a direct challenge. But some process of DDR is needed even if these groups agree to support the agreement, in order to avoid the potential instability caused by a high number of unemployed but still armed combatants who could add strength to new spoilers. In southern Sudan the agreed DDR process for 'other armed groups' was highly significant for stability in the region and therefore for the stability of the overall agreement. The timeframe of one year set out in the agreement was seen as far too optimistic and a south–south war was widely predicted (Young, 2013, p. 14). DDR only became possible when the SPLA and the South Sudan Defence Force (SSDF) signed the Juba Declaration in 2006, and agreed to 'immediately integrate their two forces to form one unified, non-partisan Army under the name of SPLA'.[41] Tensions later arose due to poor implementation and resistance from parts of the SSDF (ibid., p. 121) but it was enough to ensure stability in the short-term. Intra-communal divisions, even latent ones, should ideally be considered when designing a DDR programme, otherwise it can significantly reduce its effectiveness. The split in the Free Aceh Movement (GAM) following the signing of the Memorandum of Understanding, for example, meant that a significant number of former combatants were excluded from reintegration benefits which were for GAM fighters only (Lara Jr & Champain, 2009). Reintegration is in several of the cases omitted from the process and combatants are therefore supposed to demilitarize and demobilize without being provided with any specific incentives or assistance. The agreements for Eastern Slavonia, Macedonia, Papua New Guinea–Bougainville, Senegal and Northern Ireland included no provisions for reintegration. In other cases, the reintegration programme and the incentives provided are very vague. Integration into the armed forces is, for example, the only incentive provided in the case of Mali.

An agreement that does not require the rebel army to disarm and demobilize, or does not properly reintegrate combatants, can still be sustainable. However, such stability may come at the expense of 'human security', i.e. the security of individuals and, more broadly, the extent to which their rights are protected.

Possible Trade-Off with Human Security

Authors who stress the need for human security, as opposed to merely state security, argue that in order to ensure a sustainable peace, individual security should be prioritized and not just in the sense of physical security. There must be a space for reconciliation and human rights (Kaldor, 2007b). The assumption in the 'security first' literature appears to be that human security will follow from the creation of macro-security. But this is by no means guaranteed if stability is ensured either by strengthening the central army or by leaving security in the autonomous region to the former rebel forces. If the army is to ensure security, then significant reforms would be needed. However, one thing that stands out from the analysed agreements is the lack of security sector reforms at the central level. This is much more commonplace in agreements that do not include provisions for territorial autonomy; these almost always include fairly detailed reforms of the armed forces. Liberia's 2003 Accra Peace Agreement and the 1992 General Peace Agreement for Mozambique even disbanded the army, and specified that a new army was to be created out of the former fighting forces (see also McFate, 2011). One of the reasons the central government often sees autonomy as an attractive solution is that it allows the central institutions to remain largely unreformed. However human security can also be undermined if local security is in the hands of the autonomous authorities; either if they do not have sufficient capacity, in which case violence and instability are likely to continue, or if such capacity is built on a lack of rights and freedoms for the inhabitants. The literature on rebel governance has demonstrated that rebel-held territories are not *terra nullis*; forms of governance may be found and these sometimes include citizens' participation (see e.g. Arjona et al., 2015; Mampilly, 2011). However, the 'men with the guns' will tend to play a dominant role and are likely to continue to do so in the post-settlement period, if the rebel forces are merely legalized. The risk is that a police state (within-a-state) is essentially created. It has been argued that the Oslo Declaration for Israel–Palestine was only about security, in a narrow sense, not about peace: the main objective was for the Palestinian Authority to deal with the threat posed by Hamas (Roy, 2002). However, they lacked both the capacity and legitimacy to ensure internal security. As Perlmutter (1995, p. 65), put it, 'The West Bank cannot be run by the Palestinian police, an estimated 15,000, and Arafat's security services.' This may be an extreme case, but a lack of security sector reform and the difficulty of ensuring a transition from an armed movement to an effective force under civilian control are common features. Moreover, as will be further discussed in the following chapters, these agreements frequently include significant compromises when it comes to individual rights and the rights of 'Others'. In the longer-term this risks undermining the legitimacy of the agreement, which means that internal security will be more difficult to ensure and the overall stability of the agreement is therefore in danger.

Conclusion: Security, But Not Necessarily as We Know It

Lack of trust is a key obstacle when it comes to security. The signatories to the peace will not necessarily trust each other to abandon violence for good, or they may fear that more hardline elements gain the upper hand and reignite the war. This chapter has not diminished such concerns, but it has suggested that the resulting commitment problem does not mean that a security guarantee from a third party is a necessary condition for a successful peace agreement – except possibly in the most severe conflicts, if the joint state is to be maintained. In other conflicts, the commitment problem can be addressed through various forms of phased approaches and conditionality, and by granting autonomous powers to the weaker party. Third party involvement will help this process, and may indeed be necessary in some conflicts, but it does always need to be 'robust' or even armed.

This strategy for addressing the commitment problem, and more generally the fears and grievances underlying the conflict, has implications for the security sector reforms that are possible. Conflict resolution cannot simply be regarded as state-building, at least not based on a 'standard model'. The creation of a monopoly of force, in the sense of strengthening the army, is often not realistic and pursuing it can lead to failure. Instead what we see are a range of often messy security strategies, including joint commands, slow integration of armed forces, and autonomous powers over regional forces. This may not be ideal, but it is not an ideal situation. Not only effectiveness matters, we need to consider legitimacy as well, and a strengthened army is unlikely to prove acceptable. What is often needed instead is a form of decentralized state-building; the autonomous authorities have to be able to address the risk of spoiler violence within their own community. This however comes with two possible complications. Firstly, a lack of capacity, since central governments are fearful of ensuring sufficient resources for the autonomous territories and the former rebel forces may be ill-equipped for such a task. Secondly, if they are able to ensure internal order, the risk is that they do so at the expense of human security; at the expense of the rights and freedoms of their inhabitants, especially those that do not belong to the dominant ethnic groups in the region. We seldom find intra-communal – let alone intra-regional – consensus on the meaning of legitimate institutions, and a very narrow agreement could struggle to ensure long-term stability. These issues will be further addressed in the following chapters.

─ 3 ─

POWER

Who governs; who will enjoy political power after the settlement and who will find themselves excluded? This routinely proves a significant stumbling block during negotiations and will also impact on the longer-term sustainability of the deal. Peace agreements are compromises, even if the parties do not necessarily negotiate from equal strength, and the sharing of political power would seem to be the obvious outcome. Bieber and Keil argue that 'there seems to be no alternative to some form of power-sharing arrangements in post-ethnic conflict societies' (2009, p. 338). Such an arrangement addresses elite interests in power and prestige and also appears to ensure a more inclusive form of government, which is often a key underlying demand in intra-state conflicts.

Power-sharing may be hard to escape, but the specific arrangements vary significantly, both in degree and form. In non-territorial conflicts, a transitional power-sharing government seems to have become the dominant settlement model. This arrangement is to create the conditions for free and fair elections, including the building of effective institutions (Gutteri & Piombo, 2007). We have for example seen this in settlements signed in Nepal (2006) and Burundi (2000), and it also forms the framework of the ongoing attempts to find a solution to the Syrian war.[42] However, power can be shared in different ways, and both the conflict context and the rest of the agreement impact on the specific power-sharing model that is acceptable to the conflict parties. The two previous chapters demonstrated that the large majority of settlements in separatist conflicts include provisions for territorial power-sharing (autonomy), and a considerable number also guarantee a degree of military power-sharing. Authors have pointed to the need for combining territorial autonomy with power-sharing at the centre if it is to ensure stability (Cederman et al., 2015; Wolff, 2009), but although the leaders of separatist movements will often insist on a guaranteed share in political power at the centre, they may accept – or even prefer – for their power to remain localized. Moreover, such territorial power-sharing is likely to be the preferred option of the central government as it avoids significant reforms at the centre.

Power-sharing is by no means a panacea. It will often meet significant local resistance; it is usually ethnically-defined, cumbersome and rigid, and may become unworkable. There are several examples of failed power-sharing arrangements, but none more catastrophic than the collapse of the power-sharing Arusha Accord which preceded the Rwandan genocide. Power-sharing was pushed by the international mediators, but it was rejected by Hutu hardliners who chose extreme violence to make sure that it was never realized (Kuperman, 2000). Both the specific design of the power-sharing arrangement and the nature of intra-communal power struggles therefore matter.

This chapter first introduces the most well-known model of power-sharing, Lijphart's consociational democracy. This form of power-sharing is found in some of the analysed agreements, but political power-sharing is much less prevalent than we might have expected. In order to explain this we need to view peace agreements as a package: territorial and military autonomy will sometimes be an acceptable substitute for (political) power-sharing. However, such a substitution does impact on the resulting peace. The chapter then discusses the criticism of the consociational approach, possible ways of addressing these shortcomings, the potential of hybrid power-sharing models, and the effect of third party involvement. The findings support key conclusions from previous chapters. Political power-sharing is by no means included in all separatist agreements, but tends to be included in the more violent cases *unless* the emphasis is on separation. It is possible to ameliorate some of the problems associated with power-sharing – a degree of flexibility can for example be provided by third party involvement – but the system will always retain some rigidity. This impacts on its effectiveness and long-term sustainability, but power-sharing is in many cases the best system that can be hoped for. Finally, the success of power-sharing arrangements is strongly affected by, and in turns affects, intra-communal dynamics and intra-communal capacity.

Consociational Democracy

Power-sharing is not a uniform model; in fact, it comes in a variety of forms, ranging from approaches that appear premised on the belief that 'good fences, make good neighbours', and emphasize strong group protections and separation, to approaches that stress the need for cross-ethnic appeals and reduced importance of identities (Caspersen, 2004; Sisk, 1996). However, the dominant model, and the only one found in the analysed agreements, is Lijphart's consociational approach.

Lijphart argues that the accommodation of ethnic differences can be achieved through elite cooperation in institutions that explicitly recognize the ethnic divisions and make them the basis of rules for decision-making, territorial division of power and public policies. The consociational model assumes the stability and primacy of ethnic groups; this is a reality that cannot simply be wished away. The objective of the model is to avoid majority domination, and this is ensured by four institutional elements (see e.g. Lijphart, 1977):

1. A power-sharing government; a so-called grand coalition with representatives from all main groups.[43]
2. Minority (/group) veto on issues that can infringe on national interests.
3. Proportionality (or parity) in the electoral system and in the civil service.
4. Ethnic autonomy (territorial or non-territorial).

In later formulations, Lijphart (2004) has described the mutual veto and proportionality as secondary characteristics, but this does not fundamentally alter a system that is intended to provide solid guarantees for minorities and explicitly recognizes ethnic groups and their legitimacy. Another possible variation relates to the degree of ethnic autonomy included, which may amount to little more than the maintenance of pre-existing arrangements (Tonge, 2014, p. 40). Security is not afforded much importance in the consociational literature (McGarry & O'Leary, 2008, p. 383), but provisions related to both territory and security have the ability to affect the functioning of the consociational institutions, as will be further discussed below.

Proponents would argue that the consociational approach addresses many of the demands of the parties to a separatist war: it guarantees them a share in power, it recognizes the legitimacy of ethnic demands, and it accommodates claims to self-determination. The consociational model is not intended to reduce the importance of ethnic identities – these may in fact be strengthened – but it addresses fears of being outvoted and therefore, it is argued, temptations to take up arms (see e.g. Lijphart, 1977; O'Leary, 2013a).

Consociational Solutions to Separatist Conflicts

Only five of the agreements can be described as consociational: the agreements signed in Bosnia, Serbia & Montenegro, Sudan, Northern Ireland and Macedonia. Although these agreements share key consociational characteristics, they differ significantly, especially when it comes to the degree of territorial autonomy included and whether the agreement is intended to be permanent. These differences reflect variations in the conflict context, including the intensity of the conflict and the depth of divisions; the relative bargaining power of the groups; the preferences of third actors and the degree of their involvement (see also Bieber, 2013).

Bosnia's post-war structure has been described as a prototypical consociational system (Belloni, 2007, p. 3). The Dayton Peace Agreement created a system that is highly complex, with several layers of power-sharing, and extremely decentralized with few powers reserved for the central government. The consociational institutions include, firstly, the joint state institutions such as the Presidency, the Council of Ministers and the Parliament. In these institutions we find the classic consociational features of grand coalitions, minority veto and parity of representation. Ethnic autonomy is, moreover, also a defining feature. The country's two entities were constituted as ethnically-defined units: Republika Srpska as a Serb unit and the Federation of Bosnia and Herzegovina as a Bosniak–Croat unit. Within the bi-national Federation a complex system of power-sharing exists with minority veto, parity of representation and ethnic autonomy. The veto provisions at the central level combined with the high degree of decentralization meant that power gravitated towards the more majoritarian, homogeneous institutions in the entities, the ten cantons that make up the Federation, or even the municipalities (Caspersen, 2004, p. 573). Hayden characterized the central government as a 'customs union with a foreign ministry' (2005, p. 243), while the first head of the international civilian administration, Carl Bildt, described Bosnia as 'the most decentralized state in the world' (quoted in Belloni, 2007, p. 44).

The Belgrade Agreement for Serbia & Montenegro was however to create an even more decentralized consociational structure. Serbia

& Montenegro was defined as a union of two member-states and the agreement even included provisions for rotating seats in international organizations. Serbia and Montenegro were also to be represented equally in the executive; no member state could be outvoted in the assembly and representatives from Montenegro were to be over-represented. The agreement is actually weak on details,[44] but the central core is clear: this is a union of two states of equal standing. Cooperation between the two entities is intended to be minimal and, despite the creation of a Supreme Defence Council and the denial of Montenegro's request for separate representation in international organizations (Van Meurs, 2003), it comes closer to a confederation than a federation. The union is moreover only an interim agreement: either side can, as mentioned in chapter 1, call a referendum on inde-pendence after a period of three years.

The Comprehensive Peace Agreement for Sudan also sets out an interim consociational agreement with extensive territorial auton-omy. In the interim period, Sudan was to be ruled by a form of collective presidency consisting of a president and two vice-presidents, with the President representing the North and the First Vice-President the South. A Government of National Unity was to be appointed by the President, in consultation with the First Vice-President, 'reflecting the need for inclusiveness, the promotion of national unity, and the defense of national sovereignty' (Ch. 2, art. 2.5.1). Limited veto rights are granted to the First Vice-President, for example over the declaration of war or a state of emergency. Double majority provisions also exist in the legislature for issues concern-ing the interests of the states as well as constitutional amendments. However, the provisions are ambiguous and the implementation of the agreement made it clear that the Sudanese People's Liberation Movement (SPLM) was the weaker party in the power-sharing arrangement (see e.g. Rolandsen, 2011, pp. 559–60; Sriram, 2008, pp. 137, 140). Territorial autonomy is ensured by granting southern Sudan extensive powers, including a separate army. A limited level of local power-sharing is provided for in the South, with 15 per cent of the seats in the legislature reserved for 'other Southern political forces', until the holding of elections (art. 3.5). The agreement also includes limited provisions for personal or non-territorial autonomy: for non-Muslims in Khartoum and for Muslims in the South (Ch. 2, art. 2.4.6 and art. 6.4). Finally, the agreement promises proportion-ality in the civil service.

These three agreements combine extensive political, territorial and military power-sharing and the result is a 'minimalist' central state (see Bieber, 2013). This very much represents the extreme end of the power-sharing spectrum. The remaining two agreements however demonstrate that political power-sharing does not have to have a strong territorial dimension nor does it have to include military power-sharing.

The consociational institutions in Northern Ireland's Belfast Agreement are centred on a power-sharing executive, consisting of a First Minister and a Deputy First Minister and up to ten Ministers. The First Minister and Deputy First Minister are elected by the Assembly, voting on a cross-community basis, which in effect means that the First Minister is a Unionist and the Deputy a Nationalist, while the rest of the cabinet seats are allocated in proportion to party strength. Other key decisions in the legislature are also to be taken on a cross-community basis (Strand 1, art. 5, 15, 16). The agreement moreover ensures a degree of non-territorial autonomy, related to language rights, education and the media (Strand 3, Economic, Social and Cultural Issues, art. 3–4). This is essentially a continuation of pre-agreement arrangements (Tonge, 2014, p. 40). The Belfast Agreement also includes a crucial trans-border framework in Strands 2 and 3. Although the agreement does not include territorial autonomy, primarily due to the lack of geographic concentration of the two communities, it does therefore have an important territorial dimension (see McGarry & O'Leary, 2006a).

The Ohrid Agreement for Macedonia is the least consociational of the five agreements. This agreement includes provisions for double majorities in the case of the Law on Local Self-Government, laws directly influencing minority interests and certain constitutional amendments. These must have the support of 'a majority of the Representatives claiming to belong to the communities not in the majority in the population of Macedonia' (art 5.1). This ensures a limited minority veto. The agreement increases the powers of local government and 'municipal boundaries will be revised within one year of the completion of a new census' (art. 3.2), thereby creating more homogeneous units. This can therefore be seen as territorial autonomy, albeit without legislative powers (see Bieber, 2013). Non-territorial autonomy is moreover ensured through minority rights in the fields of culture, language and education (Annex C, art. 6). Finally, proportionality and non-discrimination in the civil service and especially in the police are to be prioritized (art. 4). What is missing from this agreement is a grand coalition. However, power-sharing executives including both ethnic Macedonian and Albanian parties have been the norm since 1991. This is a majoritarian government and the

Albanian representatives are selected by the Macedonian-dominated government (Tonge, 2014, p. 42), but it nevertheless approximates a consociational settlement.

Although there was an element of international pressure in all of these cases, the insistence on a consociational agreement very much came from the conflict parties themselves. Bieber argues that 'the weak central institutions and extensive group protection mechanisms' in Bosnia's Dayton Agreement 'reflect the involvement of the wartime parties' (2013, p. 314). Power-sharing institutions tend to be demanded by conflict parties that fear being outvoted, either now or in the future. But the sharing of political power at the centre is not always demanded and not always offered. Whereas a transitional power-sharing government is the preferred remedy in non-territorial conflicts, most of the agreements analysed in this book do not include political power-sharing. What they do include is territorial, and in some cases, military power-sharing (see table 3.1). Specific conditions are required, however, for such solutions to be feasible, and this affects the nature of the peace that follows.

Table 3.1. Forms of Power-Sharing in Peace Agreements

Consociational agreement (Political power-sharing)	Bosnia
	Macedonia
	Serbia & Montenegro
	Sudan
	UK–Northern Ireland
Only territorial and (some) military power-sharing	Indonesia–Aceh
	Israel–Palestine
	PNG–Bougainville*
	Philippines–Mindanao*
	(Indonesia–East Timor)
	(Russia–Chechnya)
Only territorial power-sharing	Bangladesh–Chittagong Hill Tracts*
	India–Bodoland
	Mali
	Moldova–Gaugazia*
	Niger
	Russia–Tatarstan
	Ukraine–Crimea
No power-sharing	Croatia– Eastern Slavonia
	Senegal–Casamance

*Limited guaranteed representation in central bodies.

When Political Power-Sharing is not Needed, or not Wanted

In some separatist conflicts, political power-sharing is not needed; or rather autonomy is all that the parties can agree on. One of the biggest obstacles to a full-blown power-sharing agreement will be the resistance of the majority group to share power. As Horowitz (2002) has argued, a majority group will be very reluctant to accept to share power when they could rule on their own in a majoritarian system. Majority acceptance of political power-sharing has been argued therefore to depend on the existence of 'appropriate incentives' (Anderson, 2013, p. 365). The agreements for Macedonia, Northern Ireland, Serbia & Montenegro and Sudan were all signed by representatives of majority groups, and these cases demonstrate that such incentives can come in a multitude of forms, including fear of losing majority status in the future (Northern Ireland), international pressure, and an attempt to preserve territorial integrity (Sudan).

Nevertheless, there is little doubt that majority groups would prefer not to share power, and autonomy presents an attractive alternative. It allows the separatist group self-determination, but without requiring the majority to 'cede as much decision-making power at the centre' (O'Leary, 2013b, p. 392). But when is autonomy an acceptable substitute for the separatist group? One condition is that the community must be geographically concentrated. Although it is possible to define autonomy in non-territorial terms, it is exceedingly difficult to imbue this with the kind of state-like characteristics that is possible with territorial autonomy. Even if it has a territorial basis, autonomy on its own still does not provide the same safeguards as a fully-fledged consociational system. Some autonomy arrangements are guaranteed by the constitution, and it would not be possible to change without the consent of the autonomous regions. This is for example the case in Moldova–Gagauzia and PNG–Bougainville. In those cases, we could argue that we are dealing with limited political power-sharing; enough to protect a level of self-government. However, the level of Gaugaz autonomy guaranteed by the Moldovan Constitution is less extensive than what is provided for in the Law on the Special Legal Status of Gagauzia. The widespread use of ambiguity in peace agreements limits the use of constitutional guarantees, and it is noticeable that constitutionally-protected autonomy is primarily found in agreements that also include political power-sharing, such as in the case of Bosnia, Sudan and Macedonia.

In some cases we also find limited guaranteed representation at the central level; not enough to provide for veto rights or an actual share in power, but enough to ensure that interests are heard. In the case of Bodoland, this is primarily done through the establishment of consultation mechanisms, and the Bougainville Government can also demand to be represented in any international negotiations that could affect its constitutional status and powers (Wolff, 2009, p. 39). The Government of Bangladesh is to establish a ministry on Chittagong Hill Tracts Affairs and appoint a Minister 'from among the tribals' (art. 19), while the Governor of Gagauzia 'shall be appointed as a member of the Government of the Republic of Moldova' (art. 14.4). The Philippine Government similarly promises that at least one member of cabinet and one official in each government department and constitutional bodies shall be from Mindanao. These appointments are to be made on the recommendation of the Head of the Autonomous Government. In addition, the Head of the Autonomous Government is to participate as ex-officio member of the National Security Council on all matters concerning the autonomous region (art. 65–6), and the region shall also be guaranteed a seat in Congress (art. 68). However, the implementation of these commitments in 2001 stipulated that the autonomous region should only be represented 'as far as practicable' and Tuminez (2007, p. 82) argues that 'Moro representation in the central political bodies remained extremely weak'.[45] Such representation therefore offers only very limited protection against domination. A more powerful way to protect autonomy arrangements is to allow the region its own coercive forces, i.e. military power-sharing. This introduces a de facto veto, even without a formal one in the central institutions.

Wolff (2009) argues that whether power-sharing at the centre is included in settlements depends on the importance of the separatist region to the centre. But this is only one of the factors of importance. An analysis of the peace agreements points to two different conflict contexts leading to autonomy without power-sharing at the centre:

1. *Agreements with a focus on separation.* The breakaway regions are focused on independence and want as few ties as possible to the centre. This includes Israel–Palestine, East Timor (if the referendum had not ended in independence) and Bougainville. As O'Leary (2013a) has argued, territorial pluralism can be seen as the end of the power-sharing spectrum; what we get are de facto independent entities. In these cases, the centre is also happy not to share power; it has either accepted the option of independence – although not necessarily the specific territory to which this

applies – or it is worried that a power-sharing system would threaten the existing political system. The latter view is especially likely where the breakaway territory is small, if the state is unitary, or based on a homogeneous identity.

2. *Conflicts in which the separatist movement has limited bargaining power.* The breakaway region is relatively small and the conflict does not threaten the state as a whole and/or the separatist group has recently been weakened, such as in the case of the Chittagong Hill Tracts or Aceh. Moreover, the centre is insistent on maintaining a majoritarian and unitary structure for the central state. In the more intense conflicts this includes some autonomy over the coercive forces, but this does not extend to separate armies. It therefore grants some protection against majority domination, but does not give an effective veto.

The fact that such agreements are adopted does not guarantee, of course, that they will work and some of these arrangements have experienced significant problems, many of which I would argue are linked to a lack of power-sharing. Firstly, the autonomous powers have, as discussed in the previous chapters, often been highly ambiguous for example regarding the coercive forces. Combined with the lack of political power-sharing, this has left the central government with considerable power when it comes to implementing the agreement and minority groups have frequently complained that core aspects have been left unimplemented. We have for example seen this in Niger and in the Philippines–Mindanao. Similarly, in the case of Crimea, one of the grievances that helped fuel the renewed outbreak of conflict was the gradual erosion of the region's already limited autonomy (Sasse, 2014). Secondly, the absence of local power-sharing has in a number of cases led to tensions. This will be further discussed in the following chapter.

While political power-sharing is therefore not a necessary condition for successful peace agreements, it would appear that some form of power-sharing – territorial or military – is needed in separatist conflicts, if the state is to be maintained. Without political power-sharing, the stability of territorial autonomy seems to depend on fairly moderate divisions and a degree of trust between the parties. The centre has to refrain from eroding the autonomous powers granted, or the separatist forces must be unable to remobilize. The lack of complex power-sharing also affects the quality of peace within the autonomous region. Territorial autonomy without central or local power-sharing therefore comes with significant limitations and will only be acceptable to the conflict parties under certain circumstances. The consociational approach however also has its share of detractors and its empirical record is mixed.

Limitations of Consociational Power-Sharing

The consociational system has been criticized for its 'uncritical acceptance of the primacy and permanency of ethnicity' and for entrenching divisions that would otherwise be more fluid (Taylor, 1992, p. 2). It has been argued to simply freeze the conflict, to provide a 'temporary lull' (Norris, 2005, p. 2). The resulting risk of breakdown is increased by its tendency to produce deadlock (Brass, 1991, p. 10; Reynolds, 2000, pp. 168–9): the need for consensus means that it is only a contentious issue away from complete immobility and is therefore 'inherently unstable' (Oberschall & Palmer, 2005, p. 80). A consociational system only works as long as the elites are prepared to compromise, but such willingness to moderate may be in short supply, especially if the elites do not agree on the legitimacy of the state. Even if the elites do want to compromise, critics argue that they may not be able to, since they are likely to face outbidding from within their own community, and be accused of selling out (Horowitz, 1985). A consociational agreement is therefore unlikely to last.

Proponents of the consociational approach would counter that the model has evolved over the years and many of the weaknesses of traditional consociational theory have been addressed (see e.g. McGarry & O'Leary, 2006a; O'Leary, 2013a; Wolff, 2009). Few proponents of consociational democracy would in any case argue that this is a perfect system of governance, or even just a good one. Many would agree that consociational democracy tends to be cumbersome and expensive, but would counter that it is often the best possible outcome; the alternative in case of deep divisions is not a 'normal' majoritarian system but the continuation of violence. O'Leary (2013a, p. 15) reminds us that power-sharing should be considered 'in the light of possible alternatives'.

Roeder's alternative approach, which he terms 'power dividing', is a majoritarian model which empowers 'multiple majorities, each construing the public interests somewhat differently, in separate, independent organs of government'. It ensures the right of ethnic and other groups 'through universalistic, individual liberties' (2005, p. 52). This would make for a more effective system, but it is hard to see why a minority group fearing majority domination would ever accept such a system – since presumably the majority group would constitute the majority in each of the 'multiple majorities' that are meant to balance one another. In separatist conflicts, groups are already far too mobilized and divisions too deep for such a system to offer a realistic solution. We may in other words have to accept a less than effective system in order to get a peace agreement. But is it possible to ensure that it does not become so ineffective that it breaks down and war breaks out anew? Is it possible to make consociational democracy less rigid, less prone to deadlock and entrenched ethnic identities?

Five Consociational Experiences

None of the five consociational agreements outlined above has collapsed and renewed separatist violence has largely been avoided. This is quite an achievement considering the bloody and very protracted nature of some of these conflicts. However, the central institutions have generally been weaker than intended. In Bosnia and Northern Ireland, we have seen prolonged periods of deadlock and resulting external intervention, while Montenegro and South Sudan chose to exit the system and become independent. Finally, the agreements have been accused of entrenching the ethnic divide and in at least one of the cases, Macedonia, we have seen a resurgence of majority ethno-nationalism (Holleran, 2014). There are significant differences however between the content of the agreements and these institutional differences have affected the functioning of the consociational approaches and the extent to which it has been possible to address the problems raised by the critics.

One of the most important criticisms of consociational democracy is that it freezes and *entrenches* ethnic identities. However, the proponents of 'liberal consociationalism' argue that this is not an inherent problem. This approach, primarily associated with McGarry and O'Leary, holds that consociational structures can be based on self-determination rather than predetermination (see e.g. McGarry & O'Leary, 2006b, pp. 270–6).[46] Instead of being predetermined by the peace agreement or constitution, the groups represented in the power-sharing institutions are based on electoral success. The Belfast Agreement is the clearest example of liberal consociationalism. Instead of using ethnic quotas for the allocation of cabinet seats, as seen for example in the Bosnian Presidency, these are allocated according to party strength. The St Andrews Agreement from 2006 extended this principle to the election of the First and Deputy

First Minister, with the largest party nominating the former and the second largest party the latter (McEvoy, 2013, p. 268). The Ohrid Agreement similarly goes out of its way to avoid the naming of the Albanian minority, referring instead to 'Representatives claiming to belong to the communities not in the majority in the population of Macedonia'.

Despite these non-ethnic formulations, the conflict parties will be fully aware who will end up holding, and sharing, power as a consequence. It could therefore be argued that liberal consociationalism is purely cosmetic, that it has little actual impact on the functioning of the system. Moreover, it is almost impossible to guarantee sufficient levels of group protection without somewhere mentioning the groups that are meant to enjoy this protection. The Belfast Agreement is in fact based on a mix of predetermination and self-determination (McGarry et al., 2008, pp. 62–3). Elected deputies designate themselves as Unionist, Nationalist or Other, and this designation forms the basis of the cross-community decision-making. Notwithstanding the non-ethnic formulations, both the Belfast Agreement and the Ohrid Agreement are frequently criticized for reinforcing sectarian divisions (Bieber, 2005, p. 120; McCann, 2015).

I nevertheless agree that defining institutions in non-ethnic terms could make a difference, and gradually reduce the rigidity of the system. Even if it is completely clear who will be sharing power when the agreement is signed – and this is indeed a necessary precondition for the initial agreement – a less ethnically-defined text will allow for flexibility in case voters stop voting along ethnic lines. Initially it may be largely symbolic, but symbols are of huge importance in separatist conflicts and fewer ethnic symbols may gradually create a space for alternative identities to emerge. In the case of Northern Ireland, the power-sharing institutions are deliberately nationally impartial and the Ohrid Agreement also creates a framework for Macedonia as a civic state (see also Bieber, 2005, p. 109). This kind of flexibility is important for an approach that is often criticized for its lack of flexibility and viewed as being unsuitable beyond the immediate cessation of violence.

The other key charge against the consociational approach, its propensity for deadlock and immobility, has been a problem in several of the cases. Bosnian deputies would, especially in the immediate post-war period, use their veto powers to block any legislation that would increase the powers of the central state, or indeed create the central institutions outlined in the agreement. As a result, only ten laws were passed in the first year of the State Parliament's existence, and an average of only five laws a year in the period 1998–2000 (Caspersen, 2004, p. 581). One obvious way to address this problem would be to limit the mutual veto. McEvoy (2013, p. 254) argues that although the mutual veto can help foster cooperation among elites, an unlimited veto right risks leading to tensions and stalemates. She therefore argues that the parties should agree on which policy issues will be subject to veto (ibid. p. 260), and points out that in Northern Ireland, where the veto powers are more clearly defined, the use of veto has not been particularly contentions. Parties have instead relied on absenteeism, but although McEvoy argues that this is now less of a problem (ibid. p. 268), boycott of the power-sharing institutions represents a recurring threat of collapse (McDonald, 2015b). Absenteeism has also been a significant problem in other cases. In Serbia & Montenegro, parliamentary sessions were 'often repeatedly cancelled because many MPs from Montenegro did not attend sessions' (Bieber, 2013, p. 317).

Another way of reducing the risk of immobility would be to increase the power of the centre. Zahar (2005, p. 129) argues that a weak centre is one of the dynamics that underpin elite intransigence, as it provides them with an institutional basis for entrenching their power and leaves the central government unable to implement its policies (Bieber, 2013). Moreover, if the centre is weak the elites have little to lose from using their veto powers; it has little actual impact and they can continue to rule undisturbed from their ethnically-defined regions (ibid., p. 324). Strengthening the centre and limiting the territorial autonomy to municipal decentralization, such as in Macedonia, would therefore appear to have its advantages: the Ohrid Agreement maintained the central state as 'the sole and unchallenged (at least de jure) legislator' (ibid., p. 320).

Although it therefore appears possible to address some of the key shortcomings of the consociational approach, the problem is that such tweaking of the model reduces the degree of group protection provided and this will not be acceptable in all cases. Liberal consociationalism does not offer the group recognition that is often being sought in separatist conflicts; it may protect against being outvoted but does not offer the validation that a more ethnically-defined agreement would. Moreover, the possibility of moving towards a less group-based system may create fears that the majority group will manipulate the system in order to water down the consociational guarantees. In the case of Macedonia, some ethnic Albanian parties are for example complaining of a lack of rights and arguing for a more ethnically-defined system. The resurgence of Slavic Macedonian nationalism has made the civic nature of the institutions increasingly fictitious (Bieber, 2005).

Similar concerns regarding group protection could be raised in case veto powers are restricted. Nationalist parties in a strong bargaining position would, in any case, likely be unwilling to limit their own powers following an intense intra-state conflict. Veto powers were curtailed in the case of Macedonia, but this reflected the relative weakness of the minority group: they were not in a position to demand further concessions. Formal veto powers were also limited in the case of Sudan, but this did not reflect a strong centre: the SPLM was more interested in the effective veto provided by extensive territorial and military autonomy, and in 2007 they withdrew from the Government of National Unity, in protest at the slow implementation of the agreement (Brosché, 2008, p. 237), thus bringing the eventual break-up of the state a step closer. Territorial autonomy based on decentralization to municipalities also reduces the level of minority self-rule: the municipalities are clearly subordinate to the central state and the representation of minorities is fragmented (Bieber, 2013, p. 320). It is therefore unlikely to prove acceptable following intense conflicts, and/or cases of significant minority bargaining power. The municipal decentralization that international actors pushed for in post-independence Kosovo (Bieber, 2013) has not been enough to satisfy Serb demands for self-rule, and a 2015 EU-brokered agreement allowed for the creation of an association of Serb majority municipalities; thereby moving closer to an autonomous region.[47] Moreover, with power concentrated at the centre, deadlock will severely affect governance across the system and could therefore lead to its complete unravelling. In the case of Northern Ireland, direct rule from Westminster can be imposed when the power-sharing institutions are unable to function. But this is a case of sub-state consociational democracy, and deadlock would represent a significant risk in other cases.

Consociational agreements that are less ethnically-defined and less prone to immobility therefore appear to depend on fairly moderate divisions. At the other extreme we find another trend: consociational agreements as part of an interim agreement. In these agreements, secession is a built-in option in case the institutions turn out to be unworkable.[48] But are there alternative models of power-sharing that are less prone to dangerous deadlock and more adaptable in a post-conflict context? The following sections examine Horowitz's centripetal or integrative approach, which is the main power-sharing alternative, and possible hybrid arrangements.

Centripetal Approach

Horowitz's (1991) centripetal approach seeks to transcend the ethnic divide by creating a number of institutional incentives for cross-ethnic appeal. These incentives are to 'make moderation pay' and include:

1. An electoral system in which a candidate's election depends on attracting votes from outside their own ethnic group. This can be achieved through a territorial distributive requirement, such as the requirement in Nigeria's 1979 Constitution that the winning presidential candidate had to secure a plurality of votes nation-wide plus at least 25 per cent of the vote in no less than two-thirds of the nineteen states (ibid.) Or through the Alternative Vote (AV), which is a preferential system that requires the winning candidate to secure either an absolute majority of first-preference votes or a majority after the transfer of lower-preference votes from elimi-nated candidates (ibid.). It is assumed that voters may be swayed to cast lower preferences across the ethnic divide, and candidates that adopt a more moderate position are therefore advantaged.
2. Non-ethnic federalism, based on ethnically-mixed political units. This is argued to promote inter-ethnic and cross-unit alliances, resulting in more moderate attitudes and fluid identities (ibid., p. 141; Horowitz, 1985, pp. 617–21).
3. 'Ethnically blind' public policies that can help reduce sectarian distance rather than augment it (Harris & Reilly, 1998, p. 141).

Critics argue, however, that what Horowitz prescribes is essentially a majoritarian system with insufficient minority protection (Lijphart, 2002, p. 47; Reynolds, 2000, pp. 159–60). Minority representatives are highly unlikely to get elected in the AV system, and minority communities will therefore simply have to hope for more moderate majority representatives, also after the election campaign is over. As O'Leary argues, centripetalists 'prioritise better behaviour by repre-sentatives from majorities rather than the direct election of minori-ties' (2013b, p. 387). This moderating influence depends, moreover, on two conditions. Firstly, the demographic situation has to be such that first-preference votes are not enough for (majority) candidates to win; otherwise there is little incentive for them to campaign for lower-preference cross-ethnic votes. Secondly, candidates must feel confident that adopting a more moderate position will not cause them to lose significant support from within their own community.

McCulloch (2013) therefore concludes that the centripetal approach is only suitable in cases of moderate divisions.

The lack of guaranteed group protection makes it hard to explain minority acceptance, but even majority support is hard to explain: why would a majority group 'voluntarily accept institutions that enhance the power of minority groups at its own expense' (Anderson, 2013, pp. 364–5)? Similarly, why would nationalist parties accept a system designed to undermine their bases of power? The theory consequently lacks an explanation of local acceptance. Horowitz recognizes this 'implementation problem' but counters that it also exists for the consociational approach, and believes that this can be overcome with the assistance of outside forces. In other words, the centripetal structures should be imposed by third parties and once implemented they will be 'self-sustaining and require minimal intervention' (O'Leary, 2013a, p. 33). Consociationalists are less than impressed with this argument and argue that continuous intervention would be needed since the political systems will be rigged towards 'unrepresentative moderates' (ibid., p. 34). Critics also point out that the centripetal approach lacks an empirical record. Even the few cases that the proponents use to support their argument are contested. McCulloch (2013) argues that rather than promoting moderation, the centripetal approach has in fact fostered outbidding and polarization. In the case of Sri Lanka, a preferential system (the Supplementary Vote – a form of truncated Alternative Vote) has been used for presidential elections. Horowitz argued that this would result in a situation where 'prudent presidential candidates could hardly ignore Tamil interests' (quoted in McCulloch, 2013, p. 99) and it was hoped that this would bring a negotiated settlement closer. However, the legitimacy of the system was not accepted by Tamil voters and candidates, and they generally boycotted the elections. As a result, the 2005 elections were not won by the more moderate candidate that promised a peace agreement, but by the hardline candidate who rejected a compromise with the Tamil Tigers and resumed the war four years later (McCulloch, 2013).

It is indeed striking that all the power-sharing agreements that were signed in separatist conflicts since 1990 are consociational. Not a single one follows Horowitz's framework. Similarly, if one looks at failed peace proposals, such as the ones put forward in the cases of Abkhazia, Cyprus, Nagorno Karabakh and Western Sahara, it is hard to find centripetal measures. This could of course simply be due to lack of imagination and a tendency to copy 'blueprints' from other conflicts, but it also speaks to the problem of local acceptance.

Hybrid Models of Power-Sharing

O'Flynn and Russell concede that consociationalism may be the more feasible option in the case of deep divisions and memories of recent violence, but maintain that 'even where it is not possible to opt for integration in the first instance, it should remain a fundamental objective actively pursued by policy makers in a determined fashion' (2005, pp. 5–6). Consociationalism could gradually give way to a more centripetal solution and such hybridity could conceivably add flexibility to a power-sharing structure. However, existing literature on interim power-sharing governments alerts us to the difficulty of moving beyond the initial set-up. As Manning argues, 'there is little reason to suppose that elite beliefs and strategies or the distribution of political power ... can easily be changed' (2007, pp. 54, 57). Jarstad (2008a) similarly points to the constraining effects of rule by the former warring parties.

The case of Northern Ireland offers some support for a hybrid model of power-sharing. The preferential Single-Transferrable Vote (STV) was adopted, instead of the PR electoral system that consociationalists usually advocate. This system is argued to have led Sinn Fein to moderate its position (McGarry & O'Leary, 2006b) and also helped the pro-settlement Ulster Unionist Party (UUP) beat the rejectionist Democratic Unionist Party (DUP) in the crucial 1998 election (Wolff, 2005). Unlike Horowitz's preferred Alternative Vote, the STV system is proportional and the elections took place within a consociational arrangement; the sharing of power was therefore already guaranteed. Wolff (2005) argues that stability in deeply divided societies requires both moderation *and* inclusion, and the use of STV in Northern Ireland suggests the promise of combining the best of the two power-sharing approaches. However, other authors view the two approaches as less than complementary. Oberschall and Palmer (2005) suggest that the British and Irish governments had intended for the Belfast Agreement to give greater priority to inter-communal integration – illustrated for example in the terms of reference for the human rights commission – but that this was obstructed by the consociational institutions which encouraged sectarian divisions.

The Dayton Agreement for Bosnia provides an even clearer example of a mixed model and the problems associated with moving away from a consociational structure. The consociational elements in the Dayton Agreement are undoubtedly the most visible and arguably the most important. However, it also contains some centripetal elements.

81

Firstly, the autonomy provided for in the Dayton Agreement is not ethnically-defined; it acknowledges the congruence of ethnicity and territory but does not protect this connection and the architects of the Dayton Agreement were hoping for the ethnically-exclusive nature of the entities to be undermined by the return of refugees and IDPs to their former place of residence (Caspersen, 2004, p. 573). Secondly, even though the Dayton Agreement creates a highly decentralized structure it does not prevent the central state from acquiring additional competencies; according to the Constitution this can be done on the vague grounds of sovereignty and independence (Annex 4, art. III, 5a). Strengthening the central institutions does not undermine the consociational structure, per se, but it does undermine the power of the entities and could be seen to favour the largest community (Belloni, 2004, p. 335). Thirdly, the consociational institutions were counterbalanced by more centripetal institutions, such as the Constitutional Court, which is based on ethnic parity but decides by a simple majority (Caspersen, 2004, p. 573). Crucially the Court included international judges who together with the judges from one group were able to outvote the two others. It therefore constituted a significant departure from the consociational guarantees found elsewhere. The Constitutional Court was authorized to determine if the veto right could be used in the central institutions; if it genuinely concerned vital interests. This was hoped to counteract the threat of deadlock (Hayden, 2005, p. 244).

The ambiguity in the agreement allowed the international administration in Bosnia to push for centripetal reforms. The most successful part of this strategy was the strengthening of the joint institutions: a number of significant reforms were agreed to – or more frequently imposed by the High Representative (Bieber, 2006b). From 2003 these reforms crucially included the sensitive field of security: a statewide system of identity cards was introduced, the entity intelligence agencies were dissolved, a joint command for the armed forces was created and the entity defence structures were dissolved (Bieber, 2006a, p. 19). Imposing these reforms did not lead to backlashes, but it also did not prove lasting: since 2006 when the OHR became a lot less willing to impose institutional reforms, the strengthening of central institutions and the weakening of the entities have come to a halt (Bieber, 2013, p. 316), and are now being reversed (Lyon, 2015).

Other attempts to move away from a consociational structure have proved equally challenging. In 2000 the Constitutional Court ruled that the ethnically exclusive nature of the entity constitutions was unconstitutional. This decision was supported by the international and Bosniak judges, while the Croat and Serb judges dissented. The

Constitutional Court intended for a less ethnically-defined structure to emerge in the entities, but the amended entity constitutions simply introduced power-sharing and minority vetoes for all three groups. The amendments were imposed by the OHR, but they were based on an agreement that had been reached earlier and they faced virtually no opposition (Bieber, 2006b, p. 129). Refugee returns were also hoped to enable a move away from the consociational structure. But even though the number of returns increased after a concerted international effort,[49] it has not been enough to alter the demographic balance of the entities (O Tuathail & Dahlman, 2004). This failure to alter the demographic balance of Bosnia also affected attempts to create a centripetal electoral system.

The OSCE imposed a draft election law for the 2000 elections which included a preferential system for the election of delegates to the House of Peoples and for the Republika Srpska (RS) presidency. The centripetal measures contained in this were limited – even though Horowitz had been consulted on measures to foster inter-ethnic moderation – but they still backfired (Belloni, 2004, p. 340). The new rules for the election of House of Peoples deputies were intended to make electoral success dependent on cross-ethnic support, but they were fiercely rejected by the Croatian Democratic Union (HDZ), which argued that it would mean that the Croat deputies would effectively be elected by Bosniak voters (ibid., p. 344; see also Kasapović, 2005, pp. 17–18). This resulted in a prolonged standoff between the HDZ and the international administration and this actually helped the nationalist HDZ consolidate its powerbase (Caspersen, 2004, p. 582). The introduction of a preferential system for the RS presidency also did not manage to moderate ethnic exclusivism: the entity was simply too homogeneous and divisions too deep for it to work (ibid.). Both preferential systems were therefore left out of the final election law.

Centripetal elements, and more generally ambiguity, can help add flexibility to a consociational agreement, especially in cases of significant third party involvement. Bosnia today looks very different from what it did in 1996. But hybrid versions come with limitations (see also Belloni, 2004). Unless third parties are prepared to impose a full-scale revision of the consociational system, which would come with significant risks of a backlash, the core of the system is likely to remain unchanged. In the case of Bosnia, reforms strengthened the central state, but they did not do away with ethnic representation and an extremely complicated system of grand coalitions, minority vetoes and proportionality. The nationalist parties have tirelessly worked against any provisions in the Dayton Agreement that could reduce their share in power, and the consociational institutions have given them the powers to do so. This illustrates the difficulty of introducing centripetal elements into a predominantly consociational system; the power structures tend to acquire permanence, even if they were intended to be transitional.

Conditions for Successful Power-Sharing

Getting the political institutions right is crucial when it comes to securing stability, but this is not simply a question of choosing 'the best' institutions. Institutions can only go so far, and their functioning depends on the specific conflict context.

Moderate Divisions or International Involvement

One of the key limitations of political power-sharing is that it only seems to work properly in the case of relatively moderate divisions; elite consensus is needed (see e.g. McEvoy, 2013, p. 273). Tonge (2014, p. 194) argues that 'consociation has only rarely worked to end any conflict defined as high-level'. In a number of conflicts, divisions are simply too deep for power-sharing to be a viable solution (Kaufmann, 1996; Rothchild & Roeder, 2005); not because power-sharing is not needed, but because it is not enough, *and* it implies too much of a tie to the centre. In cases where the separatist forces have achieved de facto independence, and which are marked by deep mistrust, the separatist forces will be reluctant to accept any links to the centre. Thus the 'Basic Principles' that form the basis of the Nagorno Karabakh talks do not include any mention of political power-sharing.[50] The 2001 'Basic Principles for the Division of Competencies between Tbilisi [Georgia] and Sukhumi [Abkhazia]' envisaged a limited form of power-sharing in the form of an Abkhaz Vice President, but the Abkhaz side refused to receive the document (Francis, 2011). Even extensive territorial autonomy, which can be described as the extreme end of the power-sharing spectrum (O'Leary, 2013a, p. 31), is rejected as insufficient.

The need for moderate divisions raises the paradox that power-sharing may only work where we already find the moderation that the institutions are meant to create (see also Spears, 2002). In the absence of elite consensus on the legitimacy of the state and the institutional set-up, third party involvement appears to a necessary, albeit not sufficient, condition (see also Bieber, 2013). Third parties can guarantee the terms of the agreement and mediate when deadlocks are encountered. The literature on power-sharing has traditionally focused on local elites voluntarily entering into an agreement, and third party involvement was not a central concern. This now appears a crucial omission (see also O'Leary, 2013b). Power-sharing approaches are needed *particularly* where local willingness to compromise and inter-communal trust are in short supply, but the absence of such conditions makes it difficult to secure an agreement and to make it work.

The five power-sharing agreements analysed above all include varying degrees of external involvement. This involvement has succeeded in addressing the trans-border nature of the Northern Irish conflict, has maintained stability and enabled significant reforms in the case of Bosnia, and has played an important role in dispute resolution. Deadlocks in the Northern Ireland power-sharing institutions caused by absenteeism have for example been resolved via inter-party bargaining chaired by the British and Irish governments (McEvoy, 2013, p. 271), and the imposition of direct rule has on occasion saved the agreement from collapse. The international role in the case of Macedonia and Serbia & Montenegro was more limited once the agreements had been signed, but third parties still played a role in dispute resolution, and NATO monitored the military implementation of the Ohrid Agreement (Bieber, 2013, pp. 314–15). While international involvement may be able to solve some problems, such as lack of trust and compromise willingness, it is likely to create others. In the case of Bosnia, international intervention and the power-sharing system have become conflated (ibid., p. 316). This has created insecurity and may have made it even more difficult to move beyond the wartime divisions and power structures. The opportunities and limitations of third party involvement will be further examined in chapter 7.

Power-sharing, often billed as the model to adopt 'when nothing else works', may therefore require fairly moderate divisions, a relatively weak separatist force, or significant and sustained third party involvement. This points to the constraints on maintaining a common state. Consociationalists would however maintain that this does not 'render institutions obsolete' (McEvoy, 2013, p. 273). The consociational institutions, with their safeguards, allow the elites to gradually learn to trust the other side. In the case of Northern Ireland it has frequently been argued by critics of the Belfast Agreement that it empowered the more extreme parties, as illustrated by the growth of Sinn Fein and the DUP (see e.g. Oberschall, 2007, p. 172). Yet what has been striking has been the working relationship between the DUP's late Ian Paisley and Sinn Fein's Martin McGuiness, which became cordial to the extent that they were even dubbed 'the Chuckle Brothers' (Bolton, 2014). This suggests the potential transformative power of consociational institutions, if the conditions are right, but it also alerts us to the importance of political contestation within the conflict parties.

Intra-Communal Dynamics

In some of the early literature on consociational democracy, we find arguments regarding the need for 'structured elite predominance' and 'monolithic representation'. The elites have to be sure that they can cooperate in a grand coalition without finding themselves outbid by more extreme rivals from within their own ethnic group (see e.g. Nordlinger, 1972). Such a situation is however very rarely found in cases of separatist conflict: ethnic groups are not homogeneous and if competing parties, factions or paramilitary organizations do not already exist, then they are likely to emerge in response to the signing of a peace agreement, and leaders will in any case have to manage potential rivals from within their own ranks.

This presents problems both for the initial signing of a power-sharing agreement and for its functioning. Lijphart appears to argue that even if leaders adopt extreme positions, in a bid to defeat radical challengers and attract popular support, the incentive of exercising power will lead them to moderate once an election is over. But as Wolff rightly observes, 'political leaders who gain power on a confrontational platform in order to maximise votes from within their own ethnic community not only contribute to polarisation of society, but also create expectations and a climate of adversarial "no-compromise" post-electoral politics' (2005, p. 67). The centripetal approach is also vulnerable to outbidding. Unless there is a moderate core of voters, hardliners are likely to triumph at the polls (McCulloch, 2013, p. 100). Extremists who are unwilling or unable to attract cross-ethnic support may also revert to violence (Wolff, 2005, p. 67). In the cases analysed, the resistance to power-sharing institutions did sometimes take violent forms, such as the Omagh bombing in Northern Ireland, but political means were also used. One of the key problems for implementation of the Ohrid Agreement has been lack of popular support from the Slavic Macedonian majority; the incumbents consequently fear outbidding and this has made cross-community cooperation difficult (Bieber, 2005, pp. 108, 120).

In the case of extensive ethnic autonomy, outbidding is moreover not only a question of political dynamics, but also a question of capacity. The leaders who support the power-sharing institutions have to be able to police their own community, both literally and figuratively. Schneckener is therefore right when he concludes that if consociational democracy is to succeed, 'conflict group leaders' must be able to 'contain radical opponents and paramilitary groups' and forge links with moderate forces on the other side (2002, p. 224). The ability to do so can come to depend on specific leaders. The death of John Garang in the case of Sudan and the ascendency of the separatist faction of the SPLM for example made it very difficult for the power-sharing institutions to work as intended (Rolandsen, 2011, p. 559).

The importance of intra-ethnic dynamics renders the consociational approach vulnerable. What is crucial, however, is that the nature of intra-communal dynamics is not independent from the content of the agreement and the peace process. The ability of leaders to take followers with them in compromise and police their own community depends on them being regarded as legitimate representatives by their own community and it depends on their capacity. Both of these are strongly affected by the kind of agreement that is on the table, and the process that led to it. This will be further explored in chapter 6.

Conclusion

Power-sharing may be the 'international community's preferred remedy for building peace and democracy after civil war' (Rothchild & Roeder, 2005, p. 5), but it does not represent a uniform model. On the contrary, we see a degree of trade-off between different kinds of power-sharing: territorial, military and political. Or rather, central governments will prefer to limit power-sharing to its territorial, and if need be, military forms, thus reducing the need for power-sharing at the centre. Separatist movements may have a greater interest in power-sharing at the centre as it provides for stronger guarantees against recentralization (and possibly more prestige for the leaders), but they are often not in a position to insist on this. In some conflicts, the leaders of separatist movement may also oppose the ties to the centre and the recognition of the state's legitimacy that such an arrangement implies. Political power-sharing is therefore far less frequent in territorial conflicts than we might have expected.

The political power-sharing that we do find follows the consociational model, with only a few elements of the main rival, the centripetal approach, encountered. These agreements demonstrate some developments compared to the original formulation of consociational democracy: they are less explicitly ethnically-defined, there are some attempts to make them more flexible, and they have a more pronounced international dimension. This affects their functioning and suggests that it may be possible to address some of the shortcomings identified by the critics of the approach. However, the deeper the divisions the more constrained is the ability to do so, or it comes to rely on significant third party involvement. Similarly, a hybrid model can provide some flexibility, but it is hard to move beyond the core consociational structure unless there is a very high degree of third party involvement.

Consociational agreements are associated with both short-term and longer-term negative consequences, including a lack of rights for 'Others', as will be discussed in the following chapter. However, in many conflicts it is the best that can be hoped for, if the state is to be maintained. The success of such an arrangement depends to a considerable extent on intra-communal dynamics and capacity, but these are also affected by the agreement itself, as well as by the specifics of the peace process. This interaction of context, content and process will be further explored in chapters 6 and 7.

—— 4 ——

JUSTICE

This may not be a just peace, but it is more just than a continuation of war. (Bosnia's President, Alija Izetbegović, signing the Dayton Agreement, quoted in Holbrooke, 1999, p. 311)

The end of the Cold War ushered in a belief that human rights should be a guiding norm of international relations, and a cornerstone in a more peaceful world. Several world leaders argued that the respect for human rights was necessary for sustainable peace. The UN Secretary General Kofi Annan (2004) declared that 'justice, peace and democracy are not mutually exclusive objectives, but rather mutually reinforcing imperatives'. But not everyone shares this optimism. Several authors point to the tensions between peace, democracy and justice, and the difficulty of moving beyond wartime dynamics (see e.g. Jarstad, 2008b; Manning, 2007). An anonymous international official claimed that the insistence on human rights in the case of Bosnia had prolonged the war and warned 'the quest for justice for yesterday's victims of atrocities should not be pursued in such a manner that it makes today's living the dead of tomorrow' (Anonymous, 1996, p. 257). Weiner (1998, p. 440) has argued that these are 'genuine dilemmas' in the sense that we have to choose between distasteful alternatives. An unjust peace may be the best that can be achieved.

This chapter analyses the provision for human rights in peace agreements and the possible trade-offs involved. But it also examines the effects of the 'core agreement': the ways in which it constrains the inclusion of human rights provisions and their effectiveness. The previous chapters found that the agreements reached in separatist conflicts are very much about group rights. Autonomy and power-sharing arrangements are ethnically-defined, at least in their effects,

and one of the primary aims is to ensure self-government and protection for minority groups. Security arrangements are also often
group-based and predicated on the need to prevent a recurrence of
inter-communal violence and ensure sufficient protection for minorities. The question is where this leaves the rights of individuals. The
groups nominally engaged in conflicts are not unitary actors and the
leaders of these groups cannot always be presumed to be representative: a claim to self-determination may, somewhat paradoxically, be
an authoritarian claim. The leaders on both sides of the conflict
frequently owe their position to the use of violence and the removal
of alternatives (see Caspersen, 2010). Moreover, these group-based
arrangements tend to be exclusive; they ensure rights and protections
for the dominant groups, but where does this leave smaller or marginalized groups who were not involved in the peace talks? The issue of
past abuses is even more controversial. The violation of human rights
was a central feature of many of these separatist conflicts but addressing such abuses could lead to renewed instability.

This chapter finds that almost all the agreements include references
to human rights, and many also list rights and freedoms that are to
be protected. Writing agreements in the language of human rights is a
simple way to confer international legitimacy onto an agreement (Bell,
2000), but the commitment is vague and remains rhetorical in many
cases. In fact, the agreements are surprisingly illiberal. This reflects a
trade-off between peace and justice, but also the group-based institutions that form the core of agreements, and the narrowness of the
peace processes. The same factors help explain why past abuses are
so rarely addressed. The chapter concludes by discussing the implications of this lack of prioritization of human rights. It shapes the post-
settlement regime, both centrally and in the autonomous territories; it
may impact negatively on longer-term stability and it certainly affects
the quality of peace. Although human rights provisions in the agreement do not determine the post-settlement phase, the ability to introduce human rights at a later stage is likely to be severely constrained.

Overarching Rights and Institutions

Bell (2000, p. 198) argues that human rights serve two purposes in
peace agreements: they legitimize the deal, both internally and exter-
nally, and they help integrate the polity. Given the international
emphasis on human rights as a precondition for peace one would
expect most agreements to make at least rhetorical reference to

human rights. However, the effective enforcement of human rights is a different matter. Not all conflict parties are interested in integrating the polity, and the negotiating leaders may also fear that human rights provisions will weaken the mechanisms for group protection that they have negotiated, or indeed their own access to power and spoils. Human rights institutions are part of the political bargaining (ibid., p. 159), and will be significantly affected by the rest of the agreement.

If we look at the peace agreements, we do find frequent references to human rights (see table 4.1). Even the extremely short Khasavyurt Accord for Chechnya, which includes hardly any institutional mechanisms, expresses the will to 'protect unconditionally human rights and freedoms ... proceeding from the 1948 Universal Declaration of Human Rights and the 1966 International Covenant on Civil and Political Rights'. Human rights are in fact explicitly mentioned in all but two peace agreements: the Bodo Accord (India) and the Belgrade Agreement (Serbia & Montenegro).[51] But we need to look beyond the rhetoric and a number of these agreements only make fleeting and

Table 4.1. Human Rights in Peace Agreements

	Language of human rights	Human rights institutions
Bangladesh–Chittagong Hill Tracts	X	
Bosnia	X	X
Croatia–Eastern Slavonia	X	
India–Bodoland		
Indonesia–East Timor	X	
Indonesia–Aceh	X	X
Israel–Palestine	X	
Macedonia	X	X
Mali	X	
Moldova–Gagauzia	X	
Niger	X	
PNG–Bougainville	X	X
Philippines–Mindanao	X	
Russia–Tatarstan	X	
Russia–Chechnya	X	
Senegal–Casamance	X	
Serbia–Montenegro		
Sudan–South Sudan	X	X
Ukraine–Crimea	X	
UK–Northern Ireland	X	X

very general references to human rights. The Oslo Declaration for Israel–Palestine for example only mentions 'political rights' and 'just peace settlement' in the preamble.

We find more specific overarching rights, for example in the form of a bill of rights, in thirteen of the agreements, although this again includes very general commitments to 'the exercise of fundamental freedoms in particular freedom of speech and expression' (Senegal) or to the 'the Universal Declaration of the Human Rights from 1948 and of the African Charter on Human and Peoples' Rights from 1981' (Niger). While such references may be symbolically important, they have to be backed up by human rights institutions in order to have a significant impact on the actual functioning of the peace agreement. More well-developed human rights institutions are found in only six cases: in Bosnia, Indonesia–Aceh, Macedonia, Papua New Guinea–Bougainville, Sudan and Northern Ireland.[52] Here we find references to specific rights – these are either listed or references are made to rights protected in the constitution or in named international treaties – and the agreements also promise the creation of human rights institutions, or the monitoring role of existing institutions is specified. These institutions include constitutional courts, human rights courts, or a human rights ombudsman (see Bell, 2000). Human rights may be the 'chic language' (ibid., p. 297) in which to write peace agreements, but only a minority of the agreements therefore go beyond rhetoric when it comes to the protection of human rights. This is despite the fact that future-oriented human rights provisions are said to be fairly easy to agree on – the difficulties tend to arise during implementation (ibid.).

When are Human Rights Institutions Included?

One thing that stands out is the high degree of international involvement in all of the six agreements that include human rights institutions. International mediators pushed for human rights to be prioritized and frequently drafted the provisions. Szasz (1996) even argues that in the case of Bosnia almost none of the human rights provisions originated in Bosnia itself. It is therefore unsurprising that international conventions constitute a key mechanism for human rights protection in several of these cases. The European Convention on Human Rights (ECHR) applies directly in domestic law in the case of Bosnia and is to be fully incorporated in the case of Northern Ireland, while the legal code for Aceh is to be redrafted on the basis of the United Nations International Covenants on Civil and Political

Rights and on Economic, Social and Cultural Rights (art. 1.4.2) and the Comprehensive Peace Agreement for Sudan lists international treaties, including the International Covenant on Civil and Political Rights, that must be complied with fully (Ch. 2, art. 1.6.1).

International involvement, and the pursuit of international legitimacy, is however clearly not the only factor of importance.[53] Other agreements that were the result of extensive international involvement, such as the Erdut Agreement for Eastern Slavonia, do not include the creation of human rights institutions. Domestic demands for human rights, or in many cases the rejection thereof, also matter. And one factor of crucial importance here is the nature of, what Bell (2000) terms, 'the deal' and the type of conflict that we are dealing with.

In most separatist conflicts, group rights not individual rights are the main concern. The experience of discrimination was a mobilizational force in a number of these cases, but since these violations were largely based on ethnicity, the problem was perceived as reflecting a lack of minority rights and particularly a lack of self-determination, rather than a question of individual rights. These grievances are in most of the agreements addressed through territorial autonomy, i.e. through group-based institutions, which reduces the need for centralized human rights protections. In contrast, if we look at agreements signed in non-territorial conflicts where autonomy is not part of the solution, we find a much greater emphasis on human rights. For example, both El Salvador's and Guatemala's peace settlements (1992 and 1996) include a separate, detailed agreement on human rights; South Africa's 1993 interim constitution has a whole chapter on 'fundamental rights' (Ch. 3); and Burundi's 2000 agreement includes an extensive charter of rights and human rights institutions.

The leaders of separatist movements may in fact be against effective human rights institutions if territorial autonomy is granted, as such institutions would constrain their autonomous powers. This could be used as an instrument for undercutting the group protection guaranteed by the agreement or, more cynically, threaten their powerbase. The leaders of armed movements may not be interested in this kind of scrutiny. Bell (2000, p. 196) suggests that in the case of Israel–Palestine, the PLO negotiators did not want to limit Palestinian autonomy further by conditioning it on human rights as policed by Israel, and they were also worried that it would have limited their capacity 'to control dissident political forces'. Moreover, the central government would in many cases reject those kinds of constraints on their power, and may even lack an interest in such protections in the autonomous territories. Israel, for example, had no self-interest in including human rights in the Oslo Declaration as Israelis were explicitly excluded from the ambit of the Palestinian Authority (ibid.), and appear to have preferred a lack of constraints on the PA. As the late Israeli Prime Minister Rabin put it when selling the agreement to his party, 'I prefer the Palestinians to cope with the problems of enforcing order in the Gaza. ... They will rule by their own methods' (Roy, 2002, p. 10).

Human rights protections will only be considered relevant when the agreement foresees an element of coexistence. However, human rights institutions can act as a counterweight to group-based institutions, and there are situations that would lead the central government to push for such provisions. Two of the six agreements that include human rights institutions (PNG–Bougainville and Sudan) are interim agreements. In these cases the central government is keen to emphasize integrative measures; to strengthen the centre at the expense of the separate institutions and thereby hope to avoid eventual secession. Similarly, in the case of Bosnia, human rights institutions were intended to 'claw back the unitary state from the separate entities' (Bell, 2000, p. 196). It would therefore appear that the central government is more likely to insist on human rights institutions in case extensive powers are devolved to the separatist regions, even if it would also constrain their own rule.

Conversely, if there is no territorial autonomy, or only very limited autonomy, then the separatist leaders are much more likely to push for human rights as a means of ensuring equality. In the case of Northern Ireland, individual rights were, in combination with the power-sharing provisions of the agreement, seen as protection against future domination and discrimination (ibid., pp. 194–5). But the central government will often be reluctant to concede to such reforms. The limited degree of autonomy reduces the risk of secession, and hence the need to tie the region to the centre, and emphasizing human rights in the agreement would not only constrain the central government but would also mean recognizing past abuses, at least by implication. This runs counter to the argument quoted above that human rights protections are fairly easy to agree on; it implies that they will only be found in the case of limited autonomy *if* the separatist forces have sufficient bargaining power. This helps explain the lack of such provisions in cases such as Eastern Slavonia (where the Serbs were effectively defeated), Bodoland, the Chittagong Hill Tracts and Senegal. Limited autonomy is itself often the result of weak bargaining power and the lack of human rights provisions in many of these agreements is therefore not that surprising.

Effectiveness of Human Rights Institutions

The inclusion of human rights institutions in a peace settlement is of course no guarantee of their effectiveness. Szasz (1996, p. 306) has argued that there were two reasons for listing international instruments as the principal means of providing substantive rights in Bosnia. Firstly, it avoided the over-reliance on 'mere recitation of established rights' which would invariably have been interpreted in light of previous Yugoslav constitutional instruments. Secondly, the negotiators were under tremendous time pressure and this provided a time-efficient solution. However, provisions agreed under time pressure and without a basis in local legal traditions may not be particularly effective. Bell (2000, p. 231) warns that since there is often a lack of focus on human rights in negotiations, the provisions lack the details that are needed in order to make them effective, and she argues that the more international involvement, the less 'human rights friendly' the agreement will be.

There is a great deal of variation when it comes to the level of detail included in the six agreements, but all are lacking when it comes to specific enforcement mechanisms. The least detailed provisions are found in the case of Bougainville, where no new human rights institutions are created, and the agreement simply points to the existing Supreme Court as final court of appeal for human rights (art. 127). In the case of Aceh, the agreement promises the creation of an impartial judicial system in Aceh, including a Human Rights Court (art. 2.2.), but no further details are provided. Human rights institutions are more detailed in the Ohrid Agreement for Macedonia, which provides for additional powers for the Public Attorney who is to protect the constitutional and legal rights of citizens (art. 77). The agreement for Sudan includes a long list of rights protected by the agreement (Ch. 2, art. 1.6), and provides for the establishment of both a Constitutional Court and a Human Rights Commission (Ch. 2, art. 2.11.3 and 2.10.1.2). However, details regarding enforcement are lacking. Human rights play an even more central role in the Belfast Agreement for Northern Ireland, but it is similarly vague on the details; for example on the precise functioning of the Human Rights Commission and the Equality Commission which are to be established (Strand 1, Safeguards, art. 5). Human rights institutions and mechanisms abound in the Dayton Agreement for Bosnia but even here the mechanisms for enforcement are unclear. In particular, there is a 'security gap', since no one has an explicit mandate to arrest human rights violators, which is necessary as a last resort if human rights are to be enforced (Bell, 2000, pp. 221, 227). Only the entities were able to effectively enforce human rights protections, but they refused to take on this task (ibid., p. 227); the extensive autonomy provided for in the agreement therefore made it impossible for human rights protections to 'claw back' the unitary state.

This suggests that the effect of such institutions may be limited. Moreover, human rights institutions will often replicate the group-based institutions and therefore not provide a counterbalance. For example, in the case of Macedonia, one-third of the judges on the Constitutional Court and the Ombudsman are elected by the Assembly and must enjoy the support of minority representatives (art. 4.3). Similarly, in the case of Northern Ireland, the new human rights institutions are to reflect 'the community balance'. These provisions are of course meant to safeguard the rights of minorities, but they also mean that human rights provisions are less likely to qualify the group-based nature of the agreement. Bosnia constitutes a partial exception as the judges representing the three 'constituent nations' on the Constitutional Court are joined by internationally appointed judges. This was meant to reinforce the Court's integrative effect but it was, as argued in chapter 3, not able to undo the consociational provisions.

Human rights protections are therefore rarer than expected in peace agreements and effective enforcement mechanisms rarer still. Human rights provisions are part of the bargaining. They reflect, and are constrained by, the rest of the agreement. Similarly, if we look at security sector reforms, then these were, as argued in chapter 2, driven primarily by concerns for stability and group protection, and only one agreement mentions human rights in this context. The agreement for Mindanao stipulates that the autonomous police must respect 'the inherent human rights of the citizens' (art. 76e). The autonomous police force was however never created and the Philippine army and police continued to commit human rights violations in the region (Amnesty International, 1997). The holding of elections is another way to signal a concern for human rights and most of the agreements either include a timetable for elections or the promise of future elections is clearly implied. However, as will be argued below, such elections will rarely lead to a change in power; they typically constitute the autonomous institutions, but they also serve to legitimize the agreement *and* the power of its signatories. The impact of the 'core deal' is even clearer if we look at the rights of non-dominant groups.

Rights of Excluded Groups

Both power-sharing and autonomy arrangements typically grant power to the representatives of 'significant communal groups'. In order to protect individuals against the abuse of powers by majorities (centrally or locally), liberal consociationalists recommend two remedies: strong human rights regimes and local power-sharing (Wolff, 2011, p. 168). However the narrowness of most peace processes pulls in a different direction. The leaders included in negotiations are typically the ones who are viewed as 'veto players': the leaders who have the ability to obstruct a peace agreement if excluded, and to make it stick if brought on board. These leaders, who may not even be representative of their communities, will be keen to protect their own power as well as the rights of the groups they claim to represent. Sizeable groups will consequently find themselves excluded from the peace process and their interests and needs largely ignored in the resulting settlement.

If we first look at the rights of women, then it is striking that only a handful of agreements even mention gender equality. The Belfast Agreement for Northern Ireland includes 'the right to equal opportunity regardless of gender' and 'the right of women to full and equal political participation' and, pending devolution, the UK Government is to promote inclusion, including the 'advancement of women in public life' (Strand 3, Rights and Safeguards and Equality of Opportunity). While the agreement for Sudan states that 'The equal right of men and women to the enjoyment of all civil and political rights set forth in the International Covenant on Civil and Political Rights and all economic, social, and cultural rights set forth in the International Covenant on Economic, Social and Cultural Rights shall be ensured' (Ch. 2, art. 1.6.2.16). Other agreements (Indonesia–East Timor, PNG–Bougainville, Philippines–Mindanao) state that women *may* enjoy guaranteed seats in the local assemblies and the agreement for the Chittagong Hill Tracts guarantees women three out of twenty-two seats in the regional council (art. C.3). Eighteen are explicitly reserved for men(!); with only the gender of the chairman not being specified. Women were actively engaged in the Hill people's struggle for autonomy, but women were excluded from the peace talks and the accord makes no provisions for their rights (Mohsin, 2003, p. 54). Elsewhere women's rights are mentioned only in the preamble (Mali) or the agreement makes reference to international treaties that include gender rights, but does not point to these specifically (e.g. Bosnia). And that is about it. Even though women are disproportionately affected by the consequences of war, they are rarely represented in the talks and their rights and interests are not included in the peace agreements. Two exceptions are worth mentioning. The Northern Ireland's Women's Coalition was included in the Northern Irish talks, even if only at the margins (Powell, 2008, pp. 26–7). This inclusion is reflected in the agreement, not only in terms of references to women's rights but also in the inclusion of victims' rights and reconciliation. Their involvement, moreover, placed women's political participation 'firmly on the map of electoral politics' in Northern Ireland (Fearon, 2013, p. 33). Women were also included in the peace talks in Sudan, but their inclusion was symbolic: they were expected to 'follow the party line and their perspectives and experiences were overlooked' (Gardner & El-Bushra, 2013, p. 14). Thousands of women had joined the armed struggle in southern Sudan, but this involvement was discounted by the leaders of the SPLM/A and they were not regarded as 'appropriate participants for negotiations' (ibid.). Although the agreement makes some general references to equal rights for women, this does not go beyond rhetoric.

The exclusion of women is symptomatic of a more general tendency. Peace agreements are typically the result of political bargaining between the dominant communal groups, and the post-settlement institutions become based on these. Such arrangements likely result in a lack of rights for groups that are not part of the power-sharing arrangements, or that find themselves as minorities in ethnically-defined autonomous regions.

Individual rights are, as noted above, not given a prominent place in most of the peace agreements and the rights of 'Others' are even less clearly defined. In the case of Bosnia, 'Others' are mentioned in the preamble of the Dayton Agreement, but power-sharing arrangements and electoral rules are based on the three constituent nations. The three-person Presidency for example consists of a Bosniak, a Serb and a Croat (Annex 4, art. V). In Sudan, there are quotas for 'Others' (i.e. not SPLM or NCP) in the southern Sudan assembly and government, but their influence is likely to be minimal with only 15 per cent of the seats (Ch. 2, art. 3.5.1). In Khartoum, a special commission is to ensure that the rights of non-Muslims are not adversely affected by the application of Sharia law (Ch. 2, art. 2.4.6), while Muslims in the South may be governed by personal laws (including Sharia) when it comes to 'personal and family matters including marriage, divorce, inheritance, succession and affiliation' (art. 6.4). References to cultural rights are also found in the case of Mindanao and the possibility for guaranteed representation of minorities in the region is mentioned, but Sharia law is also to be introduced (art. 152). Finally, in the case of Gagauzia the agreements holds that one Vice-Chairman of the regional assembly is to be of another ethnic origin than Gaugaz (art. 10.2). The rights of minorities within the autonomous regions may be more developed when this minority is part of the dominant group in the state as a whole. This is most notably the case in Israel–Palestine where Israelis are explicitly exempt from the jurisdiction of the Palestinian Authority. In the Chittagong Hill Tracts, there are reserved seats for non-tribal representatives, but they are still under-represented. The Bodo Accord provides land and language rights for non-tribal communities, and the government can also appoint five (out of forty) members of the Autonomous Council from groups which 'could not otherwise be represented' (art. 3.b) but they are not guaran-teed a share in power. Complex power-sharing (Wolff, 2009) does not appear as the dominant model, and the rights of 'Others', i.e. those not belonging to the main ethnic groups, are particularly limited.

Dealing, or Not Dealing with Past Abuses

If future-oriented human rights institutions tend to be left out of peace agreements, then this is even truer of institutions that are to deal with *past* violations of human rights. Settlements are in most cases concluded between the leaders who control the armed groups and in order to bring these leaders on board, and for them to take their followers with them in compromise, it may be necessary to include amnesties as part of the agreement. This would mean that war crimes will largely go unpunished, although other accountability measures are possible. However, scholars are increasingly arguing that such policies are legally constrained. Another issue of great contention is the issue of refugee returns. Refugees and IDPs can often become pawns in the negotiations as both sides are aware of how their return could potentially alter the demographic balance and thereby the political balance of power. The return of refugees moreo-ver raises important questions about security and capacity.

War Crimes

For peace to be possible, it is frequently necessary to conduct nego-tiations with the very people who caused violence to break out in the first place and who have, in many cases, benefited from it in terms of power and profits. 'You can't make peace without Milosevic', was how the US envoy, Richard Holbrooke, summed it up during the Bosnian peace talks (quoted in Anonymous, 1996, p. 253). But these leaders are unlikely to agree to a peace settlement if they know that they could subsequently be prosecuted for war crimes. If peace is not possible without such actors, then they have to be provided with enough incentives to be brought on board. This often comes in the form of amnesty arrangements and, frequently also, promises of access to power and spoils (see also Sriram, 2008); in essence enabling these leaders to achieve some of their goals through political rather than military means.

Amnesty arrangements for the top leaders are often the ones that cause the greatest controversy, but amnesties are also relevant for the rank-and-file. The process of DDR is usually based on amnesty arrangements for at least the majority of rebel forces. They will not face prosecution for their involvement in the conflict if they agree to disarm and demobilize. In other cases, the former illegal armed forces are simply legalized and transformed into an autonomous coercive force. This is one of the incentives to convince the combatants to abandon the armed struggle and therefore presents an important piece in the puzzle. But if DDR involves blanket amnesties, then it also means that the perpetrators of terrible human rights violations will walk free and, in some cases, return to the same towns and villages as their victims (International Crisis Group, 2000). Such arrangements could foster short-term instability and may also damage the prospect of longer-term reconciliation.

Amnesties used to be commonplace in peace agreements; they were seen as significant tools in the mediator 'toolbox' (Sriram et al., 2014, p. 8) and the UN in a number of cases 'pushed for, helped negotiate, and/or endorsed the granting of amnesty as a means of restoring peace' (Scharf, 1999, p. 507). But amnesty arrangements have faced increasing criticism and UN mediators now receive explicit instructions that blanket amnesties cannot be endorsed.[54] Some authors have in fact suggested that there are now significant constraints on the granting of amnesties and that justice may therefore be required at the 'expense of peace' (ibid.). International law in the area is, as Bell (2000, p. 259) argues, 'complex and developing', especially in cases of intra-state conflicts, and the main arguments will therefore only be briefly summarized.

In a few narrowly defined situations there is an unquestionable legal obligation to prosecute, regardless of other considerations, but in intra-state conflicts this only covers acts of genocide.[55] Amnesties could in such cases be invalidated by either the state's domestic courts or by an international forum (Scharf, 1999, p. 514). Greater uncertainty prevails when it comes to 'serious violations' of Protocol II of the Geneva Convention. This protocol prohibits a list of acts, including: violence to the life, health and physical or mental well-being of persons; cruel treatment such as torture; outrages upon personal dignity, such as rape (art. 4.2). There is a growing argument that such abuses provide a basis for universal jurisdiction, i.e. perpetrators can be arrested and tried internationally. This argument was bolstered by the creation of the International Criminal Court (ICC) which deals with 'war crimes' committed after 1 July 2002.[56] But the question is if prosecution is mandatory in such cases and amnesty therefore prohibited. Grono argues that the ICC prosecutor can only stop prosecution if it is in the interest of justice. Only if a peace agreement with robust accountability mechanisms has been concluded can the ICC prosecutor decide not to pursue war crimes suspects (Grono, 2006). Scharf is, however, more sceptical and points to ambiguous provisions in the ICC Statute, such as the ability of the UN Security Council to request the court not to commence or to defer proceedings in case of a 'threat to peace'. He therefore concludes that amnesty has not been removed as a bargaining chip; 'the duty to prosecute is far more limited than the substantive law establishing international offences' (1999, p. 526). Although it therefore remains contested if amnesties can legally be granted in cases of serious violations of international law, we would expect the instrument to be used less frequently.

Amnesty should, in any case, not be equated with impunity. It is possible for amnesty arrangements to be combined with other mechanisms for accountability, such as truth commissions, compensation for victims, or lustration (for example preventing former members of certain armed groups from holding public office) (ibid., p. 512). It has been argued that following bloody intra-state conflicts, such accountability mechanisms are actually better suited than prosecutions. They can help mediate the peace–justice divide; perpetrators may not go to prison but victims are not forgotten about and could receive compensation. Sriram (2007, p. 583) argues that when it comes to peace and justice, it is not simply a question of either/or, a range of tools are available.

Amnesties in Peace Agreements

Somewhat surprisingly, amnesties are still found in a majority of the agreements, either explicitly or de facto. General amnesties are found in five agreements: Chittagong Hill Tracts, Aceh, Niger, Bougainville and Senegal. These amnesties either come with no conditions or only depend on the rebel forces surrendering their weapons. Similar arrangements, although not referred to as amnesties, are found in Mali (art. 7A) and in Mindanao (art. 2.19) where combatants from the separatist movement are to be integrated into the armed forces, without any conditions attached to this. In the case of Bodoland we also find a general amnesty, except in cases of 'heinous crimes' (unde-fined) (art. 18) and amnesty was in Bosnia granted to returnees expect in cases of 'serious violation of international humanitarian law' (Annex 7, art. 6). 'Other armed groups' are in the case of Sudan to be integrated into the coercive forces of the two sides, with no conditions attached. The SPLM and NCP had apparently wanted to give them-selves blanket amnesty for crimes committed during the war, but were told by the international mediators that this would be illegal under international law and could therefore not be enforced (Young, 2013, pp. 112–13). However, the two separate armies are maintained and no retributive process is alluded to in the agreement. This amounts to a de facto amnesty.

Of the remaining agreements, four were non-violent and amnesty therefore less relevant, which leaves five agreements without clear amnesty arrangements: Croatia, Israel–Palestine, Macedonia, Northern Ireland and East Timor. In the first case, Croatia, the lack of amnesty is explained by this essentially being a defeat of the Serb sep-aratist forces; there was therefore no attempt to try to integrate their armed forces or provide incentives for the leaders to compromise. The Declaration of Principles for Israel–Palestine does not include amnesties but the signing of the agreement was, as is often the case in Israeli–Palestinian talks, preceded by prisoner releases (Bell, 2000). In Northern Ireland there is also no explicit amnesty arrangement, but the agreement does include the 'early release' of prisoners. While similar to amnesty, this can be revoked, in case of new crimes, and is conditional for the first two years (ibid.). Recently, it has however come to light that letters were also sent to more than 200 republi-can paramilitary suspects, informing them that they were no longer wanted by the police (BBC News, 2015a). This happened outside the peace agreement and without the knowledge of the Unionist negotia-tors. The conflict in Macedonia was a fairly low-level conflict and amnesties were therefore not a pressing concern, especially since the National Liberation Army was not included in the talks (Popetrevski & Latifi, 2004). However, mechanisms for prosecutions are not set up either. Finally, in the case of East Timor, the autonomy arrangement, which was one of the options in the independence referendum, is silent on both amnesties *and* prosecutions. This is perhaps unsurprising given that the architect behind this option was the Indonesian Government, i.e. the conflict party responsible for the vast majority of human rights violations.

The inclusion of war crimes prosecution is extremely rare in these agreements. Only in the case of the International Criminal Tribunal for the Former Yugoslavia (ICTFY), which covers the cases of both Bosnia and Croatia, was a detailed mechanism set up. This is however not part of the agreements; the ICTFY was created during the war, in 1993, and one of the goals was to deter further human rights abuses. The ICTFY is not mentioned in the Erdut Agreement for Eastern Slavonia, but is included in Bosnia's Dayton Agreement, which bars anyone indicted by the ICTFY from holding public office. This provision had not been included in previous peace proposals (Szasz, 1996, pp. 313–14). It has however been argued that de facto amnesty was granted, even in this case. The US negotiators at Dayton made clear that cooperation with the ICTFY was 'not a show stopper' (Anonymous, 1996, p. 256). There are also speculations that Serbian President Slobodan Milošević had received implicit reassurances of non-prosecution (Scharf, 1999, p. 511). In any case, the NATO forces which were charged with the military implementation of the agreement were not tasked with arresting suspected war criminals.[57]

In the other agreements, prosecution is hinted at or implied in only two cases: first in the case of Bodoland, since amnesty was not granted in regard to 'heinous crimes' and, second, in the case of Mali where a Commission of Internal Enquiry was to look into abuses during the conflict. But it is not clear if prosecutions were intended to result from this Commission and it never became functional.[58] The rest of the agreements are silent on any form of retributive justice, thereby reinforcing the impression that amnesty is the defining principle, not just for combatants but also for their leaders. Mohsin (2003, pp. 54–5) laments that despite massive violations of human rights in the Chittagong Hill Tracts, including torture, kidnappings, rapes and massacres, the accord makes no reference to these abuses and no accountability measures are included. She attributes this to the powerful position enjoyed by the Bangladeshi military.

Amnesties are justified as a necessary trade-off. Without them, combatants would be more reluctant to disarm, some leaders would refuse to sign peace agreements, and subsequent prosecutions would threaten, what is at best, a fragile peace. In the case of Northern Ireland, Tony Blair argues that the peace process would probably have collapsed without the letters to republican paramilitary suspects; they were 'essential to getting Sinn Fein on board' (BBC News, 2015a). Similarly, during the Dayton peace talks, there were fears that the issue of war crimes would derail the talks when the ICTFY formally asked the US to make the surrender of indicted suspects a condition for an agreement, and when an anonymous ICTFY official stated 'we cannot deny that (Milosevic) is a suspect' (Anonymous, 1996, p. 257). However, the negative consequences of granting amnesties could outweigh the pragmatic benefits, as will be discussed below.

The peace agreements also include exceedingly few examples of alternative forms of transitional justice. In the case of Aceh, a Truth Commission is to be established (no further details) and political prisoners and civilians with 'demonstrable loss' are to receive compensation (art. 3.2.5). Given the lack of detail, Mali's Commission of Inquiry (art. 14) could also be interpreted as a truth commission,[59] and within its remit is to evaluate the damages and compensations due to victims of the conflict (art. 14), while the agreement for Niger promises a Day of Commemoration, 'in memory of the victims of the conflict' (art. 15). The issue is postponed in Northern Ireland pending a report from its Commission for Victims and Survivors, but the agreement does mention victims and their suffering and promises support for community initiatives. The Casamance agreement urges 'intra-communal forgiveness and reconciliation' and a group of Casamance officials, village chiefs and religious leaders are to develop 'dynamics of forgiveness and reconciliation' paving the way for the return of ex-combatants (art. 3.3). The peace agreement for Bougainville includes a commitment to reconciliation both within Bougainville and between Bougainville and Papua New Guinea, but is silent on specific mechanisms (art. 14). The Comprehensive Peace Agreement for Sudan is equally vague: the parties are to 'initiate a comprehensive process of national reconciliation and healing throughout the country' (Ch. 2, art. 1.7). A truth and reconciliation commission had been suggested but this was rejected by the two conflict parties (Young, 2013).

The absence of accountability in the agreements is striking, although we have seen a movement away from de jure amnesties. This reflects a trade-off between peace and justice but it again also reflects the territorial solution found in the majority of these agreements: the focus on separation limits the need for peaceful coexistence and therefore for reconciliation. And it mirrors the narrowness of the typical peace process. Domestic demands for accountability most often come from NGOs (Sriram, 2007, p. 590), such as the Women's Coalition of Northern Ireland which pressed for the inclusion of victim's rights and reconciliation. But in most peace talks such groups are excluded. This is also true for representatives of the last group this chapter focuses on: refugees and internally displaced people.

The Return of Refugees

Separatist conflicts are about territory and one of the frequent consequences of the violence, and often of deliberate policies of intimidation, is that a large number of people were displaced from their homes. Territories were 'ethnically cleansed' in an attempt to homogenize them, create 'facts on the ground' and make control easier. If refugees and IDPs are allowed to return home, then this can at least be partly undone, but such policies are likely to be fiercely contested. The controversy stems not simply from a reluctance to admit past wrongs, although that is certainly part of it, but more importantly it relates to territorial control and power.

The right of refugees to return to their home country is clearly established in international law, but international law does not otherwise provide much guidance. Human rights instruments are silent on the obligation of states to facilitate returns and do not formally establish a right to return to a specific locality. The problem is that rights for refugees and IDPs, insofar as they exist, are individually framed and do not therefore address the problems presented by mass movements as a result of war and conflict (Bell, 2000, pp. 233, 236, 242). The right of return is important in its own right, as one way of addressing the suffering caused by the conflict. Moreover, if refugees and IDPs are denied the right to return, it could cause future instability. However, the return of refugees is likely to be opposed locally and therefore presents short-term security problems.

A significant number of the agreements analysed in this book do actually include the right of return. Such provisions are included in the agreements for Bangladesh–Chittagong Hill Tracts, Bosnia, Croatia–Eastern Slavonia, Indonesia–Aceh, Macedonia, Mali, Senegal–Casamance and Sudan. In some cases this specifies a positive obligation on the part of the state. For example, in the case of Casamance, 'The State engages to take all measures in order to facilitate the returning home of refugees and displaced persons' (art. 4.2). In Mali, a fund is to be established to facilitate return and returnees are to have guaranteed seats in the National Assembly (art. 11 and 54). However, the agreements tend to lack detail. For example, in the case of Aceh, returns are to happen 'within the shortest possible timeframe', but no mechanisms are established: the agreement simply calls for international assistance. It is also striking that a number of agreements in violent conflicts do not mention refugees/IDPs. This is the case in India–Bodoland, Israel–Palestine, Niger, PNG–Bougainville, Philippines–Mindanao. The assumption may be that refugees will return once violence ends and security is re-established, without specific action being needed. The 1995 agreement for Niger, for example, mentions that the needs of displaced persons will be taken into account when assessing the needs of a conflict area (and applying to donors for funds) (art. 20) but is otherwise silent on their rights or the need to facilitate their returns. But returns are often highly sensitive and even if the right of return is included in an agreement, the implementation of this is often fraught. Moreover, the lack of capacity in the formerly contested territories is, as mentioned previously, a common problem and this will make returns very difficult.

Refugee returns cannot simply be perceived as humanitarian issues; they can significantly affect the territorial and security provisions of an agreement and resistance to their implementation must therefore in many cases be expected. The International Community had high hopes for refugee/IDP returns in Bosnia; this was to weaken the ethnic autonomy contained in the Dayton Agreement. The agreement therefore has a whole annex devoted to returns (Annex 7). However, the enforcement mechanisms were very weak (Bell, 2000) and the local resistance considerable. The nationalist leaders had no intention of allowing 'minority returns' that would undermine the ethnic homogeneity on which they based their power. In the Chittagong Hill Tracts (CHT) a separate agreement on refugees was signed, which promised a grant to returning refugees along with educational and employment opportunities. The land belonging to the returnees would also be restored to them. However, this land is often occupied by Bengali settlers, whose right to remain in CHT remains fiercely contested. The agreement provided no mechanisms for settling this issue and these disputes over land have led to several cases of violence, 'ranging from harassment to murder' (Mohsin, 2003, pp. 49, 72). The return of refugees should ideally be linked to the overall agreement and include proper enforcement mechanisms, but this will not always be feasible. Refugee returns are particularly contentious in the case of interim agreements – with the final status of the territory still being unresolved – and where refugee/IDP numbers are so high that they can significantly affect territorial control. One example of this is Israel–Palestine.

There are 4.6 million people registered by the UN as Palestinian refugees and the right of return has long been one of the most contentious issues in the Israel–Palestine conflict. The Palestinian side argues that the refugees and their descendants have a right to return to their place of origin. Israel however refuses to take responsibility, arguing that it was the Arab attack on Israel in 1948 that led to the Palestinian displacement. Their return would moreover alter Israel's demographic balance and threaten its Jewish identity (Hovdenak, 2008, p. 32). The Oslo peace declaration postponed the refugee issue until the final status negotiations, but the acceptance of the two-state solution implied that the PLO was ready to also compromise on the right of return, since an unlimited right of return would not be compatible with a continued Jewish majority in Israel (ibid.). However, the Palestinian negotiators were constrained by domestic opinion (Usher, 1999, p. 36), and therefore needed at least symbolic concessions from Israel (Hovdenak, 2008). They needed Israel to acknowledge responsibility for the displacement and accept the right of return in principle, even if not in practice. These demands however fell on deaf ears and this was one of the reasons for the breakdown of the agreement (ibid.).

The return of refugees has also been one of the main stumbling blocks in the Nagorno Karabakh peace talks. The war resulted in up to 700,000 Azeris fleeing Nagorno Karabakh and its surrounding districts. The Azerbaijani Government insists on their return and argues that the issue illustrates Nagorno Karabakh's complete lack of legitimacy; the entity was founded on ethnic cleansing. The Armenian side counters that Armenians also had to flee during the war and argues that the return of the refugees would present a significant security threat (see e.g. Conciliation Resources, 2011).[60] The underlying problem is however again one of territorial control and demographic balance. The outcome of the proposed referendum on the status of Nagorno Karabakh would practically be determined by the areas included in the vote and on whether or not returns are allowed. When it comes to refugee returns, the general trend is therefore similar to other human rights provisions: whether due to lack of attention or direct resistance from the conflict parties, it tends not to be prioritized.

Implications: Stability Now, Justice Later?

The focus in these peace agreements is clearly on stability, and this is seen as best achieved through the creation of group-based institutions that tend to empower the leaders in control of the armed groupings.

Lack of rights for 'Others' has however resulted in tensions and violence in a number of cases. In the Chittagong Hill Tracts, there have been recurrent episodes of violence between the tribal communities and the Bengali settlers; with the latter complaining about being second-class citizens and the former insisting that there was an unwritten understanding about the withdrawal of the settlers (Mohsin, 2003, pp. 51, 73). In Bodoland, the rights of non-tribal communities have also proved explosive. The area under the control of the Bodoland Territorial Council, following the 2003 agreement, is not homogeneous and non-Bodo communities feel under-represented (Institute of Peace and Conflict Studies, 2012). In 2012, these tensions turned to extreme violence leaving forty-two people dead and 150,000 displaced. The catalyst was the alleged removal of a signboard from a mosque, which the Bodoland Territorial Council claimed was an illegal structure occupying forest land (Samrat, 2012). Like many other settlements, the 1996 agreement for Mindanao was also an exclusive settlement, which left indigenous groups, Christian settlers and some of the traditional Muslim clans feeling unrepresented. They saw their interests threatened and needs unmet and this contributed to the growing unrest and violence in the region (Lara Jr & Champain, 2009). Even the more succesful agreement for Aceh has been troubled by lack of inclusiveness: the marginalization of certain ethnic groups, in particular those residing in the central highlands, has led to localized violence (Lara Jr & Champain, 2009). If these groups are relatively small, such tensions may not directly threaten the peace agreement, but it does mean that groups that could potentially have supported the agreement are now more likely to oppose it. For a fragile peace agreement this weakening of the peace constituency could prove fatal.

However, rights for minorities within autonomous entities do present a genuine dilemma and potentially difficult trade-off. Such rights could undermine the protections that have been negotiated for the main ethnic group: the territorial autonomy would be constrained and the share in power reduced. This is particularly problematic when these groups are seen as representatives of the dominant group. In the case of the Chittagong Hill Tracts, the Bengali settlers complain of their second-class status, but the tribal community sees them as a major cause of their plight, and complain that their 'ethnic' autonomy does not go far enough. Promised powers have not been devolved, the over-representation of the tribal community on the District Council has been weakened, and the acquisition of tribal land continues to be a problem (Amnesty International, 2013a; Mikkelsen,

2015, pp. 316–17; Mohsin, 2003, p. 71). If the 'Others' were small, non-dominant groups, the effect would perhaps be minimal, but the conflict parties, especially the numerically weaker one, are likely to fear that it could water down the principles of ethnic autonomy and power-sharing, and be manipulated by the majority group; a majority candidate could, for example, pose as 'Other', thereby upsetting the power-sharing balance. The 2009 ruling by the European Court of Human Rights (ECtHR) against Bosnia, in the Sejdić and Finci case, illustrates how human rights provisions that may initially have appeared unimportant can challenge power-sharing structures. The ECtHR ruled that the Bosnian Constitution violates the European Convention on Human Rights (ECHR) due to the lack of political rights for 'Others'. The Dayton Agreement gave the ECHR priority over all other law in Bosnia, but the local parties have failed to agree on how to amend the Constitution and the international administration is not willing to impose such fundamental reforms. If a court is able to overrule power-sharing institutions (and their decisions) based on human rights, then this would weaken group protections (O'Leary, 2013b) and it would also undermine the decision-making power of popularly elected officials. This is particularly problematic as the court in question is an international court.

It could therefore be argued that the lack of rights for smaller and marginalized groups is an unfortunate but often necessary consequence of a peace agreement that builds its institutions on (the main) identity groups. However this is not the only reason for the lack of prioritization of such rights: it also serves to consolidate the powers of the signatories and reflects an assumption of homogeneity within the communal groups, and sometimes even within the autonomous region. This state of affairs would be less problematic if it were only temporary; if human rights could be promoted at a later stage. But the ability to do so is likely to be severely constrained.

One possible mechanism for change is the holding of elections. In the early 1990s, the hope was that holding elections would bring moderates to power, which would make it easier to implement the agreement and gradually introduce human rights provisions (see e.g. Paris, 2004). Elections in Bosnia were therefore to be held no more than nine months after the Dayton Agreement came into effect, but the expected victory for the moderate forces did not result. Although slightly weakened, the nationalist parties maintained their grip on power. This is hardly surprising: voters knew them, they were well organized and they controlled much of the resources, whereas their more moderate rivals had very little time to get organized. In a still fearful atmosphere, their promise to staunchly defend their communities also had popular resonance (Caspersen, 2004). Early elections are clearly problematic but they nevertheless remain the norm in peace agreements. All the nine agreements that schedule elections do so less than three years after the agreement comes into effect; seven of them planned elections within the first year, and elections for the new autonomous government in Mindanao were held only a week after the signing of the agreement. The purpose of these elections is however rarely to effect a change in the holders of power. In Mindanao, the chairman of the MNLF won unopposed and the candidate from the Free Aceh Movement (GAM) also won convincingly when Aceh elected the head of its autonomous institutions eight months after the peace agreement.[61] This was attributed to GAM's superior organization and the legitimacy that it derived both from the settlement and the years of struggle (Aspinall, 2008). These groups will also typically hold power in any transitional period so postponing elections will not necessarily make a difference (see also Manning, 2007). In the case of Sudan, this was guaranteed through an exclusive agreement, which assigned power to the two negotiating parties: the NCP and the SPLM/A. Many of the agreements so entrench the powers of the leaders who negotiated the peace that elections are unlikely to result in a transfer of power. In the case of Aceh, it has been argued that GAM's political machine 'has become so strong ... that losing at the polls is unlikely, even if it fails to deliver' (International Crisis Group, 2013b, pp. 9, 11). The leaders empowered by the agreement therefore constitute an important constraint on post-settlement reforms and the institutions themselves are, as argued in chapter 3, unlikely to simply 'wither away'.

It is important to realize that not all separatist forces are the same and their hold on power cannot be equated with an abuse of power. Some rebel forces manage to develop fairly effective governance structures, some include citizens' participation, and some clearly enjoy popular legitimacy (see Arjona et al., 2015; Mampilly, 2011). However, following violent conflicts, we are dealing with former armed movements that will find transition to civilian politics difficult and may not be the most natural democrats (see e.g. Sriram, 2008). At the central level, the armed forces are similarly likely to have been empowered by the violent conflict and may be reluctant to accept reforms, especially if it involves any kind of accountability for abuses committed during the conflict. We therefore find similar constraints, but also potential threats to long-term stability, when it comes to dealing with past abuses.

Some of the amnesty arrangements are implicit or granted behind closed doors, but this can still impact negatively on stability, both in the short- and long-term. The revelation of the secret letters caused a political crisis in Northern Ireland (BBC News, 2015a); the letters were secret precisely because such an arrangement would have been unacceptable to the Unionist negotiators. This points to a more general problem with amnesty arrangements: it might succeed in bringing some spoilers on board, but it can create new ones, or at least increase opposition to the peace process (see also Sriram, 2008, p. 186).[62] Amnesties can also cause problems for the longer-term sustainability of the agreement. The roots of the conflict are left unaddressed and the 'leaders of groups responsible for atrocities will not only go free, but also be given power in any future state' (Sriram, 2008, pp. 181–2). Territorial self-government and power-sharing institutions are typically left in the hands of the 'men with the guns', who are possibly not the best to make the necessary transition and support peaceful and democratic developments. In terms of the wider implications, amnesties signal to leaders involved in other separatist conflicts that they do not have to worry about human rights abuses; amnesty beckons as long as they eventually agree to a peace settlement (Grono, 2006).

It is hard to get away from the fact that negotiations often require concessions to 'unsavoury groups' (Sriram, 2008, p. 182) and this will frequently involve implicit amnesties. However, is it possible to make this only a short-term price; can justice be served at a later date? Here it may matter if the amnesty is de facto or de jure, as the former is clearly a lot more flexible. Not mentioning prosecution, and giving warlords a share in power, is not the same as granting amnesty explicitly and could open up for a rethink at a later stage. Bell (2000) argues that full accountability measures are rarely part of a peace agreement, and argues that such an agreement should be seen as transitional. The problem is that various ways of building in flexibility such as sunset clauses (no prosecutions for a specified time period) may not be acceptable to the leaders or will make them so determined to hold on to a political and, especially, military power that the agreement is rendered even less flexible as a result. The only case where we see this kind of sequencing is Bosnia, where war crimes suspects were largely left in peace initially, but pursued much more forcefully later on. However in this case the framework was already in place and the international actors were the key driving force. These conditions are not found in the other cases. And it still took thirteen and fifteen years, respectively, from the signing of the Dayton Agreement till

Radovan Karadžić and Ratko Mladić were finally arrested. Once an agreement has been put in place, it is hard to depart significantly from its basic principles, including on justice.

Alternative forms of accountability will likely prove less controversial than retributive justice and may be easier to introduce at a later stage. In the case of Bougainville, a process of restorative justice within Bougainville has been launched, despite a lack of detail in the peace agreement, and hailed as a success (Reddy, 2008). The prime minister of Papua New Guinea and the leader of the autonomous region have, moreover, broken an arrow in a reconciliation ceremony (Australia Associated Press, 2014). But such efforts crucially serve the strategic interests of both sides. An independence referendum is to be held by 2020, as long as Bougainville meets certain conditions, including 'good governance' which is defined to include democracy and respect for human rights (art. 313a). The Bougainville leadership therefore has an interest in implementing human rights provisions and ensuring intra-communal unity, while the PNG Government seeks to convince the inhabitants of Bougainville of the benefits of remaining within a common state. Nevertheless, the slow pace and inclusivity of the peace process also mattered. The Australian Foreign Minister, Alexander Downer, commented that 'oodles of patience' were required (Reddy, 2008, p. 120). Intra-communal reconciliation preceded disarmament (ibid.) and it took four years before elections to the autonomous government, which were assessed as 'free and fair', were held. The peace process was also broad from the beginning, with women playing an important role (ibid.).

Conclusion

While human rights are mentioned in most of the agreements, the commitment tends to be vague and largely rhetorical. This reflects the 'core deal' of territorial autonomy, as well as the power motives of negotiating leaders and the narrowness of the process. Putnam has argued that 'human rights provisions in settlements correlate only weakly, if at all, with the quantity and quality of human rights protections during and after implementation' (2002, p. 238). But although we do find several examples of unimplemented human rights provisions, such as Aceh's Human Rights Court and Commission for Truth and Reconciliation (Amnesty International, 2013b, Hadi, 2008), this may at least in part be explained by a lack of detail and a lack of genuine commitment. The articles on human rights in Aceh's Memorandum of Understanding were simply 'too vague to be effective' (Hadi, 2008), given the resistance they faced. There are also examples of human rights measures being implemented in the post-settlement phase, even if they were not included in the peace agreement or only mentioned in very vague terms, such as the reconciliation process in Bougainville. But such provisions are unlikely to significantly undermine the core deal or the powers of the leaders. If human rights are not included in the peace settlement, the obvious risk is that they will never be prioritized, especially given the considerable obstacles most of the agreements create for individual rights and the rights of non-dominant communities. Moreover, it is undoubtedly easier for both domestic forces and third parties to push for human rights in the post-settlement phase if the conflict parties have already agreed to them in principle, and especially if details and enforcement mechanisms are included in the agreement. Otherwise, the chic language of human rights will more often than not remain an unrealized potential.

— 5 —

A POST-COLD WAR BLUEPRINT
FOR PEACE?

'Nothing is agreed until everything is agreed' is a common refrain from international mediators (Merikallio & Ruokanen, 2015, p. 294). This points to the difficulty of reaching a settlement but also illustrates that peace agreements should be seen as a package. We can break a peace agreement into its component parts and analyse each in turn, but the different mechanisms interact and the effect of each depends on the agreement as a whole. Whether human rights are emphasized for example depends on the degree of separation included in the agreement and extensive territorial autonomy may substitute for power-sharing at the centre. While the individual parts are crucial, and often present stumbling blocks during negotiations, it is the agreement in its entirety that counts; this determines if it will be accepted in the first place and whether it will enjoy popular legitimacy and prove sustainable. Specific elements, such as the lack of prosecution of war crimes, may for example be regarded as illegitimate, but other aspects may make up for this and therefore result in the agreement as a whole being seen as legitimate. Or the reverse: individual elements are regarded as legitimate, but the whole is not. Similarly, the preceding chapters have touched on the potential risk of ambiguous provisions, and while ambiguity in one area may be manageable, the effect of cumulative ambiguity is more likely to be destabilizing. Likewise, the intra-communal dynamics and capacity which have been stressed throughout the analysis are affected by the agreement as a whole. These issues will be further explored in this chapter.

Viewing the agreements as packages also raises the question of what kind of peace we are dealing with. Is it possible to identify a post-Cold War blueprint for peace settlements and does it reflect the much-maligned 'liberal peace-building' (see e.g. Richmond, 2009).

The second part of the chapter discusses how important this package is for the post-settlement period: How much path dependency should we expect? The chapter finds that the post-Cold War 'peace package' in separatist conflicts is in fact much more illiberal than existing literature implies; although it is based on 'Western' conceptions of the state, its liberal elements are often negligible. Although it is possible to ensure some flexibility, most drastically through interim agreements, it is difficult to depart significantly from wartime dynamics and the resulting core deal. In other words: the content of the agreement matters.

Trends: Simple Autonomy, But Some Creative Potential

One of the clearest trends that can be noted in the twenty peace agreements is the preference for autonomy as a solution to self-determination conflicts: it was included in all but one agreement. The degree of this autonomy varies significantly but it is territorially-defined in all but two cases. This could be seen as unsurprising. A claim to self-determination is at the core of these conflicts and these claims are predominantly made on behalf of groups that are territorially concentrated, thereby presenting territorial autonomy as a fairly straightforward compromise that will protect the territorial integrity of the state, while recognizing the legitimacy of the demand for (internal) self-determination (see e.g. Ghai, 2000). Territorial autonomy is however also occasionally proposed in non-separatist conflicts. For example, the Lusaka Protocol for Angola (1994) and the General Peace Agreement for Mozambique (1992) both included elements of territorial autonomy for rebel-held areas (in the latter case as a transitional measure), and territorial solutions are also increasingly prescribed for Syria (Reuters, 2016). Territorial autonomy can recognize 'facts-on-the-ground', provide reassurances for rebel forces, and it reduces the need for reform and cooperation at the centre.

Yet what is noticeable is that this autonomy in many cases stands on its own; it is almost *the* solution to separatist conflicts. The autonomous regions are generally not part of a federal structure, with federalism having become delegitimized by the Soviet and Yugoslav collapse, and power-sharing either centrally or locally is only found in a minority of the cases. What we therefore tend to find is not so much 'complex power-sharing' (Wolff, 2009), but rather 'simple autonomy'. Moreover, almost all agreements lack a focus on, or an

115

understanding of, intra-communal divisions and of the need for sub-state capacity.

The autonomy arrangements tend to be ethnic in their effects, in the sense that they empower a particular group within the region. This is most frequently the local majority group, such as the Acehnese in Aceh; although the favoured group can be a minority, such as the tribal groups in Bodoland. One apparent trend is, however, that the ethnic character of these arrangements is de facto rather than de jure. This is most notable in the Ohrid Agreement for Macedonia, which studiously avoids mentioning the Albanian minority. But it can even be observed in the case of Bosnia, where the autonomous powers of the two entities are not ethnically-defined. They function as ethnic units, due to the congruence of territory and ethnicity produced by the war, but the hope was that this would be gradually reversed. This kind of arrangement can offer some scope for flexibility, but it can also foster intense resistance to change from nationalist forces. It can moreover cause difficulties, if the arrangement is based on a lack of recognition of the heterogeneity of the autonomous region and, oftentimes, of the separatist group itself.

Recent literature has made much of the importance of security, and in particular security institutions, for sustainable peace. Yet the analysis found that although security issues play a central role in all the agreements signed following violent conflicts, many of them depart from the idea of creating strong security institutions that can ensure sufficient harm to anyone violating the agreement (Toft, 2009). The commitment problem identified by, for example, Walter (2002) is in most cases not addressed by robust third party security guarantees, but instead through the use of phased approaches and by granting autonomous powers over coercive forces. Legitimacy is as important as effectiveness when it comes to security provisions. One of the important functions of these autonomous forces is to ensure intra-communal stability. This is however associated with potential complications: these forces may not have the capacity to ensure local stability, or they may only be able to do so at the expense of individual rights and freedoms. This problem was further highlighted in chapter 4, which found that the reference to human rights was in most cases rhetorical and appeared to constitute an attempt to ensure international legitimacy rather than an attempt to genuinely affect the post-war political order.

The dominant model for international peace-building in the post-Cold War era has been described as 'a peace from IKEA: a flat-pack peace from standardised components' (Cooper et al., 2011, pp. 1997–8). This standardized package of liberal peace-building is seen by its critics as an attempt to impose a Western understanding of the state, based on security, democracy, rule of law, human rights and free markets (see e.g. Mac Ginty & Richmond, 2013). Hayden also laments that the range of solutions proposed in intra-state conflicts is 'extremely limited'. He identifies a uniform model of 'mini-states connected by a central government of very limited powers' (2005, pp. 227–8). Some authors however point to greater creativity, such as interim agreements (Weller, 2008) and complex power-sharing (Wolff, 2009). Bell (2008, p. 236) argues that a new Law of Peace is rapidly evolving, which includes 'a more fluid concept of statehood with fuzzy sovereignty'.

Some clear trends can be identified in the peace agreements analysed in this book: a focus on territory, in particular in the form of territorial autonomy; and a focus on group rights, rather than individual rights, with human rights relegated to the symbolic level. However, the agreements reflect the specific conflict context, such as the strength of the separatist forces, the demographic balance, the intensity of the conflict and the extent of international involvement. We can therefore at most talk about blueprints, in plural, rather than one standardized package. Some of the agreements do try to blur sovereignty, such as the crucial trans-border dimensions in the Belfast Agreement. But this kind of ingenuity is only found in a few cases, and we still see a great deal of international reluctance and central government refusal when it comes to attempts to fudge sovereignty or indeed contemplate a change of borders. This is particularly a problem for the most protracted conflicts where autonomy is not enough to sway the separatist forces to accept a compromise solution. We also see some attempts at rethink as far as the definition of groups are concerned. This should be welcomed, but it is constrained especially in more severe conflicts and remains the exception. When it comes to individual rights what is striking is how illiberal many of these agreements are. Elections may be held, but they generally tend to reinforce, and legitimate, the powers of the agreement signatories. The emphasis is on ethnic groups and their rights, individual rights are either ignored or largely symbolic, the central state is rarely required to introduce significant reforms, and the 'men with the guns' tend to be empowered at the expense of other actors and groups. Several agreements were negotiated in 'Western bubbles' (Mac Ginty & Richmond, 2013, p. 763) and almost all of them made use of international mediators, but although they can perhaps be said to be 'Western' when it comes to the emphasis on self-governance and the importance of territory (Dalsheim, 2014), they do not generally embody liberal values.

Critics of the liberal peace point to its often illiberal outcomes and Richmond (2009) regrets that the post-Cold War moral capital, its emancipatory claim, has been squandered, while Barnett and his colleagues more pragmatically argue that 'compromised peace-building' may be the best that can be hoped for (Barnett et al., 2014). But the above analysis suggests that these ideals are squandered much earlier. Not during the implementation phase, which the debate usually focuses on, but when the peace settlement is negotiated (see also Selby, 2013). Part of the reason is the 'core deal' of these agreements, territorial autonomy and power-sharing, which creates genuine dilemmas and trade-offs between individual rights and minority protection. However, the lack of prioritization of human rights also reflects that the narrative of ethnic groups engaged in conflict tends to be accepted by the international mediators. The local leaders are accepted as representative leaders and the focus of the talks is on providing security and political rights for the groups they claim to represent, and positions of power for the leaders themselves. This is also linked to the narrowness of the process. Groups and actors advocating human rights are simply not included in the talks.[63]

In conclusion, although there are some examples of creativity, especially when it comes to sovereignty and to group definitions, and the agreements are written in the language of human rights, the effect of this remains limited and the dominant model is a fairly standard autonomy arrangement. If we wanted to argue that the glass is half-full, rather than half-empty, we could point to tensions and potential included in the agreements, and the possibility of addressing 'softer' concerns in the peace-building phase. Bell (2008) notes the tensions in peace agreements and a progressive reading of the new 'Law on Peace' hinges on such post-settlement flexibility. But the problem is that the 'core deal' and the actors empowered by it will limit what is possible later on. Overlooking the content of the peace settlements, and instead viewing peace-building as a distinct phase, skews the debate. In order to assess the possibility of moving beyond the initial settlement, we have to look at the agreement as a package. We need to examine the effects of its combined ambiguities and this is when it may matter that these agreements use the language of human rights and that they tend to favour civic over ethnic categories. This could create a space, albeit a small one, for a more liberal peace to emerge.

The Whole Package

All of the agreements rely on a mix of institutional mechanisms. At the core of most of them is territorial self-governance but this is combined with, for example, security sector reform and (limited) human rights provisions. The tendency to combine different conflict resolution measures has already been pointed to in the literature (see e.g. Wolff, 2009), but what has not been explored in detail is how these different provisions interact. The different elements of an agreement interact in ways that affect both the initial acceptance, or rejection, and the longer-term sustainability of an agreement. The interaction of the separate institutional elements, such as the provision of territory and power, will have an impact on whether 'good enough governance' or a 'legitimate peace' is achieved (see Themner & Ohlson, 2014).

Territory and Security

Provisions on territory and security are particularly closely linked. It is no coincidence that the NATO forces in the case of Bosnia had to ensure not only the military but also the territorial provisions in the Dayton Agreement. Territory is not only symbolically important, as a recognized homeland; territorial control also provides the community with a sense of security against a central government whose intentions may still not be trusted. The popularity of territorial autonomy therefore helps explain the relative lack of reforms of the central security institutions. What is emphasized is the creation of autonomous coercive forces and only the agreements for Mali, Niger and the Philippines–Mindanao were to lead to an integrated army, while the agreements for Serbia & Montenegro and Sudan include the creation of a joint military command. The former three cases were characterized by sizeable rebel forces and fairly limited or ambiguous autonomy arrangements, which may have led to a greater need for such reforms. The latter cases are interim agreements and the joint commands only constitute a weak tie to a centre, while separate forces are maintained. Police reforms were only central in Northern Ireland and Macedonia, i.e. cases of non-territorial autonomy and limited territorial autonomy, respectively.

Due to these dominant security arrangements, security *within* the autonomous regions becomes a crucial issue but one that has not received much attention in the literature. Separatist groups, and

119

frequently also the autonomous regions resulting from the settlements, tend to be viewed as homogeneous, but this is very rarely the case. Factions vie for dominance both during the war and after it has ended (see e.g. Bakke et al., 2012). In order for peace to be sustainable intra-communal stability has to be ensured and within the newly created autonomous territories this often falls to the separatist leaders; they have to ensure that other armed groups abide by the agreement and they have to provide law and order. However, they may not have the capacity or the inclination to do so. One problem concerns a lack of resources. If the question of resources is not properly addressed by the agreement, or if the promised resources never appear, then the local leaders may be unable to ensure stability. Ill-thought out territorial autonomy or the failure by central governments to properly implement an autonomy agreement can undermine local security and thereby threaten the overall agreement. The Mindanao region, for example, became almost a byword for anarchy: the autonomous government lacked fiscal autonomy and did not control the local police and armed forces, even though this was part of the peace agreement. This lack of capacity contributed to a failure to provide basic public services and an inability to defeat the more extreme MILF (Lara Jr & Champain, 2009, p. 11). Similar problems were seen in the case of Israel–Palestine. The Palestinian Authority did not manage to ensure internal security and this was a contributing factor in the collapse of the agreement. This inability can, in part, be explained by the lack of territorial contiguity, which made effective administration difficult (Newman, 1995–6, p. 76), and the serious economic decline caused by Israel's 'closure policy' (Roy, 2002).

Tasking former armed movements with internal security is common in peace agreements (see also Podder, 2014), but such hybrid political orders present significant challenges, even if the degree and form of pre-existing (rebel) governance vary between the cases (see e.g. Arjona et al., 2015). Sriram (2008, pp. 138–9) describes how in Sudan the SPLM/A struggled to transform itself from a military movement into an institutionalized party with the capacity to rule and ensure order. Yasser Arafat was accused of spending most of the international funds received by the PA shoring up his regime, rather than benefiting the Palestinian population (Perlmutter, 1995, p. 64). Tuminez (2007, p. 83) similarly describes the leader of the MNLF, who came to govern autonomous Mindanao, as 'an incompetent administrator with exorbitant habits' and argues that overall the Moro leaders 'appeared more interested in their own self-enrichment than the development of their people'.

Transitional challenges will exist for all armed groups, but such capacity problems can be reinforced by the peace agreement itself. Lack of resources and incomplete implementation is one problem, but another is that the autonomy arrangements typically recognize the separatist leaders as representative of the community as a whole, with few if any provisions for diverging interests, or indeed for other communal groups within the autonomous region to be represented. In South Sudan, the SPLM managed to reach an agreement with other armed groups, but the new institutions were dominated by the SPLM. This led to instability before the independence referendum and more seriously to the outbreak of a bloody civil war in the newly independent state (see e.g. Wolff, 2013). Similar problems of lack of inclusivity and broader legitimacy were found in the case of the Palestinian Authority and the Mindanao autonomous region (see e.g. Lara Jr & Champain, 2009; Perlmutter, 1995). We therefore see important interactions between territory and security, and also between territory, security and (political) power.

Political Power, Territory and Security

Chapter 3 already discussed how territorial autonomy is a possible solution when power-sharing at the centre is not acceptable to the dominant group. This is especially likely to be the case if the separatist group is relatively small, while the dominant group constitutes a majority. Territorial autonomy in that case provides the minority group with, an extent of, self-rule and some protection against majority dominance without requiring the dominant group to cede much power at the centre (O'Leary, 2013b, p. 392). Territorial autonomy can therefore substitute for a guaranteed share in central political power. Without this share in power, and the minority veto that usually accompanies it, the minority group is however more vulnerable to recentralization and loss of autonomous powers. There was for example nothing to stop the gradual undermining of territorial autonomy in the case of Crimea; apart from the Russian intervention in 2014, that is. A domestic exit option can be said to exist in cases of very high levels of territorial autonomy, including separate coercive forces, which give the separatist leaders a de facto veto against recentralization.

The interrelationship between power-sharing and territorial autonomy also affects the performance of the arrangement (Bieber, 2013). A low degree of territorial autonomy would alleviate fears of secession, but could lead to increased contestation at the centre,

121

and present a risk of dangerous deadlocks. Blockages will have less impact on the overall structure of governance in cases of high degrees of territorial autonomy, since other levels of government can continue to function undisturbed. The downside is that leaders have few incentives to invest in such 'thin states' and this could lead to a 'centrifugal minimalist state' (ibid., p. 322). In both Bosnia and Serbia & Montenegro, 'the limited competences gave rise to a level of compliance with the state institutions' decisions that was lower than what was formally foreseen' (ibid.). In the case of Sudan, the SPLM withdrew from the power-sharing government in 2007 (Brosché, 2008) and only rejoined once a new agreement had been reached that included a rotating seat of government (between Khartoum and Juba) (BBC News, 2007). Even though power-sharing institutions are meant to tie autonomous regions to the centre, and counteract centrifugal tendencies, they will struggle to perform this function in cases of very high levels of autonomy. The stateness problem has been institutionalized, and in the case of Bosnia it took heavy-handed international involvement to counteract this dynamic (Bieber, 2013, pp. 320–2).

The interaction between power-sharing and security has generally not been considered by the power-sharing literature, but it is crucial. The central institutions in the 'thin state' described above are typically unable to enforce their decisions: the central security structures are too weak (ibid.). This adds to the centrifugal tendencies. Power-sharing agreements are moreover highly dependent on the ability of the leaders to ensure stability within their own communities. Intra-communal security is, as argued above, important in all agreements but power-sharing agreements are, due to the need for consensus at the centre, even more vulnerable to spoilers and to processes of outbidding. On the plus side, power-sharing institutions can make it possible to defer vital security issues; such as decommissioning and police reform in Northern Ireland. Decommissioning nearly derailed the agreement later on, but the agreement proved strong enough to survive this challenge. Such a positive trade-off between power-sharing and security provisions depends, however, on a fairly high level of trust in the process and in the agreement, which is likely to be absent in many other cases. Political power-sharing institutions do not on their own provide sufficient guarantees. A bloody intra-state war teaches both sides that the gun rules and power-sharing institutions will likely have to be supplemented by robust third party guarantees (see Walter, 2002) or separate coercive forces.

Completing the Agreement: Human Rights and Security

Issues relating to territory and political power will often be seen as the 'central deal'. These are the institutions that determine how, or if, self-determination will be realized and the ways in which the future state (or states) will be governed. But security and human rights have a significant effect on the functioning of these institutions and can convince the population that concessions are worth it. Irwin (2013) finds that the Belfast Agreement as a 'package' was more popular than its individual parts. There would therefore seem to be very weighty reasons for prioritizing human rights and security. Yet, security is usually interpreted in 'traditional' terms with an emphasis on overall stability and group protections, and a lack of focus on public or human security. This may make it more difficult to build a sufficient peace constituency, which could undermine the sustainability of the agreement.[64] The issue of human rights in peace agreements is, as argued above, a complicated one. Even when human rights provisions are included, effective protections also depend on other parts of the agreement, in particular security institutions. It is important to note that human rights provisions can be manipulated by more powerful groups; an insistence on 'one (wo)man, one vote' can for example be a cover for majority dominance. If a court is able to overrule power-sharing institutions (and their decisions) based on human rights, then this would weaken group protections (O'Leary, 2013b). This is therefore not simply a question of peace versus justice; it is also a question of justice for whom? There is a genuine tension between protecting group rights and individual rights, but the lack of prioritization of human rights also makes it easier for the leaders to consolidate their power and establish what sometimes amounts to ethno-national fiefdoms. This suggests that it will be difficult to add human rights at a later stage.

Ensuring Flexibility

A peace agreement is, as Hampson argues, an 'imperfect road map to the future': key provisions will have to be (re)negotiated during the implementation phase, because they were left out of the original agreement, because they were too ambiguous or because they turned out to be unimplementable (1996, pp. 218–19). Ambiguity can make it easier to reach a compromise, as both sides can interpret an agreement in their favour and sell it as a victory to their followers; it can therefore be a way of turning a zero-sum game (if you win, I lose) into a positive-sum game (we both win). Henry Kissinger famously coined the term 'constructive ambiguity' to describe this technique, which he argued made it possible to reach a compromise settlement in the 1973 Arab–Israeli war. It has similarly been argued that the genius of the Belfast Agreement was that all parties could defend it as containing the elements of what they had fought for all along: Nationalists could argue that it was a first step towards a united Ireland, while Unionists could argue that it preserved British sovereignty. (Sisk & Stefes, 2005, p. 311). Flexibility is also important for long-term stability. Peace agreements are almost invariably imperfect. Negotiations are often conducted under extreme time pressure, which does not allow for a careful wording of the documents. The process is moreover usually narrow and the actors whose interests have to be accommodated, such as warlords, do not necessarily have long-term governability and stability as their main concern. Flexibility is needed in order to avoid the freezing of wartime dynamics.

Such flexibility in the design of political institutions is difficult to achieve, however, since the conflict parties will demand credible commitments and solid guarantees (ibid., p. 296). The weaker party in particular will try to secure an agreement that is as clear as possible and provides guarantees that are not easily eroded. The tendency will be for fairly rigid agreements. Excessive ambiguity and the postponement of key issues can moreover backfire. It creates uncertainty, the stronger group may be tempted to manipulate the implementation of the agreement, and both sides may feel cheated. It is therefore important to strike a balance between constructive and destructive ambiguity. This depends on both the content of the agreement, which will be discussed below, and on the nature of the peace process, which will be discussed in the next two chapters. Possible ways of ensuring flexible agreements include postponing contentious issues, interim agreements and ambiguous provisions. Incrementalism is often recommended as a conflict resolution strategy as it allows for the building of trust (see e.g. Armstrong, 1993). Partial agreements on separate issues are sometimes brought together in a comprehensive peace agreement, such as Sudan's Comprehensive Peace Agreement, which includes six agreements concluded over a period of three years. Moreover, renegotiation is invariably part of the post-settlement process. However, I will argue that when it comes to comprehensive agreements, ambiguous core provisions are likely to be destructive rather than constructive. Moreover, the analysis points to significant path dependency; it is difficult to depart from the initial, comprehensive, agreement.

Postponing Contentious Issues

Constructive ambiguity was a hallmark of the Oslo Declaration for Israel–Palestine (Elgindy, 2014), which deferred a range of divisive issues, such as the return of refugees, for future talks. The hope was that it would be easier to resolve these issues once a greater level of trust and confidence in the process had been created. However, the uncertainty only seemed to heighten insecurities and fears. Ambiguity 'succeeded only in producing confusion and eroding trust between the parties and disagreements over how to interpret various provisions led to endless delays ... renegotiation and outright lack of implementation' (ibid.). The postponement of contentious issues was much more successful in the case of Northern Ireland, where decommissioning and police reforms were kicked into the long grass. Reaching agreements on these issues proved to be extraordinarily difficult, and brought the peace process close to breaking point, but it succeeded in the end. Two things appear to have been decisive. Firstly, the mechanisms for agreeing on these issues had already been decided: it was left to independent commissions which included international representatives. Secondly, the power-sharing institutions framed and helped legitimize these talks.

This approach has been also used, with more limited success, when it comes to the division of strategic territories. In both Bosnia and Sudan, the decision on who should control contested territories was deferred for later and left in the hands of an international body. In the case of Bosnia's Brčko district the decision caused fury in Republika Srpska, but no further instability (Jeffrey, 2006). In the case of Sudan, the oil-rich region Abyei is however still disputed (Tendai, 2011). By the time the commission made its decision the context had changed, which points to the dangers of cumulative ambiguity: it now appeared clear that South Sudan was heading for independence. A number of other agreements are ambiguous when it comes to the borders of the promised autonomous regions, or leave a final decision for later, but such deferral of a highly contentious issue has often caused instability.

Postponing contentious issues can be the only way to reach an agreement, but the risk is that it creates future instability that could lead to the collapse of the agreement. Such deferral should ideally not involve – and not risk undermining – the core deal of the agreement, and the mechanisms for its resolution should be specified.

Interim Agreements

Another version of 'constructive ambiguity' involves the use of interim agreements. These agreements do not simply defer contentious issues; they create new temporary institutions. Unlike a permanent settlement, which is deliberately difficult to alter, an interim agreement builds in the promise of significant changes after a specific period of time.

In non-territorial conflicts, the use of transitional power-sharing arrangements has emerged as a dominant model. The transitional period is intended to create the conditions for free and fair elections (Gutteri & Piombo, 2007), and also avoids the freezing of a potentially dysfunctional system (Sisk & Stefes, 2005). Sisk and Stefes point to the usefulness of such a temporary power-sharing arrangement in the case of South Africa, and argue that two factors made it possible: an imbalance of power and a common vision of a future state (ibid.). This is unlikely to be found elsewhere, especially in separatist conflicts. The whole point of a power-sharing agreement, especially in its consociational form, is that it is difficult to alter; it provides solid guarantees for the minority against being outvoted. Putting a time-limit on such protections will likely prove unacceptable.

The only example of transitional provisions when it comes to the core political institutions is found in Bougainville, where the autonomy arrangement is to be reviewed every five years. The first review was meant to have happened in 2010 but was not completed until 2013. While this did not make any changes to the core deal, it did include a commitment by the PNG Government to complete and consolidate the transfer of functions to Bougainville and the payment of outstanding grants, and the Bougainville Government promised to strengthen law and order in the region.[65] Transitional provisions otherwise relate only to military arrangements. In Mindanao, the former rebel combatants were for example to be integrated into special units of the army as a transitional measure until a fully integrated army could be created. However, as discussed in chapter 2, this proved extremely contentious. The two sides had distinctly different interpretations of who should control these units, and they were therefore never created (Martin, 2011), and no significant changes to the conflict dynamics or to the 'core deal' resulted. One of the lessons from interim governments is how difficult it is to move beyond the transitional arrangement. As Manning (2007, p. 54) argues, there is little reason to suppose that the elite strategies or the distribution of political power that the agreement has established can easily be changed.

A less tested form of transitional agreement is however found in the analysed agreements: interim agreements that defer the decision on the final status of the breakaway territory. In the ideal type situation, the central government recognizes the breakaway region as a self-determination unit that has the right to independence, but the separatist forces agree to freeze the implementation of that right for a certain period. During the interim period, the separatist region is granted autonomy and continued territorial unity is 'given a chance' (Weller, 2005a, pp. 159–60). These agreements are in practice, however, often highly ambiguous and the right to (external) self-determination is not always accepted by the government.

Five examples of interim agreements are analysed in this book. The Comprehensive Peace Agreement for Sudan promised South Sudan an independence referendum six years after the signing of the agreement. This was a compromise in that the SPLM accepted the longer interim period that the NCP insisted on and also committed itself to make territorial unity attractive (ibid., p. 166). A future independence referendum is also included in the case of PNG–Bougainville. This has to be held between ten and fifteen years after the establishment of the autonomous government (i.e. between 2015 and 2020), as long as certain preconditions relating to good governance and weapons disposal are met. The agreement contains no clear commitment to work for unity in the interim period, but it does grant the PNG parliament the final say; unusually the independence referendum is therefore not legally binding. In the case of Serbia & Montenegro, either republic could request an independence referendum following an interim period of three years. No commitment to facilitate unity was included. A more ambiguous agreement was reached in the case of Chechnya. According to the Khasavyurt Accord, the final status of the republic would be determined within five years. Finally, the Declaration of Principles for Israel–Palestine is also an interim agreement which postpones a number of key issues, including borders and the 'final territorial arrangement', for future talks. These talks were to begin two years after Gaza and Jericho became autonomous (i.e. May 1996). Newman (1995–6, p. 79) argues that a 'final territorial arrangement' is an Israeli euphemism for the creation of a Palestinian state. However it does not guarantee which territory this will include, nor does it necessarily point to full independence (Cassese, 1993, p. 569).

Interim agreements have also been suggested in other protracted conflicts as a way of squaring the circle between territorial integrity and self-determination. For example, in the case of Nagorno Karabakh the current framework proposal includes a vote on the final status of the territory following an unspecified interim period. The interim agreement which was proposed for Kosovo in 1999, but rejected by the Serbian Government, hid the issue of Kosovo's final status at the end of the document: 'Three years after the entry into force of this Agreement, an international meeting shall be convened to determine a mechanism for a final settlement for Kosovo, on the basis of the will of the people' (Ch. 8, art. 1). US officials confirmed that this was to be understood as an independence referendum (Weller, 2005a). The second version of the Peace Plan for Self-Determination of the People of Western Sahara, also known as Baker II, similarly proposed an independence referendum following an interim period of five years.[66]

The benefit of an interim agreement is that it makes compromise easier. Since the final status has yet to be decided, both sides can argue that their maximalist objective will prevail. Hughes (2001, p. 32) argues that a masterstroke to secure the Khasavyurt Accord for Chechnya 'was a core ambiguity whereby the final decision on the status of Chechnya was postponed for "up to" five years'. The Chechen side had achieved de facto independence and believed that international recognition would eventually follow. However, Russia had not had to relinquish its sovereignty and had no intention to allow Chechen independence; all they wanted was a delay, a limbo in the conflict (Hughes, 2007, pp. 90–3). The hope is that the status issue will be easier to resolve once violence has ceased, tempers have cooled and trust has been re-established. An interim agreement also gives coexistence a chance to work. The central government will have to prove itself in order to preserve the common state; it will have to demonstrate its benign intentions to an often fearful minority. This kind of framework could therefore be hoped to encourage moderation. The problem is however that the underlying issue, often *the* issue that drives the conflict, remains unsettled, and violence can easily break out again, for example if it becomes clear to one side that they will not reach their goal, that independence will for example not follow from the promised referendum.

Interim agreements are typically if-all-else-fails solutions; a last attempt to reach a settlement. But certain preconditions must nevertheless be met for such agreements to be possible. If the agreement includes an independence referendum at the end of the interim period, then it is essential that both sides are willing to give unity a chance. For example, in the case of Sudan the agreement explicitly requires the two sides to make the unity of the Sudan an attractive option especially to the people of South Sudan (Ch. 1, art. 2.4.2). Related to this there must be some uncertainty regarding the outcome of the final vote. An interim agreement can be said to prejudge the final status, in particular if it recognizes the separatist unit as a self-determination unit, but the interim period is meant to provide an opportunity for territorial integrity to be maintained. Again, in the case of Sudan the leader of the SPLM/A, John Garang, had visions of a New Sudan (Brosché, 2008, p. 247) and he, along with other SPLM leaders, also had political ambitions in the North (Weller, 2005a, p. 176). Similarly, in the case of Bougainville, the community is divided over the issue of independence, with powerful factions supporting territorial autonomy as a permanent solution (Ghai & Regan, 2006). The PNG Government is therefore convinced that the common state can be maintained if (extensive) autonomy is given a chance (Weller, 2005a, p. 161; Woodbury, 2015). The referendum is in any case not legally binding. If it is completely certain from the outset that independence will be favoured, then the interim period achieves nothing. The parties might as well agree on the final status now, even if implementation is delayed. This is of course possible, as when Eritrea gained independence from Ethiopia, but it is very rare indeed that central governments agree to give up on their territorial integrity.

The preconditions for an interim agreement will however not often be met. Following a bloody war, the result of an independence referendum will in many cases be a foregone conclusion. In the case of Kosovo, it would have been abundantly clear to the Serbian leadership that an independence referendum would be overwhelmingly supported in the province. In the case of Nagorno Karabakh, the result would also be entirely predictable and merely depend on where it was held and who was allowed to vote. If a referendum is held in Karabakh only, then the result would be a resounding Yes to independence – even if Azeri IDPs returned and were able to vote. This is why Azerbaijan is adamant that a popular 'expression of will', under these circumstances, must not include the option of full independence (see e.g. Trend Agency, 2011). The modalities of the referendum were meant to be postponed for future talks,[67] but the question of 'who would vote, on what and when' has become a crucial stumbling block in the negotiations (Huseynov, 2010, p. 16). It may be possible to get the parties to agree to an interim settlement even if these preconditions are not met, such as in Chechnya, but only if the final status and the mechanisms for deciding upon it are deliberately ambiguous. Such an agreement will however cause considerable problems for the implementation phase.

The transitional nature of an interim agreement will, regardless of the specific mechanisms agreed on, significantly affect its implementation and the functioning of its interim institutions. All eyes will be on the end-game – the final status decision – and this will influence the political and military decisions made. The separatist leaders will have little incentive to cooperate, at least as far as the central institutions are concerned. They have every reason to demonstrate that the joint state is not functioning and that independence is the only option. The central government does have incentives to make the interim institutions work, as this is a chance to demonstrate the benefits of continued coexistence and this is much more easily done if the agreement is implemented, institutions are well-functioning and minority rights respected. We could therefore expect the central government to go the extra mile and ensure successful implementation. However, the government may also fear that by implementing the agreement they will create more effective institutions in the separatist region, resulting in the emergence of a proto-state that will strengthen their opponents and make secession more likely. The lack of effective institutions in the autonomous region is, as argued above, a likely source of instability, but if the central government is primarily concerned with the risk of secession, they may work hard to avoid anything that could strengthen the legitimacy of the separatist leaders. Moreover, the agreement may have been so intentionally ambiguous, in order to make compromise possible, that the central government has in fact never agreed to the possibility of independence, or they may change their mind as a result of a change in the balance of power.

The cases analysed appear to confirm non-cooperation as the dominant trend. Following the death of John Garang, the separatist faction of the SPLM became more dominant and the NCP became reluctant to implement the peace agreement, reportedly fearing that it would strengthen the SPLM and increase the risk of independence for South Sudan (Brosché, 2008, pp. 238–9). The SPLM on its part became increasingly focused on the institutions in South Sudan and the party's new leader did not run in the 2010 presidential elections. The SPLM argued that there was no need for him to run with the independence referendum only months away (*The Sudan Tribune*, 2009) and the party in the end withdrew its alternative candidate for the presidency, citing 'electoral irregularities' (BBC News, 2010). Montenegro similarly showed little interest in the union with Serbia and Montenegrin deputies rarely attended sessions of parliament (Bieber, 2013). In the case of Israel–Palestine, the issue of status was postponed for later, but divisive permanent status issues kept coming to the forefront (Perlmutter, 1995, p. 63). The interim period was meant to be distinct from the final status issue (Roy, 2002), but policies pursued in the interim would, in effect, determine or at least severely constrain the final status. The prospect of Palestinian statehood was effectively undermined by the lack of contiguity of the Palestinian autonomous territory: by 2000, the Palestinian Authority only controlled 17.2 per cent of the West Bank and between 66 and 80 per cent of Gaza in isolated, encircled enclaves (Roy, 2002; see also Newman, 1995–6). The prospect of Chechen statehood was similarly undermined by Russia's failure to deliver promised economic and reconstruction aid and by the imposition of a blockade on the entity. This lack of resources weakened the authority of the Chechen leader Mashkadov and contributed to the entity's descent into anarchy (Hughes, 2007, p. 93).

Bougainville has so far been viewed as a success story. A resumption of violence has been avoided, (most) weapons have been disposed of, and effective institutions are gradually being built in the autonomous region. Yet concerns for the future are increasing as we have entered the five-year window for an independence referendum. The ambiguities of the agreement now cause uncertainty and tensions. Several problems could lead to renewed instability: firstly, the preconditions for the referendum – good governance and weapons disposal – are ill-defined and therefore open to manipulation. What level of governance has to be achieved, and does this still apply when the PNG Government has failed to supply promised resources to the autonomous region? Secondly, how will the PNG Government react to a 'yes' vote in the referendum, which looks like the most likely outcome (Woodbury, 2015)? Making the referendum non-binding may have been necessary for the 2001 agreement, as it allowed the government to argue that PNG sovereignty had not been undermined (Ghai & Regan, 2006, pp. 599–600), but it now creates significant uncertainties that could lead to a resumption of violence. The PNG Government still has reasons to oppose secession, including the economic costs and the risk of further fragmentation (Woodbury, 2015), and the fear is that it will try to avoid holding a referendum or refuse to implement the result.[68]

A couple of lessons can therefore be drawn from this fairly untested form of peace agreement. Firstly, for it to work there must be some doubt about the outcome. Such agreements will work best in cases where the central government has an actual chance of winning over 'hearts and minds' in the separatist region. Secondly, an interim agreement is by its definition ambiguous, but the level of uncertainty should be controlled; by making the link between the interim agreement and the final status explicit, not just de facto as in the case of Israel–Palestine, and by including mechanisms for deciding on status. Moreover, significant international guarantees will in most cases be needed; mistrust and fears will otherwise pose an almost insurmountable obstacle. In the case of Nagorno Karabakh, the Armenian side fears that a promised referendum will never be held or that the process will be manipulated; that they will be cheated if they agree to withdraw their troops (see Navasardian, 2006, p. 111). The composition of the peacekeeping force and other forms of international monitoring and verification are therefore crucial. The EU will almost certainly be asked to help fund such a mission, but it is not involved in the detailed planning of the interim phase. They argue that this is because the details of an agreement are still not known,[69] but such preparations are crucial; not just for the sustainability of the agreement but for reaching an agreement in the first place.

Interim agreements rely on significant transformations being possible during the transitional period, especially if the initial agreement is based on significant ambiguities. However, uncertainty regarding the final outcome as well as the violence and years of separation that often precede such an agreement militate against this. The case of Montenegro, which was not even characterized by violence and deep divisions, demonstrates how difficult it is to undo a de facto separation. But at least this separation was peaceful, and this may indeed be the main purpose of an interim agreement.

Gradual Reforms

A final strategy for ensuring post-settlement stability is to design institutions in a way that allows for gradual change. These possible mechanisms are however also significantly constrained. The hope of liberal consociationalism is, as mentioned in chapter 3, that it will allow power-sharing to wither away once attitudes change (see e.g. Wolff, 2010). However, the system tends to reinforce itself (Manning, 2007). Power-sharing systems and other institutions designed to protect the interests and rights of particular groups will, even if not formally 'ethnic', provide incentives for elites to appeal in ethnic terms and for voters to respond to such appeals. The weakening of such institutions by human rights provisions is also likely to be resisted forcefully by the elites who benefit from the existing system. Such obstacles to flexibility are particularly significant in cases where an overall consensus on the state is missing, and in cases of extensive territorial autonomy.

132

Thus, in Bosnia, only the entities were able to effectively enforce human rights protections, but they refused to take on this task (Bell, 2000, p. 227), and the ability of human rights protections to alter the structure of the state was therefore constrained. The hope that agreements can be reformed later on – that they can for example be made more 'liberal' with a greater emphasis on human rights – appears to be widespread, but it will often prove illusory. The initial agreement is a strong determinant of what is possible later on. Nevertheless, it is conceivable that the language of human rights, the framing of institutions in civic rather than ethnic terms and the granting of de facto rather than de jure amnesties could be important. It may empower reformers to demand more change and start debates (see also Barnett et al., 2014). In order for this to happen one of two things is likely to be needed: the process must be broadened or significant third party involvement is needed. These options will be discussed in the last two chapters.

Conclusion

Unless we view peace agreements as a package, we fail to understand the degree to which they address grievances, accommodate interests and the dynamics they create. Are there any combinations that should be avoided? As the previous chapters have argued, the following factors make it hard to ensure a sustainable peace: autonomy arrangements with insufficient capacity, especially when it comes to security; simple autonomy with no recognition of the diversity of the autonomous region; or power-sharing with very high levels of territorial autonomy. It is not always possible to avoid such agreements but they are likely to be beset with problems. More generally, it is necessary to achieve a balance between the parties, in terms of what they get from the agreement (Hoffman & Bercovitch, 2011). It may be possible to reach an agreement without this, for example in the case of Senegal, but it is unlikely to prove durable.

A difficult balancing act is needed when it comes to ambiguity. This can provide much needed flexibility, but ambiguities also add to the insecurity and uncertainty surrounding the agreement and can lead to renewed instability. The danger appears to be of 'cumulative ambiguity' when several provisions, including the 'core deal', are unclear. For example, in the case of an interim agreement, there is so much uncertainty regarding the final outcome that the rest of the agreement needs to be fairly unambiguous; it can be incremental and conditional but each stage should ideally be clear, with robust guarantees. Ambiguity puts a strain on the peace process and the degree to which it can withstand it depends significantly on intra-communal dynamics, but this tends to be under-analysed in existing literature, both when it comes to capacity within the autonomous region and the ability of leaders to represent their communities. State-building has received a lot of attention in the peace-building literature, to the extent that the two are often equated, but this needs to start earlier and in separatist conflicts it must be decentralized. Central governments will often be reluctant to strengthen what they perceive as separatist institutions but this puts the agreement at risk of collapse. Former warlords have to be turned into democrats or at least civilian leaders willing and able to compromise. Although these leaders will claim to represent their respective communities, this will almost always be contested and will often rely on coercion. This presents two countervailing challenges. Firstly, these leaders have to bring their followers with them in compromise and have to be able to police, both literally and figuratively, their own community. Secondly, in order for the agreement to prove durable, for it to achieve broader legitimacy, it is necessary to widen the process, to create space for dissenting voices and empower alternative actors.

The kind of peace negotiated in these separatist agreements is not the liberal peace that has been so intensely debated. It may in some cases use the language of the liberal peace, but the content is often distinctly illiberal. This raises the prospect that the illiberal outcomes that the critics have pointed to originate much earlier in the peace process. However, the question remains if the ambiguities and omissions analysed above can be utilized to make the process more liberal at a later stage. I have already argued that the initial framework matters and constrains the ability to prioritize human rights later on, or that this will at least require extensive third party involvement. The following chapters will more fully discuss the interaction between content and process, both before and after the signing of the agreement.

Part 2

Context and Process

— 6 —

INTERNAL DYNAMICS: A RIGHT TIME FOR PEACE

Seamus Mallon famously described the Belfast Agreement as 'Sunningdale for slow learners', referring to the collapsed 1973 agreement with which it shared many similarities (Powell, 2008, p. 309).[70] Other agreements have similarly been a long time in the making. The 1996 agreement for Mindanao in the Philippines was presented as the implementation of the Tripoli agreement which the conflict parties had agreed to twenty years earlier. The 2014 agreement replaces the Autonomous Region of Muslim Mindanao with an autonomous political entity named Bangsamoro, but the core of the settlement is unchanged; only the actors are new. In the case of the Nagorno Karabakh conflict, the Armenian and Azerbaijani presidents have for more than ten years debated the same basic principles for a solution. As Zartman (2001b, p. 8) argues, 'Parties resolve their conflict only when they are ready to do so. ... At that ripe moment, they grab on to proposals that usually have been in the air for a long time and that only now appear attractive.' In many conflicts where an agreement has proved elusive, it does appear that all possible solutions have been on the table. Getting an agreement is not about suddenly finding the magic formula that no one else had previously considered. The dynamics of the conflict have to change; the timing has to be right.

The idea of a ripe moment for peace is intuitively compelling and it has been highly influential. In 1991, James Baker, the then US Secretary of State, commented on the Yugoslav conflict: 'my gut feeling is that we won't produce a serious dialogue on the future of Yugoslavia until all parties have a greater sense of urgency and danger' (Holbrooke, 1999, p. 27). The Under-Secretary General of the UN similarly argued that 'not all conflicts are "ripe" for action' and the UN should only intervene in situations where 'the investment of scarce resources is likely to produce a good return' (Marrack Goulding, quoted in Zartman, 2001b, p. 12). But the idea of ripeness does not necessarily imply that mediators should just wait for a window of opportunity to present itself and otherwise simply let the fighting continue. Third party involvement and the design of the peace process can help promote ripeness, especially if the concept of ripeness is widened to include, or even stress, intra-communal dynamics: these can pose an obstacle to peace, in the form of spoilers, but competition for power can also provide an impetus for change. These intra-communal dynamics affect the decision to start negotiations and they also impact on the content of the resulting agreement and its sustainability. Furthermore, although the agreements reached are often similar to previous proposals, there are usually some important differences. These may be fairly subtle but even symbolic changes can make the difference between a wasted opportunity and a successful agreement, and can also affect the longer-term sustainability of the agreement.

The following two chapters examine the crucial and often complex interactions between the content of the peace agreement, the nature of the peace process and the dynamics of the conflict. This chapter focuses on internal or intra-state dynamics: in particular the importance of balance and trust between the two sides, and the intra-communal balance between hardliners and moderates. The next chapter focuses on the external dimension of this interaction, in the form of third party involvement and external spoilers. This chapter will argue that despite the importance of timing for successful peace talks, this is not simply exogenous to the proposals on the table and the design of the peace process. The 'right time' for peace can, at least up to a point, be created. The right process and the right agreement can convince the conflict parties to stay on board and reduce the risk of effective spoiler activities. Such attempts will however be characterized by an important tension: between control and the ability to marginalize or defeat spoilers, on the one hand, and legitimacy and the creation of a peace constituency, on the other. The chapter stresses the importance of political contestation within conflict parties and, more broadly, intra-communal divisions – for reaching an agreement, for its sustainability and for the quality of peace – and proposes an enriched concept of conflict ripeness.

Ripe Moment for Peace

Zartman's ripe moment identifies a window of opportunity; the time when de-escalation of a conflict can begin. Negotiations may start for other reasons, for example if the parties are trying to defuse international pressure, but they will not be successful unless the conflict is ripe for resolution. The most essential element of a ripe moment is the existence of a *'mutually hurting stalemate'*. All sides realize that they cannot escalate to victory and the current deadlock is painful. This is optimally associated with an impending, past or recently avoided catastrophe (Zartman, 1995a). An oft-cited example is Bosnia where the Serb forces by 1995 were losing territory they had controlled since 1992, and the bargaining situation was thereby restructured (Touval, 1996, p. 568). However, Zartman's mutually hurting stalemate is not simply about 'objective' indicators of a military stalemate, it is very much about *perceptions*.[71] Both sides have to recognize that they cannot win and that the situation is costly. They also have to perceive that there is a *'way out'*; that a negotiated settlement is possible and less costly than the current status quo. This is the second element of a ripe moment for peace.

Zartman's concept has been criticized for treating the conflict parties as unitary actors – focusing on the balance of power between the two sides and on losses and potential gains for the group as a whole – instead of also paying attention to internal politics (see e.g. Stedman, 1991). In the original formulation of the concept, Zartman also included a third element: a *valid spokesperson*. The negotiators must be representative: they must be able to take their followers with them in compromise. The concept of a valid spokesperson goes some way in addressing the, often limited, ability of the leaders to compromise, but Zartman no longer includes this in his conception of a ripe moment since it is, as a structural element, 'of a different order than the other two defining perceptual elements' (Zartman, 2001b, p. 11). I will argue, however, that we need to include intra-communal dynamics in order to understand when negotiations start in earnest and the outcomes that they produce.

Sources of Ripeness

The context in which the analysed agreements were negotiated varied significantly: from fairly equally balanced sides, to clearly asymmetric conflicts where high costs were nevertheless being inflicted by the separatist forces, to situations of near-defeat of the separatist forces. A number of the agreements resulted from conflict contexts that closely resemble Zartman's ripe moment. For example, in the case of Sudan both the NCP and the SPLM/A had come to realize that they could not achieve victory through military means. Moreover, the NCP was facing both an external and internal legitimacy crisis as a result of the ongoing war, while the SPLM/A was weakened by internal divisions and losing regional support (Ahmed, 2009, pp. 136–8). The loss of external support is a frequent source of conflict ripeness, especially on part of the separatist movement. Another example of this is the Chittagong Hill Tracts (CHT), where India withdrew its support for the United People's Party of CHT (PJCSS), following Bangladesh's democratic transition. In fact, India added pressure on the separatist movements by 'playing the refugee card' and stopping food supplies to CHT refugees (Mohsin, 2003, pp. 15, 41). Similarly, before the signing of the Oslo Accords, the PLO had seen its bargaining position weakened following the loss of patronage from Arab states and from the Soviet Union (Lieberfeld, 1999, p. 70).

An objective military balance is not enough for negotiations to start in earnest and certainly not enough for them to conclude successfully; it has to be associated with significant costs. A military stalemate has, for example, existed for decades in the case of Nagorno Karabakh but it is a soft stalemate not a hurting one (Hopmann & Zartman, 2010). Moreover, both sides perceive the stalemate to be temporary: they believe that the passing of time will bring them closer to their maximalist goal. The Armenian side believes that their de facto independence will become increasingly entrenched which will strengthen the case for international recognition, whereas the Azerbaijani Government is equally convinced that international isolation will gradually weaken the entity and make reintegration more likely – strongly aided by Azerbaijan's vastly increased military spending (see e.g. De Waal, 2010; Özkan, 2008). Perceptions matter and the sensitivity to costs will vary between actors; non-state armed groups, in particular, may be willing to accept significant pain. Heraclides (1997, p. 700) argues that 'separatists and other committed insurgent groups tend to have a greater propensity for risk-taking. Their threshold of acceptable costs is much higher than it is for the state', and Zartman (1995b, p. 9) similarly points out that rebels 'overinvest in their attachment to ends' in order to overcome their weakness. A number of obstacles make it difficult for armed separatist groups to abandon violence and pursue a political solution. These include fears of appearing weak, distrust of both friends and enemies, and the often

140

considerably risk of internal splits. They will therefore often hold fast to maximalist goals that outside observers consider unachievable; it will be very difficult to abandon the strategy, even if it is not working and the costs are too high (McCartney, 2005). This can appear irrational, such as when the president of the self-proclaimed Serb entity in wartime Croatia refused an agreement with Croatia that would bring oil supplies to his collapsing entity, declaring 'we will just have to rely on horse power' (Caspersen, 2010). However, the constraints are significant and in order for armed groups to make the difficult transition they will need signs that there are likely tangible benefits from negotiating and a space for alternative ways of relating to their opponents (McCartney, 2005, p. 33); they need convincing that there is a 'way out'.

This however points to a more general problem with the concept of a ripe moment. It is very difficult to assess if it exists in a particular conflict. If negotiations and the resulting agreement are successful, observers will tend to conclude that the conflict was indeed ripe for resolution; if they fail, then the conflict was clearly not ripe (see also Kleiboer, 1994). The concept could be clearer when it comes to the kind of balance of power that is most conducive to ripeness, but the difficulty mainly stems from three factors that affect the existence, or not, of a ripe moment: different types and sources of power, the importance of perceptions and the significance of internal divisions.

The relative power of the conflict parties does not simply depend on military power or other forms of structural power. Bargaining positions are also affected by 'soft political power' (Philipson, 2005), including the degree to which one side is seen to embody certain moral principles (Albin, 2001, p. 142). International legitimacy is one such 'soft power' which could compensate for limited military capacity and help create a mutually hurting stalemate as well as the perception of a 'way out', even in asymmetric conflicts. Above, I described how the ripe moment in Sudan was, in part, created by the international legitimacy crisis facing the government. However, in the case of separatist conflicts, the international system is typically stacked against the separatist forces. Territorial integrity remains the dominant principle and separatist movements, especially if they take up arms, will in most cases be regarded as illegitimate, and will in some cases be classed as terrorist groups. In the case of Sri Lanka, it has for example been argued that the Tamil Tigers' (LTTE) lack of international legitimacy, manifested in its inability in 2003 to take part in a US conference to discuss development aid and reconstruction, created an asymmetry in the conflict and led the LTTE to turns its back on negotiations, despite the existence of a military and economic stalemate (Philipson, 2005). Conversely, in the case of Northern Ireland, the decision to grant Gerry Adams a US visa has been argued to have been an important catalyst for the willingness of the Republicans to start serious negotiations (Powell, 2008). Recognition of the legitimacy of the demands of these groups, if not their methods, will often be necessary for 'ripeness' to emerge. The importance of such 'soft power', which is much harder to quantify, makes it difficult to determine when a ripe moment exists, but it again attests to the interaction between ripeness and the peace process.

Zartman emphasizes the crucial importance of perceptions. This would imply that trust, or more often mistrust, is also of great significance, which is again something that can be addressed as part of the peace process (more on this below and in chapter 7). But since such perceptions are subjective, it also means that the individual leader becomes important. A new leader may perceive the conflict – and the prospect of victory – differently and the change in power could also signal to the opposing side that a 'way out' is feasible (see also Kleiboer, 1994; Stedman, 1991). Serious negotiations were in many cases spurred by a leadership change. Thus, in the case of Israel–Palestine, the change in leader on the Israeli side (from Likud to Labour) has been deemed highly significant (Lieberfeld, 1999). Similarly, the democratic transition in Bangladesh in 1991 appears to have been crucial in enabling the CHT agreement. The new Bangladeshi Government wanted to reach a solution in order to firmly establish civilian control over the army, and moreover realized that its international credibility as a democracy, and therefore foreign aid, was at stake (Mohsin, 2003, pp. 14, 39).

The above examples highlight that the emergence of a ripe moment does not simply reflect the perceptions and preferences of a specific leader, although those may be important as well. Internal politics matters. Critics of Zartman's ripe moment frequently point to the inability of leaders to act on a mutually hurting stalemate due to the fear of outbidding from more extreme rivals (see e.g. Haas, 1988). But internal rivalry does not simply constrain the ability of leaders to act on a ripe moment; it can also be the source of such ripeness. Lieberfeld (1999, p. 75) argues that both Labour and the PLO had an interest in reaching an agreement that would preserve their political dominance. Rabin had promised the Israeli voters a settlement within six to nine months of becoming prime minister and Yasser Arafat was keen to reach an agreement as soon as possible, since the PLO was facing bankruptcy and losing support to Hamas (ibid.). Zartman has described this as a 'mutually enticing opportunity' (1997, p. 197). The Bosnian Serb leaders were also not only motivated to sign the Dayton Agreement by NATO bombings and losses on the battlefield. What made the stalemate particularly painful was that their own political survival was at stake: the civilian leadership was under mounting pressure from the military leadership and from their former mentor in Belgrade, Slobodan Milošević (Caspersen, 2010). In the case of Sudan, leaders on both sides were similarly driven by personal ambitious of securing their position against internal rivals (Ahmed, 2009, pp. 136–8); for the NCP leaders, in particular, it had become a matter of survival (Rolandsen, 2011, p. 554). Internal opposition can therefore make a stalemate hurt, but these costs are not necessarily linked to the stalemate itself.

Internal dynamics can also provide a positive push for an agreement. In the case of Bougainville, women's groups have been seen as crucial in pushing the leaders to agree to a settlement. They worked hard to engage opposing Bougainville factions in dialogue. An elder argued, 'I think that we would have eventually had our peace process but ... the women were the most important ... they said "Enough is enough!"' (Reddy, 2008, p. 120). When it came to negotiating the agreement, the continued existence of internal challengers actually worked to the benefit of the more moderate forces, as it 'limited the scope for compromise on the part of the Bougainville side to the negotiations, and added to the pressure on the PNG side' (Ghai & Regan, 2006, p. 598).

A number of very different calculations, including those primarily based on internal politics, can therefore be behind a ripe moment and motivate leaders to begin serious negotiations. However, such a widened understanding of a ripe moment has implications for the type of agreement that follows and helps us understand the weakness of some of them.

Implications for Peace Agreements

If political contestation within communities or perhaps the need for international legitimacy are the main drivers behind peace talks, rather than an impending catastrophe for the community as a whole, then we would expect this to affect the kind of agreement that the leaders are willing to accept, and also their ability to do so.

The agreements for Indonesia–Aceh, Philippines–Mindanao and Bangladesh–Chittagong Hill Tracts followed regime transitions. The government held the upper hand militarily but was motivated to reach a settlement by the need for internal and external legitimacy (see e.g. Heraclides, 1997) – although in the case of Aceh, the devastation caused by the tsunami was also a highly significant factor (Awaluddin, 2008, p. 26). As Heraclides argues (1997, pp. 688–9), there can be good reasons to negotiate from a position of strength, including the more limited concessions needed to secure a deal. However, if the primary goal is to ensure a PR victory, then this would be expected to affect both the degree of concessions made and the willingness to implement them. In all three cases, the agreements were highly ambiguous when it came to the level of autonomy offered, and the governments faced vocal internal resistance. Important provisions were, as discussed in previous chapters, left unimplemented or significantly watered down.

Similarly, if the main motivation behind negotiations is to defeat potential challengers, then the risk is that the agreement becomes focused on ensuring internal control, rather than on addressing community grievances. The Oslo Accords have been criticized for reinforcing asymmetries and for being a 'wholly Israeli formula' (Pappe, in Usher, 1999, p. 35), but it has also been argued that they essentially enabled the creation of a Palestinian police state, since both the Israeli and Palestinian negotiators saw the defeat of Hamas as one of the primary objectives (Roy, 2002). The main motivation behind the willingness of the Movement of Democratic Forces of Casamance (MDFC) to abandon the armed struggle and its demand for independence appears to have been monetary. Conflict had become a business for many MDFC leaders and the government addressed these incentives by offering aid and money (Fall, 2010). This would explain the willingness to accept an agreement that offered very few concessions and did not address key grievances in the region.

Even if a mutually hurting stalemate can be said to exist, at least in the wider sense outlined above, a balanced outcome that addresses the main fears and grievances on both sides cannot be assumed. This creates potential problems when it comes to ensuring wider legitimacy and is associated with a risk of renewed violence. The risk would appear to be particularly acute if the agreement is signed with the weakest faction among the separatist forces. Such a faction may be highly motivated to reach an agreement but is likely to lack the ability to bring the rest of the community with it in compromise. In Israel–Palestine, Rabin chose to negotiate with Arafat despite his weakness, because he was willing to defer thorny issues for future talks (Perlmutter, 1995, p. 62). However, Arafat was not able to deliver Palestinian support for the agreement, and remained significantly constrained by challenges from Hamas.

Similarly, in the case of the Philippines–Mindanao, President Ramos deliberately chose to negotiate with the armed groups separately and started out with the MNLF, which was regarded as the weaker group militarily. The MNLF was seen both at home and abroad as an organization that embodied Moro aspirations, and the hope was therefore that an agreement with the MNLF would demonstrate that Moro demands were being addressed (Stankovitch & Carl, 1999). However, as argued in previous chapters, the MNLF lacked the capacity to carry the settlement and was soon outflanked by the rival MILF.

While intra-communal unity is therefore not a necessary condition for a ripe moment to emerge, or for a successful agreement to be reached, internal competition is only favourable under certain conditions and such rivalry will affect the negotiating process. The concept of a ripe moment would be enriched by stressing intra-communal dynamics and their effects on the resulting settlement. The content of the agreement, the peace process and internal dynamics are all closely linked, and all impact on the sustainability of a settlement. Spoilers are not always successful and both the peace process and the settlement can be designed in a way that makes it easier to co-opt or manage them; thereby helping to create conflict ripeness.

The Problem of Spoilers

One of the main obstacles to reaching a settlement and to its implementation is the existence of so-called spoilers. Stedman (1997) defines spoilers as 'leaders and parties who believe that peace emerging from negotiations threatens their power, worldview, and interests, and use violence to undermine attempts to achieve it'. However, the concept of spoilers has also been used to refer to actors who use extreme positions and popular appeals to outbid pro-settlement forces. An often-quoted example is that of Ian Paisley, whose firebrand rhetoric for many years constrained Unionist leaders who were contemplating a settlement for Northern Ireland.

There are plentiful examples of the dangers spoilers can pose for a peace process and for the settlement signatories. The collapse of the Oslo Accords owed much to the activities of spoilers: extreme forces on both sides denounced the agreement as a betrayal of core interests and used violence and political outbidding to undermine it. Hamas continued its violent campaign, and also secured a shock-victory in the 2006 Palestinian parliamentary elections (Jeffery, 2006).

Meanwhile, in Israel, Labour faced growing opposition from Likud which promised a harsh anti-terror campaign and rejected territorial compromise (Perlmutter, 1995, pp. 61–2). Rabin paid the highest price for his willingness to moderate when he was assassinated by an ultranationalist in 1995. Shimon Peres was appointed acting Prime Minister but was narrowly defeated by Likud's Benjamin Netanyahu in the 1996 elections. Netanyahu promised to slow the peace process, build new Jewish settlements in the West Bank, and block the creation of a Palestinian state (CNN, 1996).

The signing of a peace agreement frequently leads to splits in the separatist movement, with some factions continuing the violent struggle. In the case of Casamance, the MDFC split into an array of factions, some of which rejected the peace agreement. The leader of one such faction was killed after negotiating with the central government without prior consultation with the wider organization (Fall, 2010, p. 28). Similarly, in the case of Bodoland, two military factions repackaged themselves following the signing of the 1993 accord and escalated their violent campaign (Vandekerckhove & Suykens, 2008, pp. 459–60). In the Philippines, the split of the MNLF preceded the 1996 agreement, but the more extreme MILF rejected the settlement and a number of MNLF fighters shifted allegiance. The MILF continued its violent campaign and war was reignited in 2000 (International Crisis Group, 2013a).

Spoiler activity – or the threat of such activity – can prove detrimental, even if a formal split does not occur. The Bosnian Serb leaders repeatedly argued that they would be killed by hardliners from within their own ranks, if they agreed to a settlement (Holbrooke, 1999). Across the border in Croatia, the unwillingness of the local Serb leaders to agree to a settlement, even when it became clear that their entity was unsustainable, had a lot to do with their inability to take hardliners, in particularly paramilitary forces, with them in compromise (Caspersen, 2010). Pointing to such spoilers could of course be a bargaining ploy; an attempt to extract further concessions or avoid blame if the talks break down, but several cases do point to a very real threat.

All peace agreements are vulnerable to spoiler activity, but some agreements would appear to be more vulnerable than others. Since the issue of status remains undecided in interim agreements, a lot is still at stake, both in terms of collective and individual interests, and the uncertainty and insecurity associated with such an agreement could be manipulated by actors opposed to its likely outcome. The interim period in Israel–Palestine was argued to represent 'an ongoing invitation for Oslo's foes ... to try to derail the process, as bloodily as necessary' (Perlmutter, 1995, p. 63). In Bougainville, there are also fears that the potential for spoiler violence could rise during the referendum. Armed groups that have remained outside the peace process, and who in some cases control parts of the territory, may seek to spoil the referendum, seeing it and the legitimacy that it would afford to the ruling party as a threat to their powerbase (Woodbury, 2015). However as will be shown below, there is a complex interaction between the content of the agreement, the peace process and the dynamics of the conflict.

Examples of spoiler activity therefore abound, but the concept is nevertheless problematic. It implies that anyone opposing a peace settlement does so for illegitimate reasons, either based on an extreme ideology or on selfish interests. But this normative connotation is problematic. There may be very good reasons to oppose an agreement: it could be unjust, be based on a problematic institutional design or simply have very little chance of succeeding (see e.g. Newman & Richmond, 2006). Opposition to an agreement is, moreover, part of the bargaining process. Any leader engaged in peace talks will oppose different versions of an agreement, and some may even threaten a return to violence, or indeed actually resume violence for a period of time. For armed separatist movements, the threat of violence is their main bargaining power and we should therefore not be surprised if this is used during the talks. Peace processes will always produce spoilers, but such opposition should not be automatically dismissed as illegitimate (see also Dalsheim, 2014).

Mediators will often try to promote intra-communal unity and reduce the complexity of the conflict (see e.g. Powell, 2008, p. 25), but internal factionalization and competition is not always an insurmountable obstacle to a settlement. Violence during and after peace talks is very common but does not necessarily lead to the collapse of an agreement; nor does the existence of more extreme political rivals. Not all spoilers pose the same risk: some can be defeated or marginalized. The Bosnian Serb delegation was reportedly furious when they were shown the territorial divisions that Milošević had agreed to in Dayton, and the Bosnian Serb President, Radovan Karadžić, initially rejected the agreement. However, they had become so weak that it was enough for Milošević to threaten to have them arrested if they did not accept the agreement (Sell, 2002, p. 254). Similarly, the split in the IRA over the Belfast Agreement did lead to violence, most notoriously the Omagh bombing which killed twenty-nine people in August 1998, but it was not enough to threaten the agreement. On the contrary, it galvanized the supporters of the agreement (Powell, 2008,

p. 138). In Bougainville, the existence of potential spoilers such as the self-proclaimed King Noah Musingku is often pointed to (Woodbury, 2015, p. 14), but the threat has so far remained latent. And spoilers do of course not always remain spoilers. Powell (2008, p. 1) describes how he witnessed the swearing in of Ian Paisley as First Minister of Northern Ireland and Martin McGuiness as Deputy First Minister. Sworn enemies, and former spoilers, were now sharing power. If anyone ten years earlier had suggested that this would happen, 'I would have thought they were mad' (ibid.). The presence of spoilers, and especially their success, is significantly affected by both the content of the peace agreement and the design of the peace process.

Managing Spoilers

Stedman (1997) argues that the most effective strategy for managing spoilers depends on the spoiler type. Based on their goals and their commitment to these goals, he distinguishes between limited, greedy and total spoilers. While the first two types can be accommodated in the peace process, the total spoiler will have to be defeated. Other authors have however pointed to problems with this typology, and instead suggest analysing spoilers in terms of their capacity: what resources do they control and are they consequently able to 'spoil' effectively (see e.g. Greenhill & Major, 2007)? This analysis should include not just coercive resources, but also non-coercive ones such as economic resources and popular support, and their relative importance depends on the conflict situation: for example, are elections held or does power originate in the barrel of a gun (Caspersen, 2010)? Analysing spoilers in terms of capacity does not mean that individual leaders or their motivations are without importance, but it does give us a better way of assessing if spoilers are likely to derail a peace process, and it can help determine the best way to manage them. The following section examines how the settlement and the peace process can be designed in ways that reduce the risk of dangerous (/effective) spoiling activity, while chapter 7 will consider the potential role of third parties in this process.

Bringing Potential Spoilers on Board

The first strategy will usually be to try to convince potential spoilers to support the peace agreement; to avoid internal challengers and splits, and persuade groups outside the process that they have more to gain from being part of the settlement process than from remaining excluded. Some groups will insist, however, on demands that are impossible to accommodate and including them would make negotiations impossible. Powell (2008, p. 18) assesses that unless the DUP had walked out on the Northern Irish peacetalks, it would not have been possible to reach an agreement. However, it is difficult to determine a priori which groups will be willing to compromise on their maximalist demands. Even total spoilers sometimes agree to negotiate, and some analysts even suggest that it is not beyond the realm of possibility to negotiate a settlement with ISIS (Powell, 2015); although that would likely lead other Syrian and Iraqi groups to walk out.

Actors with the capacity to destroy an agreement must be persuaded to take part, or be defeated. Darby and Mac Ginty (2000, p. 254) describe this as 'sufficient inclusion'. A peace process cannot be built on moderates alone and the instability of overly narrow agreements has been illustrated repeatedly. The 1996 agreement for Mindanao did not include the strongest separatist force, the MILF, and although the agreement held it therefore failed to stop the war (International Crisis Group, 2013a). However, what constitutes sufficient inclusion is not static. Whether or not the spoilers are able to undermine a settlement depends on the resources they control, but this is at least partly a product of the content of the agreement and the peace process. Sufficient inclusion could also refer to the need to include negotiators who are representative of their communities. If successful, such a strategy would make it harder for groups excluded from the process to mobilize public opinion against the agreement. In Northern Ireland, it was seen as crucial that the pro-agreement parties represented a majority of Unionist voters. Following the walkout of the DUP, the Ulster Unionist Party (UUP) therefore insisted on keeping two smaller unionist parties on board (Powell, 2008, pp. 21, 25). The importance of including representative negotiators is however often overlooked, as will be further discussed below.

The key to getting spoilers on board is to address their demands; find a solution that all negotiating parties consider acceptable. But this is of course easier said than done. Some demands will be non-negotiable and the previous chapters have shown how difficult it is to reach genuine compromises on issues linked to territory, security, power and justice. Moreover, the conflict parties are not unitary actors and the groups will be internally divided in terms of their priorities and the kind of compromises that are acceptable. Agreements will therefore contain a mixture of collective and individual incentives, designed to make the leaders both willing and able to agree to a settlement. Trade-offs will be part of the deal ('win some, lose some') and 'constructive ambiguity' is also frequently used.

A few examples will illustrate the importance of the content of the agreement. In the case of Northern Ireland, the UUP was repeatedly brought back from the brink, for example when they threatened to walk out over the creation of North–South institutions. A significant watering down of these enabled the party to stay on board. When it came to the explosive issue of decommissioning, the mediators had to make use of constructive ambiguity, including an unofficial guarantee from Tony Blair to the UUP a few hours before the agreement was announced. The UUP split over the agreement but these concessions enabled the UUP's leader to take most of the party with him, at least temporarily (Powell, 2008, pp. 105–6). Ambiguity along with individual incentives can make a settlement possible, but such strategies can cause problems for the sustainability of the agreement. It can result in collective grievances not being addressed or popular expectations being disappointed once the agreement is implemented. The Mindanao peace agreement was in part made possible by offering the MNLF leaders prestigious roles (Heraclides, 1997, p. 690), but the autonomy provisions that were to address long-held grievances were ambiguous and several were left unimplemented. This was one of the reasons for the decision of some MNLF fighters to revert to violence (International Crisis Group, 2013a). Previous supporters can turn spoilers if they feel that they have been misled or cheated.

The content of the agreement matters because it addresses at least some of the motives of a (potential) spoiler. The agreement can moreover reduce their capacity for effective action, by diminishing the pool of dissatisfied militants and voters, and the agreement thereby directly affects the resources available to spoilers. A compromise will never meet everyone's demands. Some individuals and groups will be left unhappy by the agreement, but the design of the process could still convince a less determined spoiler. Mediators can for example make use of the 'departing train strategy', which hopes to persuade the spoiler that they will be marginalized if they do not support the peace process (Stedman, 1997). In Northern Ireland, Tony Blair for example stated: 'The settlement train is leaving, with or without Sinn Fein' (Powell, 2008, p. 14). Mediators could also try to convince potential spoilers by offering various inducements and reassurances (Rothchild & Emmanuel, 2010). These do not change the content of the agreement, but may enable parties, or indeed the general public, to accept ambiguities or become more convinced of the merits of the agreement. A peace dividend is often implied, but economic sweeteners can be added. Following the signing of the Mindanao agreement both parties, for example, raised economic expectations in order to sell it to the public (Stankovitch & Carl, 1999).

Despite these different options, strategies are still needed for managing spoilers whose demands cannot be accommodated and who cannot otherwise be persuaded to support the agreement.

Marginalizing or Defeating Spoilers

The parties that stay on board must be empowered, and thereby given the means to marginalize or defeat any remaining spoilers. However, the best way to do so remains contested: should the leaders be insulated, against their rivals and the general public, or should the process be broadened and opened up?

Insulating Elites

The most common strategy is to try to insulate the negotiating leaders from societal pressures. First of all, secret elite talks are the norm in peace processes. In some cases, the public has not even been aware that negotiations were taking place. For example, the Oslo back-channel talks were deliberately held far away from Israel–Palestine and a lot of effort went into keeping them secret. The circle of people involved was gradually extended but the veil of secrecy was only fully lifted when Rabin and Arafat signed the agreement on the White House Lawn (Corbin, 1994, p. 177). In most other cases, it is known that negotiations are taking place, but the talks usually happen far from any prying eyes and the content of what is being discussed is kept confidential. Press conferences were held while the Aceh peace talks were ongoing but the mediator, Martti Ahtisaari, urged the parties, 'to remain circumspect in regard to the media' and no information was leaked (Merikallio & Ruokanen, 2015, p. 296). The Indonesian Government's chief negotiator argues that this 'zip mouth policy' contributed significantly to the establishment of peace, as it prevented the media from provoking 'unhelpful debate' (Awaluddin, 2008, p. 27). US mediators brokering the Dayton accord deliberately chose a remote location: 'to discourage Balkan warlords from running off to television studios in New York and Washington every time the negotiations hit a snag' (Holbrooke, 1999, p. 204). The Nagorno Karabakh peace talks are even more secretive. The

OSCE Minsk Group, which facilitates the talks, has no spokesperson and although talks have been ongoing for more than twenty years, the populations in Armenia and Azerbaijan have very little knowledge of what is being discussed. The broad principles of the talks were released in 2006 but the mediators have refrained from disclosing any further details, including the position of the two sides or the gradual evolution of the principles (De Waal, 2010, p. 163; International Crisis Group, 2005c, p. 8). The argument in favour of such secrecy is that it is so difficult for the leaders to make concessions that any publicity would make it impossible to reach an agreement. In some cases, this lack of publicity is maintained even after an agreement has been reached, as it is feared that the news of what has been agreed to will be so explosive that violence might ensue. The leaders need time to prepare their publics. For example, the content of the recent agreement in the Nagaland (India) was not immediately made public (BBC News, 2015b).

Attempts to insulate the leaders from public pressure and potential outbidding do not stop here. It is now widely recommended in the literature that elections should not be held shortly after a peace agreement is signed. Paris (2004) famously warned against holding early elections as, in the absence of effective institutions, they would lead to instability. Lake (2010) similarly argues that well-functioning and therefore legitimate state institutions must be created first, and the most important task for these institutions is to ensure social order. The population must witness the benefits of a settlement; they must be given a stake in the peace. Roeder (2010) strikes a similar tune, but goes further, when he warns against the dangers of a polarized civil society. Stable peace requires either a pluralistic civil society, which is unrealistic following a civil war, or a 'hegemonic civil society'. This is essentially a control regime (see Lustick, 1979) which 'suppresses the expression of interests that fuelled the secessionist attempt' and therefore disenfranchises groups that 'overtly represent the (formerly) secessionist communities' (Roeder, 2010, pp. 55–6).

Such strategies starve potential spoilers of important resources: hardline challengers will not be able to mobilize disillusioned voters in early elections, and the pro-settlement parties will develop the capacity to defeat any spoilers. There are however a number of potential problems with such a strategy. Firstly, the issue of capacity should not be reduced to one of security; wider governance issues, including economic capacity, also matter. For example, the expected economic benefits of the 1996 agreement for Mindanao failed to materialize, and the region's enduring poverty is, as Rogers (2004, pp. 19–20) argues, 'an effective incubator for violence'. But there is a potential trade-off between security and economic capacity. A very significant proportion of South Sudan's budget went on military spending (Brosché, 2008), so there was not much left for economic development. The SPLM consequently faced heavy criticism for having failed to deliver a peace dividend, for example illustrated by the capital, Juba, remaining largely undeveloped with little infrastructure (Sriram, 2008, p. 139). Secondly, Roeder's argument is based on the central government emerging victorious and instituting a unitary state (Roeder, 2010, p. 56). However, empowering the signatories against potential spoilers will, in case of a negotiated settlement, often entail ensuring sufficient capacity in the autonomous region; in a sense empowering the (former) separatist forces. The leaders must have sufficient capacity (broadly conceived) to ensure local stability and, if necessary, defeat internal spoilers. Leaving this to the national police or security forces would be explosive in many post-settlement contexts. But such a strategy is not cost-free.

I have already described how in Mindanao the autonomous government lacked the capacity to defeat the MILF and the increasingly chaotic situation within the region undermined support for the settlement both in Mindanao and in the Philippines as a whole (Lara Jr & Champain, 2009). Similarly, the Palestinian Authority lacked the capacity and the legitimacy to ensure control. In both cases this lack of capacity was, at least in part, a result of the agreement. However, pre-agreement governance structures also matter. In Sudan, the SPLM lacked the money, structures and qualified individuals to implement the agreement effectively, which resulted in significant delays in disarmament and demobilization (Brosché, 2008; Sriram, 2008, p. 136). However, the SPLM had something to build on: during the war, it had created a partially effective system of governance. This was exclusive and very much focused on security but it provided 'a degree of stability of certain areas of South Sudan' (Mampilly, 2011, p. 22) and the party managed by and large to ensure internal cohesion in the post-settlement period. This was aided by the agreement which was designed to give SPLM full control in southern Sudan, and it subsequently managed to reach a deal with rival armed forces in the South. The Free Aceh Movement (GAM) was also strong enough to maintain stability in Aceh, even though the post-settlement period in Aceh was marked by continued violence and some opposition to the agreement (International Crisis Group, 2006, pp. 6–8; Lara Jr & Champain, 2009). Before the signing of the agreement, the GAM had gained control over a handful of districts and established elements of governance, including the supply of some public services (Barter, 2015). The settlement further empowered the GAM, to the extent that Aceh has now taken on 'some of the trappings of a one-party state' (International Crisis Group, 2013b, pp. 9, 11).

These examples however point to the potential costs of such a strategy. If it is to prove effective, it may result in the creation of an exclusive and even oppressive regime in the autonomous region; one that is squarely based on the former armed movement. Control rather than legitimacy becomes the defining feature. However this is not only problematic from the point of view of human security and human rights, it can also sow the seeds of future conflicts. The lack of economic development and inclusivity in South Sudan caused lingering dissatisfaction. This was held in check by the narrative of future independence (see also Caspersen, 2012), but internal divisions came to the fore once the euphoria of independence died down (Wolff, 2013).

The assumption behind these strategies is that if spoilers get the chance, they will be able to undermine a settlement. Years of violence and nationalist propaganda have made it too hard to sell a settlement. As David Owen (1995) later said about Milošević and other Serb leaders: they had to 'ride the tiger of nationalism' if they did not want to be eaten by it. If elections are held, spoilers can 'play the ethnic card' and instrumentalize fears and prejudices. The more severe the conflict, the greater the need for secrecy and for protecting the signatories from the electorate's verdict. However, such a strategy must be transitional and eventually give way to a broader process (Hoddie & Hartzell, 2010). But how do you ensure that instability will not ensue once the process is opened up, if it is indeed possible to reform the system once these leaders have been empowered? In the following I will argue that alternatives to an illiberal peace do exist, but they are contingent on specific conditions or must be part of a rethink of dominant strategies.

Broadening the Process

The alternative strategy is almost the polar opposite of the first one. Instead of insulating and isolating the negotiating parties it seeks to broaden the process and ensure a popular mandate. Support for such a strategy can be found in analyses of spoiling behaviour that argue that successful outbidding is *less likely* in a more democratic setting, since it is harder for spoilers to contest the legitimacy of elected signatories (Pearlman, 2009). A democratic system is unlikely to survive unscathed from a bloody intra-state war, and it is not feasible to very quickly create such a system, but there are other ways of promoting similar dynamics.

One option is to hold a referendum as a means to ensure the popular legitimacy of the agreement and also put pressure on the leaders to live up to their promises and implement the agreement. This strategy was used to great effect in the case of Northern Ireland: 71 per cent voted in favour of the agreement in Northern Ireland and 94 per cent in the Republic of Ireland. Such a referendum could have been a huge risk for the leaders who supported the agreement, but polls showed them that they could win 'provided they stuck together in sufficient numbers' (Irwin, 2013, pp. 297–9). The popular support for the agreement, which crucially included a majority of both communities, helped strengthen the process through an often fraught implementation process and reduced the risk of significant groups reneging on their commitment to the agreement (see also Kydd & Walter, 2002).

Why then are referenda so rarely used as part of a peace process? In some cases it is simply not feasible. In the case of continuing violence a referendum would not be safe, and would at least have to be postponed for later. The more fundamental problem is that the agreement is likely to be rejected. A population exposed to violence and years of propaganda telling them that the 'other side' is the enemy hell-bent on their annihilation could be forgiven for not being immediately persuaded by the feasibility of an agreement, especially one that, in most cases, includes future coexistence. Irwin (2013, p. 310) argues that the public in deeply divided societies is often supportive of compromise solutions, but 'those in power, who can pay for these polls do not want this truth to come out'. However this would in many cases be unduly optimistic. A referendum would be particularly risky if significant forces campaign against the agreement. In the case of the Annan Plan for Cyprus, the Turkish Cypriot voters supported the agreement, but it was rejected by the Greek Cypriots. This has been explained both in terms of the EU's mishandling of Cyprus's accession – an important carrot had gone – and the lack of support from the Greek Cypriot leaders. The referendum was meant to circumvent opposition from the Turkish Cypriot leader, and it succeeded in doing so, but 'the UN team overlooked the problems on the other side of the Green Line' where the president and government successfully campaigned for a 'no' (International Crisis Group, 2005a, p. 5). Similar outcomes could be foreseen elsewhere. For example, if an agreement were to be reached in the case of Nagorno Karabakh, a popular referendum would be an extremely risky enterprise. Antagonisms run so deep and the propaganda has been so intense that it is not surprising that polls from Nagorno Karabakh find widespread support for territorial maximalist conceptions: not just independence, but independence that incorporates the disputed territories around Nagorno Karabakh itself (Toal & O'Loughlin, 2013).

However popular opinion cannot be ignored; it may be possible to insulate leaders from societal pressures for a while, but the process will eventually have to be broadened. This broadening of the process would appear to be particularly important in the case of an interim agreement or a highly ambiguous agreement; the initial compromise and the subsequent implementation will otherwise be too difficult. The in-built uncertainty of the interim framework in the case of Nagorno Karabakh, combined with the extreme secrecy of the process, provides fertile ground for rumours and conspiracy theories, which are clearly not conducive to peace. Broadening the process does not mean doing away with elite-level, Track I approaches. Rather, by including civil society organizations, it would be possible to strengthen the process. The broadening of the process typically happens in the post-settlement phase, if at all, but it could beneficially happen already at the pre-settlement stage in an attempt to prepare the population for a difficult compromise.[72] In Northern Ireland the process was broadened at an earlier stage and this appears to have strengthened the process and helped marginalize spoilers (see Foley, 2010).

The broadening of the process can be both vertical and horizontal. The typical peace agreement, as identified in the previous chapters, is negotiated by a small group of leaders that usually only represent the dominant communal groups. This results in agreements that tend to favour these groups, at the expense of other smaller or less powerful groups. However, by incorporating these groups, and ensuring that their needs and interests are also accommodated in the peace agreement, it may be possible to build a stronger peace constituency, and thereby help strengthen moderate leaders against more extreme rivals. The 1996 agreement for Mindanao was criticized for being too narrow and therefore lacking a peace constituency (Lara Jr & Champain, 2009). The most recent agreement was the result of a broader process (Conciliation Resources, 2012), but indigenous peoples' organizations were again complaining about a lack of inclusion (Mikkelsen, 2015, p. 256). This could risk weakening the agreement. There may therefore be reasons to go beyond 'sufficient inclusion', to make sure not only that veto players are included but also that a peace constituency can be created. Or rather peace constituencies, in plural. The civil society groups to which the process is broadened will in most cases be mono-ethnic, as these are the groups with enough roots in society to have a genuine impact (Foley, 2010).

Sceptics would argue that such processes are not practical. As Powell (2008, p. 27) argues when discussing Mo Mowlam's insistence on an inclusive process in Northern Ireland: 'while an admirable goal, it was not practical politics. It is not possible to make progress in sensitive negotiations if you require parties to make compromises and reveal their true positions in public.' However, the broadening of the process could, as argued above, happen in parallel with the elite-level talks. In order for the leaders to commit to difficult compromises, for trade-offs to be negotiated, and for the leaders to even begin to imagine what such solutions would look like, a certain level of confidentiality is likely needed. The problem is that it frequently goes too far. It is in the interest of the leaders to keep the process as narrow and closed as possible, as it helps ensure their hold on power. For example, the Armenian and Azerbaijani presidents want to be in charge of every detail of the Nagorno Karabakh talks. The two (semi-)authoritarian regimes are suspicious of civil society activists, and have obstructed efforts by the international mediators to broaden the process (De Waal, 2010; Zamejc, 2013). But it does not have to be this way. The Bougainville peace process was, as mentioned in chapter 4, broadened at a much earlier stage and it proceeded at a slow pace, thereby also ensuring domestic backing for the agreement (Reddy, 2008).

The broadening of the process cannot simply be ensured by holding elections. These will rarely lead to a change in power. Consolidating the power of the signatories may strengthen the peace agreement in the short-term, but the problem is that once their power is consolidated, these leaders may be highly reluctant to broaden the process. Many of the agreements so entrench the powers of the signatories that postponing the elections is unlikely to make a significant difference; the process would have to be broadened in the pre-settlement phase.

Conclusion: Rethinking Ripeness

This chapter has highlighted the interaction between internal conflict dynamics, process and content. The right time for peace is not exogenous to the peace process and the content of the proposed agreement. Ripeness can, at least up to a point, be created. At the same time, the content of the agreement is affected by the internal dynamics: by the balance of power between the two sides, or indeed imbalance, and by the need to bring potential spoilers on board, or alternatively marginalize them. This interaction helps explain the weakness of some agreements, such as when conflict 'ripeness' originates in internal challenges, and the illiberal tendencies in many agreements.

The most commonly prescribed method for bringing spoilers on board consists of insulating the agreement signatories from popular pressures and strengthening their capacity to defeat more extreme challengers. However this typically involves a trade-off with human rights and it may also undermine stability in the longer term. Relying exclusively on the former armed movement for (local) state-building is associated with a range of problems. The SPLM/A in South Sudan has for example been argued to be 'always a military organisation first'. The armed movement was used to following dictats from leaders (Sriram, 2008, pp. 138ff) and keen to protect its power and clientelism (Podder, 2014). The starting point for former armed movements clearly varies, but the transition to civilian politics will always prove difficult. The insulation of elites must eventually give way to a broader process, but such a transformation may be difficult once the settlement signatories have been empowered. The risk of a narrow process is illustrated in the case of Israel–Palestine where control became the raison d'etre of the Palestinian Authority, and lack of popular legitimacy made Fatah refuse to reform.

However, the process could be designed differently; a broader process does not come with the same compromises on human rights and freedoms and it may even be less likely to cause instability. In the case of Bougainville we have seen a much broader, and slower, process which is less focused on security in a traditional sense. Most notably, the local police force is unarmed. This has been described as a problem by the head of the autonomous region: 'we have a police force which is not strong enough', and has resulted in the existence of certain 'no go' areas (Woodbury, 2015, p. 14). However the broader peace process, which has included an intra-communal reconciliation process, means that the agreement has, so far, survived this challenge.

I therefore propose that a more enriched conception of conflict ripeness, which is not only concerned with the start of negotiations but with the sustainability of the settlement that results, should stress intra-communal dynamics. If a ripe moment is based on narrow interests, the risk is that the settlement will be as well and this could undermine stability in the longer-term. However, this tendency can be tempered by broadening the process, thereby ensuring that wider interests and grievances are heard and an agreement that enjoys greater popular legitimacy results.

This is not to say that broadening a peace process, which may imply a reduction in the control of former armed forces, is without risks. The prospect of losing power could turn signatories into spoilers. The peace process must have gained some momentum, and not solely depend on the 'men with the guns'. This entails selling the agreement to the wider public thereby creating a peace constituency that believes in a 'way out'. Such a strategy requires resources and will typically depend on third party involvement and guarantees; this should not therefore be left for the peace-building stage but incorporated earlier. In the following chapter, I will argue that third party involvement can play a positive role in changing conflict dynamics and the involvement does not always have to be 'robust'.

— 7 —

EXTERNAL INVOLVEMENT:
OPPORTUNITIES AND CONSTRAINTS

The conflicts analysed in this book are, for the sake of simplicity, described as intra-state conflicts. But although the key drivers in most of these conflicts are internal, external factors are of often crucial importance. Most separatist movements, and in particular the successful ones, receive support from abroad: from patron states, from diaspora populations and, in some cases, from networks of organized crime (see e.g. Caspersen, 2012; Checkel, 2013). Central governments will typically be reluctant to internationalize the conflict (Fortna, 2008), but they will often be forced to do so in case of a serious threat. And even if they do not seek such support directly, their actions in these conflicts will still be both constrained and enabled by international norms, including norms of territorial integrity and human rights. It is therefore perhaps unsurprising that the peace processes frequently have a strong international dimension.

Most of the twenty agreements involved international mediators and most of the negotiations took place abroad. The degree of involvement in these talks however varied significantly: from the 'presence' of an international mediator, in Chechnya, to a strong dose of American arm-twisting, backed up by NATO air power, in Bosnia. While the spectrum is broad, the pre-settlement phase represented the height of international involvement. But this involvement did in some cases continue into the implementation phase where we again see a broad spectrum of involvement: from the deployment of civilian monitors, for example in Aceh and Bougainville, to the establishment of de facto international administrations in Bosnia, Croatia and East Timor.

Third party involvement affects both the content of peace agreements and the functioning of the institutions they have created and it *could* help overcome some of the problems identified in the preceding chapters. It has the potential to provide assurances and allay fears, provide much-needed resources, reduce the risk of immobility, introduce flexibility, broaden the process and promote human rights. There are however limits to what third parties can achieve. The literature has typically explained failures and shortcomings by pointing to the insensitivity of liberal peace-building to local culture (see e.g. Richmond, 2009); the lack of sufficiently 'robust' peacekeeping (see e.g. Doyle & Sambanis, 2000); unintended consequences (see e.g. Hultman, 2010); or the problem of ensuring an exit strategy (see e.g. De Waal, 2009). External actors will not however always be supportive of a peace agreement. Separatist conflicts are, as noted above, often fuelled by the involvement of external actors, as Russia's involvement in the conflict in Ukraine currently reminds us.

This chapter will argue that for all of these issues, there is again an important interaction between the peace process, the conflict context and the content of the agreement. The importance of context is often acknowledged. Doyle and Sambanis (2000), for example, argue that the degree of international involvement needed depends on the degree of hostility and the level of local capacity. But there is less understanding in existing literature of how the content of the peace agreement enables and constrains third party involvement. The critical peace-building literature for example largely ignores the peace settlement (Selby, 2013) and Lyons' (2010, p. 159) argument that the period immediately following the signing of an agreement is more important for post-conflict elections than the agreement's content is fairly typical. This chapter will argue that even limited third party involvement can have a positive impact on the sustainability of an agreement, and the quality of the peace it provides (see also Fortna, 2008), but the content of the agreement engenders considerably path dependency. It creates institutions and empowers specific actors and consequently constrains what even robust peacekeeping is able to achieve. The initial agreement matters. It matters for the feasibility of different peace-building strategies and therefore also for possible exit strategies.

Third Party Involvement: From Military Intervention to Support and Advice

The need for 'robust' third party security guarantees is often pointed to in the literature (see e.g. Doyle & Sambanis, 2000; Walter, 2002).

However, as discussed in chapter 2, of the twenty cases analysed in this book, only five had armed peacekeeping missions and only one of these, Bosnia, had a mandate to enforce the peace. Why is third party military involvement not more widespread? The lack of international willingness to commit troops has been discussed widely (see e.g. Stedman, 2002; Toft, 2009). But another obstacle is the lack of local willingness to accept third party involvement. The central government will in most cases be highly reluctant to accept peacekeepers. Peacekeepers imply that the government is not able, or indeed willing, to ensure peace (Fortna, 2008) and such international involvement is also generally seen as benefiting the weaker side, typically the rebel forces (Regan, 2002; Zartman, 2005). In the case of Aceh, the GAM was unhappy that only a small group of unarmed observers were to monitor the implementation of the agreement and instead demanded at least 2,000 armed observers. However, the mediators made it clear that the Indonesian Government would not countenance this (Merikallio & Ruokanen, 2015, p. 305). Similarly, the Bangladeshi Government refused the rebel demand for UN peacekeepers, and there was no external push for such a deployment (Fortna, 2008, pp. 61–2). Peacekeepers tend therefore to go to cases where the rebels are relatively strong (ibid.).

Although rebel forces are typically keener on peacekeepers, since they find themselves more exposed following disarmament, lack of trust remains an obstacle. A number of failures in the 1990s demonstrate that the ability and willingness of peacekeepers to fight is by no means assured (ibid., p. 87; see also Polman, 2004), and the leaders of Nagorno Karabakh have for example expressed their concern that peacekeepers would not be willing to use force against an Azerbaijani offensive. They cite the example of Croatian Krajina where UN peacekeepers were deployed to guarantee the ceasefire but did not intervene when the Croatian army launched a military offensive against the Serb entity. The Karabakh leaders consequently reject withdrawing forces from the districts surrounding the entity even if UN peacekeepers were to be deployed.[73] Similarly, the SPLM/A rejected a UN security guarantee and instead insisted on maintaining a separate army for southern Sudan, describing it as 'the only fundamental guarantor' (Young, 2013, p. 117). An international military presence may therefore not be acceptable to the local parties. This clearly makes the task at hand even harder and usually results in a lack of willingness to intervene.

With or without consent, the effectiveness of military involvement remains contested. Scepticism regarding the effectiveness of military intervention has been heightened after the 2003 invasion of Iraq, but as Hoddie and Hartzell point out, the instability in Iraq is not the first time military interventions have not had the intended effect. They point to cases such as Rwanda and Sri Lanka and argue that 'taken together, these examples suggest that military intervention alone is often insufficient for securing an enduring peace in the aftermath of civil war' (2010, p. 1). But this does not mean that international involvement cannot have an important effect on peace processes. Fortna has argued that peacekeeping does not have to be 'robust' – it does not have to be large and well-armed – to have a stabilizing effect on peace (2008, pp. 107–9, 173). This is because the political and economic dimensions of multidimensional peacekeeping are, at least, as important as the military aspects. Hoddie and Hartzell likewise stress the potential of 'soft intervention', which they define as 'explicitly nonmilitary incentives and disincentives available to third parties seeking to influence the trajectory of a peace process or the nature of the postconflict environment, or both' (2010, p. 14). The argument for robust peacekeeping has been very much focused on the risk of rebels 'cheating', of not disarming since they do not trust the government to stick to their end of the bargain. However, as has been argued in previous chapters, lack of government implementation of the agreement is often the biggest cause of post-settlement instability. This is not to say that security is not important, and military withdrawal tends to be among the broken promises, but lack of implementation of autonomy provisions or lack of supply of promised resources is often as important. Moreover when it comes to security, the risk of instability caused by recurrent violence and lack of order in the autonomous region appears to be more of a risk than renewed secessionist attempts. This suggests that other forms of intervention are needed.

Reaching an Agreement

Third party military action can make a negotiated settlement more likely by altering the cost-benefit calculations of the conflict parties (Regan, 2002). The threat of renewed military action undoubtedly acted as a disincentive during the Bosnian peace talks at the Wright-Patterson Air Force Base in Dayton, Ohio. The US envoy, Richard Holbrooke, argues that he was not worried about the hawkish message the negotiating venue might convey: 'I thought that reminders of American airpower would not hurt' (1999, p. 204). But such collective cost-benefit calculations cannot necessarily be assumed. The previous chapter stressed the importance of internal dynamics: leaders may not be able to compromise, even if they recognize the likelihood of an impending catastrophe. The risk of unintended consequences is also considerable. The threat of defeat could lead, for example, to greater dependence on an external patron: 'A drowning man clings to a serpent' (Heraclides, 1991, p. 40), especially if they still fear the consequences of a compromise solution. Levelling the playing field could also make the (formerly) weaker party reluctant to compromise, since an outright victory would now seem a lot more realistic.

Unlike military intervention, which was only used to push the parties to compromise in the case of Bosnia, non-military third party involvement was found in most of the cases (see table 7.1). Such intervention can also help create ripeness, is associated with fewer risks and can be carried out by both state- and non-state actors (Zartman, 2005, p. 13). For example, the peace agreement for Aceh was negotiated by the former Finnish President Martti Ahtisaari,

Table 7.1. Third Party Involvement in Negotiations

Bosnia	US, EU
Croatia–Eastern Slavonia	US, UN
Indonesia–East Timor	UN, Portugal
Indonesia–Aceh	Crisis Management Initiative
Israel–Palestine	Norwegian mediation with US support
Macedonia	EU
Mali	Algeria, Mauritania, France
Niger	Algeria, Burkina Faso and France
PNG–Bougainville	New Zealand, Australia, Fiji, Vanuatu, Solomon Islands, UN
Philippines–Mindanao	OIC
Serbia–Montenegro	EU
Sudan–South Sudan	IGAD, US
Ukraine–Crimea	OSCE
UK–Northern Ireland	US
Bangladesh–Chittagong Hill Tracts	
India–Bodoland	
Moldova–Gagauzia	*No third party involvement*
Russia–Tatarstan	
Russia–Chechnya[74]	
Senegal–Casamance[75]	

and his NGO, the Crisis Management Initiative; in Sudan the talks took place under the auspices of the Intergovernmental Authority on Development (IGAD) but with increasing involvement of the US State Department; the Mindanao peace agreement was negotiated by the Organization of the Islamic Conference (OIC);[76] while Algeria, France and Mauritania helped mediate the National Pact for Mali.

Third parties can help convince the actors in the conflict that they should start negotiating. Zartman emphasizes the importance of perceptions when it comes to 'ripe moments' and third parties can help shape those perceptions: 'parties at conflict need help. They are too taken up with the business of conducting conflict to see the need and opportunities for a way out, unless someone helps them' (2005, p. 13). They can do so through persuasion. For example, Ahtisaari tried to convince the GAM that their maximalist objective was unachievable: 'what you have dreamt about – that is to say independence – is out of the question' (Merikallio & Ruokanen, 2015, p. 292). If persuasion is not enough, third parties can also try to alter the cost-benefit calculations; make the stalemate more painful. In the case of Sudan the US did this by threatening the Sudanese Government with further sanctions, if it did not continue negotiating. The government also feared that in the absence of progress in the peace talks, the US would increase its support for the SPLM/A and other armed groups (Young, 2013, pp. 90–1), thereby altering the military balance even if not through military intervention.

Mediators also have to convince the conflict parties that there are alternatives to continued violence; that a 'way out' is both realistic and attractive. Financial incentives are sometimes used to persuade specific members of the different factions to support the agreement (Rothchild & Emmanuel, 2010, p. 129), but inducements can also be more symbolic or more targeted at perceptions. For example, Mo Mowlam, the Secretary of State for Northern Ireland, visited the Maze prison to convince the Loyalists not to reject the peace talks. This mattered because it showed that she took them and their grievances seriously (Mowlam, 2005). In the case of Aceh, the GAM was deeply sceptical of 'autonomy' as a starting point for negotiations (Merikallio & Ruokanen, 2015, p. 294), but Ahtisaari used the example of the Åland Islands, a Swedish-speaking region of Finland that has enjoyed wide-ranging autonomy since 1921, to demonstrate that autonomy can mean actual self-government (Stepan, 2013, p. 244). Negotiations therefore went ahead.

However there are clearly limits to what third parties can do if the conflict parties are not ready to negotiate in earnest. The international mediators tasked with facilitating a solution to the Nagorno Karabakh conflict regularly step up their efforts, resulting in announcements of imminent breakthroughs (see e.g. Voice of America, 2010). But these never materialize. The local leaders face significant internal constraints and the mistrust between the two sides is almost bottomless. It is therefore difficult to see what third parties would have to offer, or threaten, to convince the parties to accept a difficult compromise. Part of the problem is a lack of agreement between the three co-chairs. Pressure will only work if Russia, the US and France agree, for example, to withhold investment unless an agreement is forthcoming. In the present international climate, that seems highly unlikely. International officials involved in the talks argue that no pressure is exerted by the international co-chairs and the two presidents are in fact the ones who dictate the process.[77]

If, on the other hand, there is a willingness to reach a compromise, third parties can do a lot to help negotiate an agreement, without having to resort to strong-arm tactics. The mediators can offer reassurances in case of ambiguities and can also offer recognition for the weaker party. Merely negotiating with rebel forces on an equal footing to the central government does this symbolically, which is one reason why international mediation will often be resisted. Further reassurances, and continued third party support, can be built into the peace agreement and can therefore help convince the parties that an agreement provides an attractive, and not too risky, way out.

Importance of Content

'Robust peacekeeping' was, as argued above, rare in the cases analysed, but even peacekeeping with a more limited mandate can make aggression more costly. These peacekeepers may not have the mandate or capacity to enforce the peace, but their monitoring can make a surprise attack more difficult, and their presence can also signal that a more forceful intervention will follow if either of the parties reverts to military means (Fortna, 2008, p. 86). But such reassurances could potentially be provided by unarmed third parties. The prospect of international involvement can moreover act as a carrot, which helps convince the parties of the benefits of an agreement, and not simply a guarantee against being cheated.

In addition to a NATO peacekeeping force, Macedonia's Ohrid Agreement for example lists a range of international organizations that are invited to assist with its implementation (Annex C), such as the OSCE, which is requested to help with election monitoring, media development and police training. Importantly, the EU is tasked with coordinating the international efforts in cooperation with the Stabilization and Association Council, and the overall framework for the implementation of the agreement is therefore Macedonia's accession to the EU. Consequently, third party involvement provides both reassurances to the Albanian community that the agreement will actually be honoured and a carrot in the form of closer EU integration for the majority. The framework of EU integration is similarly found in the Belgrade Agreement that created Serbia & Montenegro. The EU insisted that Serbia's and Montenegro's only path towards closer integration with the EU was as a joint state; and the lure of EU accession managed to persuade Montenegro's leader to defer the republic's independence (Gallagher, 2003; Kim, 2005). The EU also features in the Aceh peace agreement, although in a more traditional confidence-building role. Along with ASEAN, the EU is to establish an Aceh Monitoring Mission (AMM) with the mandate to monitor the implementation of the commitments made by the parties, including monitoring of DDR, army relocation, judicial reform and human rights provisions (art. 5.2). The AMM is also charged with resolving any disputes over implementation (art. 6.1). Such monitoring helps reassure the weaker party that they will not simply be abandoned once the agreement is signed and hence be completely reliant on the intentions of the stronger side. The extent to which the third party is able and willing to use this authority is a different matter, as will be discussed below. Other agreements include similar confidence-building measures. In the case of Bougainville, the UN peacekeepers are to monitor and verify the DDR process and keep one of the keys to the double-lock securing the weapons handed over. In a number of other agreements, the international post-settlement involvement is only set out in vague terms (see table 7.2). For example, in the case of Mali, the Commission for Supervision and Implementation is to hold special sessions in the presence of and under the chairmanship of the mediator (art. 83). However the authority of the mediator in case of any disputes is not specified.[78] Similarly, in the case of Mindanao the agreement simply states that 'the OIC shall be requested to continue to extend its assistance and good offices in monitoring the full implementation of this agreement' (art. 12), but no further details are provided and no role in dispute resolution foreseen. In these cases the lack of detailed focus on the post-settlement period

167

Table 7.2. Third Party Involvement in Implementation (as per the settlement)

Bosnia	NATO force and international administration
Croatia–Eastern Slavonia	UN peacekeepers and transitional administration
Indonesia–East Timor	UN to arrange referendum and maintain 'adequate presence' until result implemented
Indonesia–Aceh	AMM
Macedonia	International organizations to facilitate, monitor and assist
Mali	Algeria to chair the commission overseeing the integration of combatants. International experts on the Independent Commission of Enquiry
Niger	Mediators part of Peace Commission which oversees DDR. Military observers to be deployed
PNG–Bougainville	UNOMB, Peace Monitoring Group
Philippines–Mindanao	Possible OIC assistance and monitoring, no details
Serbia–Montenegro	EU to be involved in dispute resolution
Sudan–South Sudan	UNMIS and international presence in some bodies
UK–Northern Ireland	Independent International Commission on Decommissioning and international experts on Commission on Policing for Northern Ireland
Bangladesh–CHT	
India–Bodoland	
Israel–Palestine	
Moldova–Gagauzia	*No third party involvement*
Russia–Tatarstan	
Russia–Chechnya	
Senegal–Casamance	
Ukraine–Crimea	

did not prevent an agreement from being reached, but it could be argued to have impacted negatively on its implementation.

Central government resistance to internationalization has already been mentioned, but rebel groups are also not necessarily interested in third party monitoring and verification. This is more likely if they are negotiating from a position of relative strength, and the agreement allows them to maintain some of this strength, and of course if they are likely to renege on some of their promises. In Sudan, John Garang, leader of the SPLM/A, did not reportedly want the proposed Assistance and Evaluation Commission (AEC) to have a strong mandate and report back to the IGAD or another international body. Young (2013, p. 107) speculates that this was because he did not want the commission to probe into matters of governance in southern Sudan and oversee elections that 'might not meet international standards'. In the final agreement, the AEC has international representation and is to conduct a mid-term review of the implementation process (Ch. 1, art. 2.4), but it does not report back to any international body. The UN Peace Support Mission (which would later become UNMIS) is to monitor and verify the agreement and support its implementation, but its authority in case of disputes is not clear, and its role is primarily focused on the process of military withdrawal and the limited process of DDR.[79]

Dictating the Agreement?

Third parties were involved in most of the negotiations and some form of third party involvement is usually foreseen for the post-settlement phase as well. But how much have these third parties otherwise affected the content of the agreements? Here we again see considerable variation.

In a few cases, the agreement is almost dictated by the mediator. Serbia & Montenegro was famously dubbed 'Solania' due to the heavy pressure exerted on the parties by Javier Solana, the EU's High Representative for Common Foreign and Security Policy (see Van Meurs, 2003). At the other extreme we find the Khasavyurt Accord for Chechnya which was simply negotiated in the 'presence' of an international official, the head of the OSCE Assistance Group in Chechnya (Hughes, 2007, p. 89). Most of the cases of international involvement fall somewhere between those two extremes. The mediators have made some proposals, and sometimes ruled out solutions, but significant parts of the agreements have been left to the conflict parties.

Most of the Dayton Agreement for Bosnia was drafted by the mediators. However, the content had developed over time and been shaped by years of negotiations, expect for the human rights provisions that were new to the Dayton Agreement and whose origins were entirely international (Szasz, 1996). The core deal – the decentralized power-sharing institutions – came from the parties themselves (Bieber, 2013). Foreign experts also played an important part in the drafting of large parts of Sudan's Comprehensive Peace Agreement and Young argues that this explains its legalism, which he finds inappropriate given the lack of well-established judicial authorities in Sudan (2013, pp. 108–9). But the core deal again came from the local parties, in fact the agreement on an independence referendum for South Sudan was negotiated directly between Salva Kiir for the SPLM, and Ghazi Salhudin for the NCP, and reportedly took everyone by surprise (ibid., pp. 93–4). In Sudan the parties negotiated directly, whereas in Northern Ireland the Belfast Agreement was primarily negotiated through shuttle diplomacy. This made for a much more directive approach. The mediators, especially the British ones, presented proposals and amended them in light of the parties' reactions to them (see e.g. Powell, 2008). In Aceh, Ahtisaari presented a framework for negotiations to the parties, according to which a solution had to be found that respected the integrity of Indonesia's borders; independence was, in other words, off the table. Some form of autonomy was the most the GAM could hope for, but Ahtisaari stressed that this should be part of a wider package which would also include the withdrawal of the Indonesian army from the province (Merikallio & Ruokanen, 2015, pp. 293–4). Due to this directive approach, Ahtisaari was reportedly given the name 'Ayatollah Ahtisaari' (ibid., p. 303). Others have argued however that the mediators let the parties 'set their own agenda' (Hadi, 2008). The mediators involved in the Oslo process for Israel–Palestine have been criticized in even harsher terms for their allegedly passive role, which allowed the asymmetric nature of the conflict to be mirrored in the talks: 'the Oslo process was conducted on Israel's premises, with Norway acting as Israel's helpful errand boy' (Waage, 2007–8, p. 62).

The extent to which the mediators take on a directive role depends of course on the conflict, for example whether or not the main parties are ready to engage in direct negotiations, but it also depends on the nature of the mediator and in particular their leverage. A US envoy, negotiating on the back of a US-led military campaign, will clearly have a lot more clout and be able to dictate solutions to a far greater extent than the representative of an NGO who has been invited by the parties, or often only one of them, to facilitate an agreement. The degree of involvement has also varied within each agreement, with the mediator's touch often being far more visible when it comes to human rights provisions than the 'core deal'.

Moreover, the mediators seem in most cases to be content with, or even encourage, a fairly narrow process. In Sudan, the mediators supported the parties in keeping civil society and other political parties out of the process, fearing that a broader process would harden positions and make the process unworkable (Young, 2013, pp. 8–9, 111, 113). Ahtisaari likewise rejected the GAM's plea for a popular mandate, 'if you don't have the courage to make the decision in the name of the people, we are all wasting our time' (Merikallio & Ruokanen, 2015, p. 294). The IGAD mediator in Sudan justified the narrow process by arguing that it 'would be tested at the ballot box' (Young, 2013, p. 109), but Young argues that democratic transition was never a major objective; elections were simply viewed as necessary to legitimize the agreement (ibid., pp. 8–9, 99). This appears to be a general trend. Mediators may insist on elections, but a vague commitment to democratic principles often suffices, and although they similarly insist that some references to human rights are included, they are worried that pushing for effective institutions would risk jeopardizing the agreement. In Sudan, the mediators proposed a reconciliation process, but this was rejected by the local parties, who were aware of their role in past abuses, and the agreement only contains a non-specific reference to the goal of reconciliation (ibid., p. 112). Although Ahtisaari insisted on including human rights in the Aceh agreement, he appears to have limited this to safeguards against future violations. He told the GAM that if they began scrutinizing past injustices, they would never achieve an agreement: 'You can't wash all your dirty linen at once' (Merikallio & Ruokanen, 2015, p. 302). The provisions therefore lack any kind of, potentially explosive, details. It is for example not specified if the Human Rights Court for Aceh would have retroactive powers and therefore be able to try cases of war-related abuses (Hadi, 2008). As argued in chapters 4 and 5, despite rhetorical references to human rights, the result is a not very liberal peace. It would appear that third party mediators play some role in this outcome.

The final, indirect, way in which mediators affect the content of the agreements is through the use of deadlines. Deadlines are used in most peace talks to maintain momentum, to focus minds and create a sense of urgency. Powell (2008, p. 31) describes how, in the case of Northern Ireland, the mediators 'wanted a dynamic approach to rush the parties into an agreement without allowing them to stop and think too much'. Reaching an agreement as fast as possible makes sense if war is raging and people are continuing to lose their lives, but deadlines are also used when a ceasefire is in place and the need for speed is less pressing. Deadlines create an artificial sense of urgency, which may make it easier to reach an agreement, but the risk is that the resulting agreement is rushed, that it lacks important details and that it is not supported by a significant peace constituency. This would not be a big problem if the gaps can simply be filled in later; if 'details' such as effective human rights provisions and broadening of the process can be postponed. However, this is often difficult, even in the case of significant third party involvement in the post-settlement phase.

Implementing the Agreement

Peacekeepers have had some success in the cases analysed in this book. Although the international presence in Bosnia has been heavily, and often rightly, criticized, it was no small feat for the stationed NATO forces to prevent a return to violence. The international presence was not as robust in the case of Eastern Slavonia and Macedonia, but the conflict context was less intractable and the peacekeepers helped avoid a return to violence. Outside of the Balkans, the arrival of Australian peacekeepers in East Timor managed to quell the violence that broke out following the independence referendum. Only in the case of Bosnia would the peacekeepers have been able to deter an attack from the main conflict parties. However it may be enough for peacekeepers to manage violent factions or splinter groups, such as in East Timor where they only needed to deter the anti-independence militias (Fortna, 2008, p. 96). This depends, however, on the main parties actually being supportive of the peacekeepers and this cannot be assumed even if they consent to the initial deployment, especially if the agreement includes significant ambiguities.

The UN Mission in Sudan (UNMIS) has faced significant criticism, in particular for failing to protect civilians in the contested regions of Abyei and South Kordufan. When fighting broke out in Abyei in 2008, the then US Special Envoy for Sudan, Richard Williamson, was scathing in his critique: 'We pay a billion dollars a year for UNMIS and they didn't leave their garrison, while 52,000 lives were shattered and nearly a hundred people perished' (Tendai, 2011). The failure of UNMIS to act was attributed to a lack of operational and resource capabilities, but also to an unwillingness of some peacekeepers to fulfil their duties. However, added to this is the fundamental problem that the main parties have consistently prevented the UN Mission from protecting civilians (Better World Campaign, 2014). In 2011, the two governments agreed to demilitarize Abyei and a separate peacekeeping mission was deployed to the area (the UN Interim Security Force in Abyei), with a mandate to use force to protect civilians. But without an agreement on the issue of status, the security situation 'remains highly unpredictable and tense' and both sides have failed to cooperate with the mission (ibid.).

Peacekeepers can make an important difference when the conflict parties are willing to cooperate and an agreement has been reached on the most contested issues. Fortna particularly emphasizes how they can assist in the difficult process of DDR and the creation of a unified army, and also monitor the implementation of the political agreement and possible human rights violations (2008, p. 100). But this stabilizing function does not in many cases depend on the potential use of coercive means. This expands the range of third party actors who could play a positive role in the post-settlement phase.

DDR and Capacity-Building

By monitoring and verifying the process of DDR, third parties can provide assurances in what is otherwise a sensitive and difficult process. Peacekeepers do not have to have the capacity to force the conflict parties to disarm; they can instead rely on their moral and political authority (Fortna, 2008). The unarmed United Nations Observer Mission in Bougainville (UNOMB) thus held a key to the double-lock to where the Bougainville forces put their weapons and also had to verify the completion of the process (Woodbury, 2015). The Aceh Monitoring Mission similarly played an important role in the DDR process, by monitoring and ultimately verifying the process. The process is, as discussed in chapter 2, invariably incomplete, but the third parties helped legitimize it.

If the process of DDR is incomplete, the risk is that it will lead to high levels of local crime and disorder which can threaten the agreement as a whole. Third parties therefore have another important function: the supply of resources and the building of capacity (see also Doyle & Sambanis, 2000). The need for local capacity, to ensure intra-communal security and provide tangible benefits of peace, has been emphasized throughout this book. Resources are needed to integrate former combatants and build an effective coercive apparatus that can help protect against spoiler violence. Resources are moreover needed to build or rebuild other state institutions, including human rights institutions, and strengthen civil society. Following years of violent conflicts, governments will often be severely strapped for cash and these resources will in many cases have to come from third parties, and most agreements call for international donors to assist with implementation. However such calls are often not heeded and even pledged support typically fails to materialize; international attention is fickle and once an agreement is signed it tends to move on to somewhere else.

173

Another problem is that the funds may be mismanaged. Rebel armies will often struggle to turn themselves into effective (local) governments and the temptation to spend the money on arms rather than infrastructure, health or education may be hard to resist. This could ultimately undermine popular support for the agreement. International donors could try to counter this by supporting, and encouraging, the transformation of armed movements into political parties capable of governing. Advice and assistance will be beneficial, but resources are also often needed, for example to provide severance packages to high-level military officers (Lyons, 2010, p. 153).

Political Provisions

The other area where third parties can help promote stability is when it comes to ensuring that the conflict parties actually implement the provisions they have agreed to. Fortna (2008) argues that the lack of peacekeepers in the Chittagong Hill Tracts meant that there was insufficient pressure on the Bangladeshi Government to honour its promises and implement the agreement. But the question is how much third parties can do if the central government fails to live up to its promises. To a considerable extent this depends on the mandate and capacity of the international presence.

Third parties were put in charge of implementation in two of the cases, Bosnia and Croatia,[80] although in the case of Bosnia the Office of the High Representative (OHR) was initially meant to assist and support the local parties, rather than implement the agreement directly. However, the parties were unable to agree on even the most basic laws and the powers of the High Representative were increased as a result. From 1998 onwards, the Dayton Agreement was increasingly implemented through decrees from the OHR (see Caspersen, 2004). In most cases, the international involvement in implementation is however much more limited.

Third parties were involved in dispute resolution in a couple of cases. This is most notably the case in Aceh, where Ahtisaari was the final arbiter if the parties failed to agree on the implementation of the agreement. The agreement authorized him to issue binding decisions (art. 6.1.), but Ahtisaari was reluctant to use these: 'it is not appropriate for a former president of a foreign power to dictate to other leaders ... how they should take care of matters in their own country'. He wanted the process to be 'guided by good dialogue until the end' (Merikallio & Ruokanen, 2015, p. 319). This appears sensible given the lack of capacity to enforce these decisions, but it does mean that the AMM was criticized for not doing enough when the Law on Governing Aceh significantly watered down the promised autonomy (Schulze, 2008). In other cases, the authority of the third party is much less clear, such as in Sudan where neither the Abyei Boundaries Commission (ABC) nor UNMIS were mandated to enforce the decision on the contested territory and lacked significant leverage. Leverage was more readily available in Macedonia, where the EU could wave the carrot of future integration in front of the government, if it became reluctant to implement certain provisions (International Crisis Group, 2011).

Naming and shaming would be an option in the case of limited mandate or capacity. After all, both sides are usually concerned with their international image and do not want to be seen as responsible for wrecking the peace. This is made difficult, however, by the ambiguous provisions in many agreements, such as when it comes to the powers that are to be under the control of the autonomous region, its access to resources, or its precise borders. This kind of ambiguity makes it harder to determine if provisions have been implemented. Another problem is that third parties are often worried that by criticizing one or more of the parties, they risk undermining the momentum of the peace process. The holding of free and fair elections in Sudan was a precondition for the next step in the implementation process – the independence referendum – but it has been argued that 'the international community largely ignored the widespread electoral abuses by the ruling parties so that the peace process could be kept on track' (Young, 2013, p. xvii).

Implementing the agreement therefore poses significant challenges and there are limits to what a third party can achieve, especially in the case of unclear mandates and ambiguous agreements. What then are the prospects of actually altering the terms of the agreement, or the dynamics that it has created? As argued previously, a peace agreement is necessarily imperfect; it is often rushed, it reflects immediate security concerns and fears, and it often downplays or even ignores human rights. Ideally, it would therefore be flexible. Can third parties help accomplish this?

Altering Post-Settlement Dynamics

The ability of third parties to change the post-settlement dynamics has predominantly been focused on two issues: the strengthening of moderate forces and intra-communal diversity, and the promotion

175

of human rights. However, while it appears that a positive impact in these areas is possible, this will be constrained by the institutions created by the initial settlement and the actors it empowered.

Promoting Human Rights and Strengthening Moderates

It is often argued that third parties can play a valuable role in monitoring human rights violations in the post-settlement phase, if need be by publicly criticizing perpetrators. Fortna (2008, p. 99) for example suggests that civilian police monitors can patrol with local forces and deter them from harassing, intimidating or killing the government's opponents. The AMM played such a role when it raised the issue of aggressive patrolling by the Indonesian army and reports of intimidation of ex-GAM members by the army's intelligence units. This ceased to be a problem once if was brought to the attention of the army's major general (Schulze, 2008, p. 38). However, Putnam (2002) warns that the effective, and sustainable, promotion of human rights relies on the existence of institutions which in the early post-settlement phase are yet to be established. Even if such institutions are included in the peace agreement, it is difficult for third parties to insist on their implementation, especially as regards past abuses, and it is harder still to insist on the introduction of provisions not already agreed to.

The case of Bougainville demonstrates that a third party can play a positive role when it comes to human rights provisions, here in the form of restorative justice. The UN mission in Bougainville was mandated to support reconciliation and it did so through logistical support, by attending and witnessing the ceremonies and, occasionally, by acting as go-between (Reddy, 2008, p. 122). But ambiguities present a significant problem for third parties, if agreed provisions are not implemented. Not only are human rights provisions often left vague, the concept of 'human rights' is itself vague and open to interpretation. This makes it harder for third parties to put pressure on the parties. In Aceh, the AMM was mandated to monitor the implementation of human rights provisions, but was reluctant to do so. One AMM official argued, 'the concept is non-existent, there are no policies and the area is weak, confused and aimless' (quoted in Schulze, 2008, p. 39). Other AMM members claimed that when they wanted to raise these issues they were 'ignored, marginalised and even silenced' (ibid.). The AMM did not therefore criticize the local parties when the promised Human Rights Court for Aceh and the Trust Commission were not implemented, or when Sharia was introduced in Aceh.

Third parties involved in the implementation of settlements will often fear that too much pressure when it comes to human rights risks causing instability, and keeping the peace processes going is typically seen as more important than addressing past abuses or ensuring democratization. Putnam cautions that implementation missions 'must be tailored to the politics of what is possible' and human rights actors must 'balance a sensitivity for the fragility of postconflict political settings against the impetus to react forcefully against all forms of human rights violations' (2002, p. 260). Schulze (2008, p. 39) comments that the reluctance of the AMM to push for the implementation of human rights provisions ironically contributed to it achieving its overall aims.

A push for human rights provisions not already contained in the agreement is even less likely. The prosecution of war criminals will be difficult at the best of times, but almost impossible if the suspects are now in positions of government. And once institutions are put in place that are based on the dominant groups in the state, it is indeed an uphill struggle for any third party intervener to reform these institutions, thereby weakening existing guarantees and positions of power, and ensure the rights of individuals and groups excluded from the process. The international implementation of the Dayton Peace Agreement for Bosnia constitutes only a partial exception. Ambiguities create difficulties for third parties with a limited mandate, but the ambiguity in the Dayton Agreement could be used by the OHR to move the agreement in a more centripetal direction, in particular through the strengthening of central institutions (Bieber, 2006a). However, as was argued in chapter 3, this did not alter the group-based nature of the agreement. In order for this to have happened, the OHR would have had to impose changes to the 'core deal' and this has been seen as a step too far, which would risk creating a backlash and also make it impossible to argue that peace has become self-sustainable.

One option for changing dynamics when faced with local resistance is to engineer a change in the local leadership. But the content of the settlement again creates significant constraints. Third parties could try to influence the dynamics of intra-communal politics, but such strategies risk backfiring. Funding moderate parties would for example create a more level playing field, but it could lead to accusations that these parties are the agents of international actors and do not represent domestic interests; hardliners could therefore unintentionally be strengthened. Moreover the problem is that the incumbent parties are typically empowered by the peace agreement. The agreement legitimizes their position and power-sharing institutions have been argued to favour more extreme parties (see e.g. Oberschall & Palmer, 2005); and most forms of power-sharing certainly favour parties that appeal exclusively to one group (Džankić, 2015). These constraints are hard to overcome. Limitations even exist in cases with a strong international mandate. The international administration in Bosnia for years tried to strengthen what were seen as moderate forces in Bosnia's Republika Srpska. However despite occasional successes the effects did not prove lasting. This is demonstrated most starkly by the conversion of Milorad Dodik. During the war, he courageously opposed the nationalist forces and was after the war seen as a possible vehicle for a moderate transformation of Republika Srpska. Significant resources were invested therefore into the promotion of his party. However, once Dodik gained power he dismayed his former international supporters by adopting a more hardline position than his predecessor (see e.g. Caspersen, 2006, 2010). The OHR also removed officials who were seen to violate the Dayton Agreement, or the spirit of this agreement, but this again failed to fundamentally alter the dynamics of Bosnian politics.

The same problem applies to international attempts to strengthen civil society organizations that are supportive of an agreement. In the case of Bosnia, there was a very conscious strategy to strengthen civil society, but this was done by supporting NGOs that did not have roots in society and therefore failed to have an impact (Foley, 2010, p. 171). Such problems are most acute where the agreement does not enjoy the support of a significant peace constituency, which again demonstrates the close interaction of content and process. This suggests that if third parties wish to affect the intra-communal balance of power, they need to do this during the negotiations – through the involvement of a greater range of actors and the avoidance of exclusive and excluding agreements – and not simply wait till the post-settlement phase.

Path dependency is considerable, even in the case of peace enforcement, and this kind of coercive implementation, in any case, comes with a range of downsides. The international approach in Bosnia has been criticized for producing the 'politics of irresponsibility' (see e.g. International Crisis Group, 1998): the local parties can adopt extreme positions and refuse to cooperate, without facing any of the consequences. They can simply rely on the third party to make unpopular decisions and will not be held to account for their unwillingness to compromise. As a result, peace does not become self-sustainable. This also means that the international administration has been unable to leave. The international presence was meant to last for one year only, but it is still there, more than twenty years after the signing of the Dayton Peace Agreement. By intervening so forcefully, the OHR has become party to the ongoing power struggle and this makes it difficult to exit.

External Spoilers

There are consequently significant limitations to what third parties can do both in the post-settlement and the pre-settlement phase. So far I have assumed that the international actors are in fact supportive of peace and stability; they may not be able to achieve their goals and their actions may have unintended consequences but they do not set out to undermine a negotiated settlement. But this cannot always be assumed. Many conflicts will include both internal and external spoilers, and the existence of external actors opposed to a peace agreement constitutes a considerable obstacle that will have to be overcome in most cases for sustainable peace to be possible (see e.g. Wolff, 2011).

Separatist conflicts are often fuelled by the involvement of external actors such as patron states, who may have an interest in ongoing conflict and contribute to its continuation, either directly (through military action) or indirectly (through support for leaders adopting maximalist positions) (see Caspersen, 2008b). There are several examples of this, including Russia's support for Abkhazia and South Ossetia; India's support for the United People's Party of the Chittagong Hill Tracts (PJCSS); Turkey's support for Northern Cyprus; Serbia's support for the Bosnian Serbs, etc. However just as the term spoiler was problematic when applied to internal actors opposed to an agreement, it can also be misleading when applied to external actors, or it certainly contains a value judgement. For example when Russia opposed Ahtisaari's plan for Kosovo's supervised independence, this was by many regarded as 'spoiling' behaviour which strengthened the Serbian intransigent position. However, both Russia and Serbia could argue that they had legitimate reasons to oppose the plan, such as the fear of an international precedent or concerns for the position of Kosovo's Serb minority.

Another problem with the concept is an empirical one. The support for separatist forces, as opposed to central governments, is often covert. Or rather patron states will at most admit to supplying resources to rebel forces, and stress their legitimate aims, but deny any direct involvement. This is the typical response, even when there is ample evidence that forces from the patron state are actually present on the ground, such as when Vladimir Putin dismissed the suggestion that the uniforms worn by Crimean separatist forces bore a striking resemblance to Russian army uniforms: 'you can go to a store and buy any kind of uniform'.[81] However, Russia's decision to annex Crimea suggests a serious challenge to the principle of territorial integrity and it is conceivable that external support for separatist forces will become less covert in the future. This example points to another difficulty with the concept: it is sometimes difficult to distinguish between an external spoiler in an intra-state conflict, and an external aggressor in an inter-state conflict. Parent states will often insist that we are dealing with the latter. Azerbaijan for example insists that the Nagorno Karabakh conflict is the result of Armenian aggression and therefore an inter-state conflict. The Azerbaijani Government consequently insists on negotiating directly with Armenia and refuses to meet with leaders from Nagorno Karabakh. Finally, it is important to note that external spoilers can also be non-state actors, such as the Lord's Resistance Army (LRA) which fought against the SPLA in southern Sudan and was notorious for its atrocities against the civilian population (Schmitz, 2013). Non-state involvement is however particularly destabilizing if backed up by a state actor. Until the signing of the Comprehensive Peace Agreement, the LRA was supported by the Sudanese Government and used in its fight against the SPLA (ibid., p. 140).

Although the concept of an external spoiler is in some ways problematic it does help to capture the significant trans-border dynamics that often characterize intra-state conflicts. This potential threat to peace agreements has been overcome in different ways and in different phases of the peace process. In the case of Sudan, the peace agreement commits the parties to 'end the presence of the foreign insurgency groups on the Sudanese soil' and to 'work together to disarm, repatriate or expel these groups as soon as possible' (Annex 1, art. 12.2 and 12.3). This was not easy, however. The LRA was initially paid off by the South Sudanese Government in exchange for not launching attacks, but this strategy simultaneously constituted an incentive for the LRA to keep going. The SPLA eventually launched a successful military offensive against the LRA, in a joint operation with the militaries of Uganda and the Democratic Republic of Congo (ibid.).

Patron states have in most cases ceded or reduced their support for rebel movements *before* an agreement is reached. India withdrew its support for the PJCSS (Mohsin, 2003, pp. 15, 41); the PLO could no longer rely on patronage from Arab states and the Soviet Union (Lieberfeld, 1999, p. 70); Serbia significantly scaled back its support for the Bosnian Serb statelet (Caspersen, 2010); and the SPLA had also lost valuable regional support (Ahmed, 2009, pp. 136–8). In some cases the patron state clearly functions as a veto power. For example, Russia is reportedly blocking any attempts at conflict resolution between Georgia and Abkhazia and any such initiatives consequently have to take place 'under the radar'.[82] The withdrawal or scaling back of support does not mean, however, that a patron state ceases to have an impact on the peace process, the settlement or its implementation. Scholars frequently argue that partisan actors can play a positive role in peace processes; they have leverage and can help deliver 'their side' and ensure that their interests and needs are addressed (see e.g. Svensson, 2009). This could explain Fortna's finding that a neighbouring country's support for rebels 'has no negative repercussions for peace' (2008, p. 117). The involvement of a 'trusted' third party in the peace process provides an implicit guarantee to the rebels against being cheated. In some cases there are also rumours of a more explicit guarantee. India was, for example, said to have provided a secret guarantee to the PJCSS, although a secret guarantee would, as Fortna points out, lack credibility (ibid., p. 135), as it would be easy for India to renege on it.

The reasons for the withdrawal of support are manifold and include changes within the external 'spoiler', most dramatically the collapse of the Soviet Union; transition within the parent state, such as the regime change in Bangladesh which resulted in a change in India's position (Mohsin, 2003); or international pressure, such as the economic sanctions and international isolation which finally led Serbia's Milošević to abandon his plans for a Greater Serbia. However, the content of the agreement also matters, even if we are dealing with an external spoiler. A patron state will often insist that key rebel demands are met and underlying grievances addressed. This is especially the case if the patron state is also a kin-state and the plight of the brethren across the border has proved to be a powerful popular mobilizer. The leaders of Armenia are, for example, vulnerable to charges of 'selling out' Nagorno Karabakh and are significantly constrained in their ability to support a compromise settlement (Caspersen, 2008b). External supporters of a settlement can, just like internal ones, risk being undermined by hardliners. But patron states will sometimes demand a role in the post-settlement state as well, or such a role is necessary in order to address rebel demands and assuage fears of being cheated. 'Sufficient inclusion' may well include external actors, both when it comes to the negotiating phase and to the solution that emerges from it.

181

When a conflict includes a patron state, trans-border elements will often have to be addressed in the agreement, especially if the patron is a kin-state. Milošević not only pushed, or even bullied, the Bosnian Serb leaders into accepting the Dayton Agreement; he was also a signatory and Republika Srpska was permitted to establish a 'special parallel relationship' with Serbia. Such links and the resulting blurring of sovereignty will however often be anathema to the parent state. The Greek Cypriot leaders have for example been strongly opposed to a Turkish security guarantee for the Turkish Cypriot population (International Crisis Group, 2005a). If the patron state has been given an important role in the peace settlement, and consequently an effective veto, the agreement will only be sustainable for as long as the patron remains supportive. The risk of a newly belligerent patron exists even when trans-border elements are not incorporated, as witnessed by the collapse of Crimea's autonomy arrangements following Russia's (covert) intervention. However, an explicit trans-border dimension would arguably make it even easier to destabilize the situation. In Gagauzia an unofficial referendum in 2014 overwhelmingly supported membership of the Russia-led Commonwealth of Independent States over closer EU integration and also backed Gagauzia's right to declare independence should Moldova lose or surrender its own independence (Minzarari, 2014). This refers to the provision in the peace agreement which grants Gagauzia the right to independence if there is a change in Moldova's status. Russia has not acted on this invitation, but it does illustrate why central governments may be reluctant to fudge sovereignty.

Finally, the involvement of patron states could also have an immense impact on the post-settlement phase. The lack of international willingness to commit troops to many intra-state wars has been mentioned above. Some authors suggest that the kind of extensive third party involvement which is needed to implement agreements in 'hard cases' will only happen if third parties have a vested interest in the conflict (see e.g. Stedman, 2002). Patron states would clearly fit that bill, but intervention by a third party with vested interests is likely to be guided by these interests, rather than the stability of the negotiated peace. One example of this is Russia's deployment of peacekeepers in the Georgian breakaway regions, Abkhazia and South Ossetia, following the signing of ceasefire agreements in the 1990s. The commitment was certainly credible, but Russia's strategic interests predominated and Georgia repeatedly asked for changes to the composition of the peacekeeping force.[83] The peacekeeping force essentially became a border guard for the breakaway regions and when Georgia launched a military offensive against South Ossetia in 2008, Russia had the perfect excuse for intervening: its peacekeepers were under attack (see e.g. Cornell & Starr, 2009).

Conclusion

This chapter has again demonstrated the important interaction of context, content and process, both in the pre- and post-settlement phase. Third party involvement affects the content of the peace agreement but is in turn constrained by it. Most conflict resolution literature is focused on the post-settlement period and this is clearly crucial for stability and should not be ignored by third parties; the job is not done once the agreement is signed. Third parties can do a lot in the post-settlement phase, and such involvement does not necessarily take the form of 'robust peacekeeping'. An unarmed observer mission is sometimes all it takes to provide reassurances and put pressure on the parties if they fail to implement agreed provisions. However, while the post-settlement phase should not be ignored, the content of the agreement should not either. This will significantly limit what is possible later on, even in the case of forceful third party intervention. It is therefore important to get it right and not simply hope, often in vain, that problems can be rectified at a later stage.

There are clear limitations to what third parties can do to ameliorate some of the negative consequences associated with peace agreements, but there also appears to be a hesitancy to push for change. If we perceive of third party involvement as a spectrum, then the cases seem to collect at either end. In most of the cases, international involvement is limited, consisting mainly of monitoring. The mandate of the third parties is restricted, or authority is not exercised even when the mandate allows for it, such as when Ahtisaari refrained from making any binding decisions in case of implementation disputes in Aceh. At the other end of the spectrum, we find what amounts to de facto protectorates, such as in Bosnia and Eastern Slavonia, where the third party effectively takes over the running of the country or the region. This leaves the middle of the spectrum, and the possibility for more effective yet less intrusive third party involvement, largely unexplored. In order to have a significant impact such involvement should however start before an agreement is reached, for example by pushing for a broader, more inclusive process, as this will be reflected in the terms of the settlement.

Finally, we can of course not always assume that third parties have benign motives. The involvement of patron states, or other forms of 'external spoilers', adds to the complexity of the conflict and will have to be addressed, often before serious negotiations can start. Such external involvement will also often need to be reflected in the peace agreement, for example by including a trans-border dimension. This is however likely to be resisted by the central government and can become a source of continuous instability.

CONCLUSION

Getting the parties in a separatist conflict to agree to a settlement is an achievement and should be celebrated as such. The obstacles to reaching a peace agreement are immense and include fear, mistrust, greed, and sometimes external interference. It therefore takes courageous leaders, who are willing to abandon their intransigent positions and take a leap into somewhat unknown territory. And it often takes mediators who are prepared to go the extra mile to change perceptions, provide reassurances, and tweak the details of the agreement so it becomes acceptable to both sides.

However, reaching an agreement is no guarantee that stability will prevail. Post-settlement violence is more common than not and this, along with the strains of a difficult compromise, could lead the agreement to collapse. This is all the more likely if the agreement does not address key grievances, if it is clearly unbalanced, or if it does not include major actors in the conflict. But even if the agreement does not collapse and stability is somehow maintained, this may come at a price. The settlement may trade justice and rights for stability and prioritize control and security over legitimacy. This clearly has a detrimental impact on the daily lives of the population, but it could also undermine stability in the longer-term.

Although each of the conflicts analysed in this book is different – with a unique set of grievances and interests, actors and conflict dynamics – lessons can nevertheless be learned: what did the agreements get right, what did they get wrong; what type of agreement is suitable in different conflict contexts; what are the alternatives? Such an analysis requires us to view the agreements as packages, since the different elements interact. The specifics of the autonomy arrangements for example affect the extent to which security can

185

be provided, and provisions related to territory, security and justice all significantly impact on the functioning of a power-sharing system.

The content of peace agreements matters. It matters for the ability to reach an agreement in the first place and for longer-term stability and quality of peace. This is not to deny the importance of context, such as the severity of the conflict or the balance of power between the two sides, or of the specific peace process, including the involvement of third parties. But context, process and content all affect each other; for example, the content of the settlement and the design of the peace process affect the risk of effective spoiling. Based on this I proposed an enriched concept of ripeness which incorporates intra-communal dynamics. Ripeness thereby becomes relevant for the sustainability of an agreement, not just for the start of serious negotiations. This requires a focus on legitimacy, not just stability, and on divisions within the groups supposedly engaged in conflict. The book demonstrated the existence of significant path dependency; it is difficult to depart from the 'core deal' in the post-settlement period, even in the case of extensive third party involvement. The agreement creates institutions and empowers specific actors – usually the negotiating elites – and this strongly affects what is possible later on. The assumption is often that details can be added later, and 'soft concerns' such as human rights addressed once the intensity of the conflict has been reduced. But this may not be feasible. Peace agreements are a chance to achieve a transformation of the existing system, and such a chance may not come back.

Peace agreements will of course never be perfect and it is easy to criticize them with the benefit of hindsight – and from the comfort of an academic position. But this book has pointed to provisions that are better avoided, possible pitfalls, and factors that mediators and others involved in finding peaceful solutions should bear in mind. This is by no means a blueprint, but an attempt to learn lessons.

Dominant Model: Simple Autonomy

The twenty agreements analysed in this book display a lot of variety, especially when it comes to the details included: some only sketch out the agreed post-settlement institutions in very broad terms, while others contain page after page of detailed provisions. The agreements also reflect considerable differences when it comes to the intensity of the conflict; the strength of the separatist movement; demographic variables such as relative size and geographic concentration of the separatist community; and the degree of third party involvement both pre- and post-settlement. Despite these differences it is still possible to identify a dominant model.

Autonomy is included in all but one of the agreements. The extent of this autonomy varies, but it is typically territorially-defined and it is also ethnic, in the sense that it empowers a particular group within the region. I have described this model as simple autonomy rather than 'complex power-sharing' (Wolff, 2009), because in many cases it stands on its own. Political power-sharing either centrally or locally is only found in a minority of the cases, and although we find some examples of ingenuity when it comes to including trans-border dimensions (see Bell, 2008; Weller, 2008) this is still relatively rare and constrained by both international reluctance and central government refusal to fudge (external) sovereignty. Attempts to depart from rigid group-based institutions are similarly constrained, especially in more severe conflicts, and remain the exception.

Security issues are central in all the violent conflicts, but many of the agreements depart from the idea of creating strong security institutions that can ensure sufficient harm against spoilers (Toft, 2009). The autonomous region is in many cases granted autonomous powers over coercive forces, such as the police and in some cases the military. This addresses the commitment problem faced by rebel forces and also the lack of legitimacy of the (central) armed forces, but it does make for a messier compromise and can, as will be further discussed below, impact negatively on human security and lead to future instability. The core deal of territorial self-government and group-based security provisions makes it difficult to prioritize rights for individuals and for non-dominant groups, and the need to make peace with the leaders of armed movements may necessitate a willingness to ignore past abuses. Although most of the agreements include references to human rights, these tend therefore to be rhetorical and aimed at ensuring international legitimacy rather than genuinely affecting post-settlement institutions. However, the illiberal nature of many of these agreements also reflects a preference for a narrow, non-inclusive, peace process and an apparent acceptance of the agreement signatories as being genuinely representative of their communities. We therefore find a dominant model that is based on territorial autonomy; prioritizes groups and group rights, rather than the rights of individuals; and reinforces the powers of the negotiating elites. Although there is tension in these agreements, and some display greater creativity and possibility for reform, Bell's new Law on Peace (2008) therefore appears largely unrealized, except when it comes to group rights within the existing state.

Two factors in particular affect the specifics of this design: the intensity of the conflict and the degree of territorial control enjoyed by the separatist forces. The longer the conflict lasts, the more violent it is and the greater the degree of separatist control, the more complex the agreement – if it is indeed possible to reach an agreement. We are consequently more likely to see interim agreements, fudged sovereignty and extensive autonomy with separate coercive forces and limited ties to the centre; such as in the cases of Sudan and PNG–Bougainville.

Implications – Beyond Separatist Conflicts

The success of a considerable number of these agreements defies the negative predictions regarding the prospect of ethnic autonomy (see e.g. Lake & Rothchild, 2005; Roeder, 2009). Ethnic autonomy can provide a sustainable solution to intra-state conflicts, even following years of violence. The analysed cases moreover suggest that recentralization, or lack of implementation of agreed provisions, is a greater threat to such arrangements than renewed separatist attempts. I am not arguing that there are no problems with ethnic autonomy – this book has pointed to plenty – but some of these problems can be addressed. These findings have implications for ongoing discussions of solutions for Eastern Ukraine. Territorial autonomy seems to be the only realistic basis for a negotiated solution in this conflict, but the lack of implementation of Minsk II points to deep concerns in Kiev that autonomy is but a step towards secession, and also a reluctance to strengthen the breakaway territories and legitimize the separatist forces (see e.g. Sasse, 2016).

The analysis has been focused on agreements reached in separatist conflicts, and agreements signed in non-territorial conflicts tend to differ in important respects. Human rights, central power-sharing and security sector reform are all likely to play a more prominent role in agreements that do not include territorial self-government. However, even conflicts that are not initially about territory can acquire a territorial dimension and this can become part of the solution. For example, the extreme sectarian violence in the Central African Republic has led some Muslim Seleka rebels to call for the creation of a new state in the north (Smith, 2014). Territorial autonomy can provide an attractive solution, especially in very intense conflicts. It recognizes control on the battlefield, provides guarantees, and avoids the need for former enemies to cooperate in a power-sharing government. There is a reason why so many peace processes keep reverting to this formula, and agreements signed in non-separatist conflicts also sometimes include forms of territorial autonomy. This was found, for example, in the Lusaka Protocol for Angola and, as a transitional measure, in the General Peace Agreement for Mozambique. Proposals for the Syrian conflict are also increasingly focused on territorial solutions. However if an autonomy arrangement is adopted, there are certain pitfalls that should ideally be avoided.

Pitfalls: Ambiguity, Lack of Capacity and Lack of Inclusivity

Autonomy arrangements are frequently the cause of tensions, with the central government and the autonomous region arguing over the distribution of powers and resources. However, I have pointed to three factors that are particularly associated with tensions, instability and in some cases collapse of the agreement.

The first of these is excessive ambiguity. While a degree of 'constructive ambiguity' may be necessary to get an agreement, and could even help ensure much-needed flexibility in the post-settlement period, it can easily become destructive. Ambiguity also presents problems for third parties, who will find it harder to 'name and shame' one of the conflict parties if they renege on their promises. Ambiguity is especially problematic if it involves the core deal or if it is cumulative. It may be possible to address a few ambiguous provisions in the post-settlement phase, but ambiguity in several areas, for example relating to both the borders and the powers of the autonomous region, risks overwhelming the implementation process.

The second factor I pointed to is the importance of intra-communal dynamics and sub-state capacity. Both are often neglected in peace agreements and are also under-analysed in the existing literature. Without sufficient capacity in the autonomous region, including the capacity to defeat spoilers, local violence can escalate and this may spread beyond the region and undermine the legitimacy and stability of the agreement. We saw this, for example, in Mindanao and Chechnya. The central government is however often reluctant to ensure enough resources for the autonomous region, fearing that it will increase the risk of secession. The former rebel movement may, moreover, not have the ability or the inclination to govern effectively.

Further research is needed into the link between pre-settlement rebel governance and post-settlement capacity, and how this is affected by the content of the agreement. However what does seem clear is that although rebel forces are by no means identical, and some are in a better position to govern than others (see e.g. Arjona et al., 2015), the transition to civilian politics will prove challenging. The agreement should be designed to support this, not create additional obstacles.

Finally, I have emphasized the problem of narrow agreements that lack inclusivity. This refers to a lack of rights for non-dominant groups and for individuals within the dominant communities. Most peace processes are narrow and the resulting agreement tends to favour the 'men with the guns', but there is also a genuine tension between the need for stability, and resulting emphasis on control, and the need for wider legitimacy. However, as the case of the Palestinian Authority demonstrated, a police force is not enough to ensure sta-bility; for an agreement to be sustainable in the longer-term, a peace constituency is needed. Capacity is crucial but it also depends on legitimacy.

Policy Implications

These conclusions have implications for mediators and others involved in finding a solution to intra-state conflicts.

Firstly, it is important to view the peace agreement as a whole and consider how the different provisions interact. If there is ambiguity regarding the autonomous region, its powers, borders and resources, then this will also impact on the effectiveness of security provisions.

Secondly, although ambiguity will be hard to avoid it should be kept to a minimum and ideally not involve the core deal. In the case of an interim agreement, which has ambiguity at its core, the objec-tive should be to keep everything else as clear as possible, including the mechanisms for deciding on status, the steps leading to this, and the ways in which this will be monitored.

Thirdly, the capacity of the autonomous region to govern effec-tively needs to be ensured, through the design of the autonomy arrangement and, if possible, by ensuring third party monitoring of its implementation. This does not simply mean empowering the former armed movement; the development of effective capacity neces-sitates reforms. Third parties can help encourage and fund this, and it can also be promoted through a more inclusive settlement.

Fourthly and finally, mediators should not simply accept the narrative of homogeneous ethnic groups engaged in conflict, but instead push for greater diversity to be acknowledged, for the process to be broadened and for human rights to be included in the agreement. While it may be necessary to make deals with warlords, and other actors with dubious democratic credentials, they should not be empowered more than what is absolutely needed to reach an agreement.

NOTES

1. See for example the oft-used UCDP Peace Agreement Dataset v. 2.0, 1975–2011, http://www.pcr.uu.se/research/ucdp/datasets/ucdp_peace_agreement_dataset/
2. For a similar analytical framework, see Wolff (2011).
3. See for example the Peace Accords Matrix, https://peaceaccords.nd.edu/ and the UCDP Peace Agreement Dataset, http://www.pcr.uu.se/research/ucdp/datasets/ucdp_peace_agreement_dataset/. Bell (2000, p. 25) uses the term 'framework or substantive agreement' to refer to essentially the same type of agreement.
4. This is more similar to the Minorities at Risk Project (2009) whose database also includes arrangements established in non-armed conflicts.
5. I have not included the 1991 Ethiopian Transitional Period Charter, since it does not specifically mention Eritrea, even if it did pave the way for its independence. I have also not included the 2003 Law of Administration for the State of Iraq for the Transitional Period (TAL) or Iraq's 2005 Constitution. It contains similar mechanisms to the peace agreements listed above, but the main driving force was not a separatist conflict, even if it did address largely undeclared separatist sentiments in Kurdistan. However, I do make a reference to this case in chapter 3.
6. In the literature, the different forms of autonomy or self-government are often treated separately with particular attention afforded to federalism. However, federalism, federacy, asymmetric federalism, etc. all share important characteristics and the following analysis will treat them under the rubric of autonomy.
7. Some years later a new law on local government was enacted which provided the possibility of some elements of (limited) territorial autonomy (Weller, 2005b, p. 67).
8. The Bodoland Territorial Area Districts are part of India's federal structure, but are in the second tier and not a federal unit.
9. The former is however unicameral.
10. The term autonomy is however not used in the Memorandum of Understanding.

192

11. There are some examples of guaranteed representation at the centre (e.g. in Mindanao) and also of ethnic quotas locally (e.g. Chittagong Hill Tracts) but not enough to qualify as power-sharing.
12. *Low level of autonomy:* mostly limited to cultural autonomy and administrative powers, although limited fiscal and legislative powers may be included. *Medium:* typically includes executive, fiscal and legislative powers but there is often a great deal of ambiguity when it comes to powers shared with the central government. *High:* includes all of the above as well as autonomy over coercive forces, such as the police and military. In these cases, the autonomous region typically controls all powers not specifically reserved for the central government.
13. This refers to the autonomy included in the Agreement on the Question of East Timor, but rejected in the independence referendum.
14. In effect, since Chechnya's de facto independence was maintained.
15. This refers to the level of segmental autonomy *within* Northern Ireland.
16. The factors leading separatist movement to compromise are further explored in chapter 6.
17. Its implementation score after ten years is 65 per cent. Peace Accord Matrix, Agreement Between the Republic Niger Government and the ORA, https://peaceaccords.nd.edu/accord/agreement-between-republic-niger-government-and-ora
18. Peace Accords Matrix, Boundary Demarcation: Mindanao Final Agreement, https://peaceaccords.nd.edu/provision/boundary-demarcation-mindanao-final-agreement
19. Brčko Final Award, http://www.ohr.int/ohr-offices/brcko/arbitration/default.asp?content_id=5360
20. http://2001.ukrcensus.gov.ua/eng/results/general/language/
21. The Indonesian Government also accepted an independence referendum for East Timor, but unlike the other cases, East Timor had already been recognized as a self-determination unit and the International Community strongly pushed for a referendum.
22. Basic Principles, http://www.osce.org/mg/51152
23. Basic Principles, http://www.osce.org/mg/51152
24. The British army's security guarantee in Northern Ireland is not a third party guarantee as the British army is, by the Nationalist side, very much seen as party to the conflict. The partisan nature of this guarantee was to some extent offset by the promise by the British Government to consult regularly with the Irish Government on security issues.
25. UN Security Council, Resolution 1031, http://www.refworld.org/cgi-bin/texis/vtx/rwmain?docid=3b00f15126
26. UN Security Council, Resolution 1037, http://www.refworld.org/cgi-bin/texis/vtx/rwmain?docid=3b00f20f40
27. Operation Essential Harvest and Operation Amber Fox, www.nato.int/fyrom/tfh/home.htm
28. UN Security Council, Resolution 1590, http://www.refworld.org/cgi-bin/texis/vtx/rwmain?docid=42bc14d44
29. UN Security Council, Resolution 1264, http://www.refworld.org/cgi-bin/texis/vtx/rwmain?page=search&docid=3b00f1e35c&skip=0&query=1264
30. Subsidiary organs of the Security Council, http://www.un.org/en/sc/repertoire/2004-2007/04-07_05.pdf#page=68, p. 193

31. Peace Accords Matrix, Agreement Between the Republic Niger Government and the ORA, https://peaceaccords.nd.edu/accord/agreement-between-republic-niger-government-and-ora
32. Author's interviews in Nagorno Karabakh, October–November 2008.
33. Although the Aceh conflict is coded as a war as a cumulative category, i.e. more than 1,000 battle-related deaths since the onset of the conflict (UCDP/PRIO, 2013, p. 9).
34. Included in the proposed autonomy arrangement.
35. De facto, not specified in agreement.
36. See also the overview of implementation in Peace Accords Matrix, Memorandum of Settlement (Bodo Accord), https://peaceaccords.nd.edu/accord/memorandum-settlement-bodo-accord
37. Peace Accords Matrix, Agreement Between the Republic Niger Government and the ORA, https://peaceaccords.nd.edu/accord/agreement-between-republic-niger-government-and-ora
38. The need for a peace constituency will be discussed in chapter 6.
39. The link between the content of a peace agreement and spoiler activity is explored more fully in chapter 6.
40. Thanks to Roger Mac Ginty for suggesting the term 'controlled collapse'.
41. Juba Declaration on Unity and Integration between the Sudan People's Liberation Army (SPLA) and the South Sudan Defence Forces (SSDF), http://peacemaker.un.org/sites/peacemaker.un.org/files/SD_060108_JubaDeclarationOnUnityAndIntegration.pdf
42. Action Group for Syria, Final Communiqué, 30 June 2012, http://www.un.org/News/dh/infocus/Syria/FinalCommuniqueActionGroupforSyria.pdf
43. McGarry and O'Leary (2006a, pp. 62–3) specify that the executive must enjoy majority support in each significant group or, in a weaker formulation, plurality support. The executive does not therefore need to include all parties.
44. Further details were provided in the Constitutional Charter that implemented the agreement.
45. In the agreement for Bodoland, it simply says that the Election Commission of India will be requested to consider seat reservation for Bodoland candidates (art. 6).
46. Lijphart (1995) has also argued that self-determination is preferable.
47. Association/Community of Serb Majority Municipalities in Kosovo: General Principles/Main Elements, http://eeas.europa.eu/statements-eeas/docs/150825_02_association-community-of-serb-majority-municipalities-in-kosovo-general-principles-main-elements_en.pdf. This is however yet to be implemented.
48. Interim agreements are discussed in detail in chapter 5.
49. Data available from http://www.unhcr.ba
50. Basic Principles, http://www.osce.org/mg/51152
51. The Constitutional Charter, which implemented the agreement, does however contain detailed human rights provisions.
52. These are also found in the Ukrainian Constitution, but not in the chapter relating to Crimea, which simply mentions that the Autonomous Republic of Crimea can participate in ensuring the rights and freedoms of citizens (art. 138). This is the part of the constitution most comparable to the other peace agreements.

53. And the international push for human rights is, as will be argued in chapter 7, often limited.
54. United Nations, Guidance for Effective Mediation, http://peacemaker.un.org/mediationapp#MediationOverview
55. To constitute genocide the abuse must be committed with the specific intent of genocide, and be targeted at national, ethnic, racial or religious groups (Scharf, 1999).
56. The Rome Statute for the ICC incorporates a Protocol II-based list of serious violations in intra-state conflicts.
57. UN Security Council, Resolution 1031, http://www.refworld.org/cgi-bin/texis/vtx/rwmain?docid=3b00f15126
58. Peace Accords Matrix, National Pact, https://peaceaccords.nd.edu/accord/national-pact
59. Peace Accords Matrix, National Pact, https://peaceaccords.nd.edu/accord/national-pact
60. The recent ECtHR ruling that the rights of Azeri IDPs have been violated by their inability to return has made this position harder to sustain. See http://www.asil.org/blogs/european-court-human-rights-rules-rights-refugees-displaced-nagorno-karabakh-conflict-june-16
61. The older generation of GAM leaders actually supported a candidate from outside the movement, since they feared that GAM candidates were unprepared to hold power in their own right (Aspinall, 2008).
62. The issue of spoilers will be discussed in detail in chapter 6.
63. The role of international mediators in the promotion of human rights, or lack thereof, is further discussed in chapter 7.
64. This will be further discussed in the following chapter.
65. Joint Review of Bougainville's Autonomy Arrangements by Government of Papua New Guinea and the Autonomous Government of Bougainville, 26 October 2013, https://bougainvillenews.files.wordpress.com/2015/03/joint-review-of-autonomy-arrangements-jsb-and-rc-approved-joint-resolutions.pdf
66. Report of the Secretary General on the situation concerning Western Sahara, Annex 2, http://www.arso.org/S-2003-565e.htm
67. Author's interview with former OSCE official, 11 November 2015.
68. Its reaction to Australia's decision to establish a diplomatic mission in Bougainville is ominous: Australians were banned from travelling to the autonomous region (Lasslett, 2015).
69. Author's interview with EU official, 10 November 2015.
70. Seamus Mallon was deputy leader of Northern Ireland's Social Democratic and Labour Party (SDLP).
71. This sets the concept apart from much of the quantitative literature which emphasizes the crucial importance of opportunity for conflict, based on the relative capacity of insurgents vis-a-vis the state (see e.g. Fearon & Laitin, 2003).
72. There is some understanding of this among international officials involved in the Nagorno Karabakh talks and the EU has initiated a programme of civil society involvement. Author's interview with EU official, 10 November 2015.
73. Author's interviews in Nagorno Karabakh, October–November 2008.
74. Although there was OSCE presence at the final talks.

75. International presence at talks, but the Senegalese Government had significantly limited the involvement of neighbouring Guinea Bissau and Gambia (Fall, 2010, p. 26).
76. The 2014 agreement was negotiated by Malaysia, the International Monitoring Team and the International Contact Group, which includes both states and international NGOs. See http://www.c-r.org/where-we-work/southeast-asia/international-contact-group-mindanao
77. Author's interview with former OSCE official, 11 November 2015. Author's interview with EU official, 10 November 2015.
78. The UN Development Programme also assisted the government with the DDR process (Lode, 2002), but this is not included in the agreement and it appears to have only played a supporting role.
79. UN Security Council, Resolution 1590, http://www.refworld.org/cgi-bin/texis/vtx/rwmain?docid=42bc14d44
80. The international administration in East Timor was not mandated to implement the agreement, which contains no details on independence.
81. President of Russia, 'Vladimir Putin answered journalists' questions on the situation in Ukraine', 4 March 2014, http://en.kremlin.ru/events/president/news/20366
82. Author's interview with EU official, 10 November 2015.
83. See e.g. Press Conference by Georgia, 31 October 2007, http://www.un.org/press/en/2007/071031_Georgia.doc.htm

REFERENCES

Ahmed, E., 2009. The Comprehensive Peace Agreement and the dynamics of post-conflict political partnership in Sudan. *Africa Spectrum*, 44(3), pp. 133–47.

Albin, C., 2001. *Justice and Fairness in International Negotiation.* Cambridge: Cambridge University Press.

Al-Khatteeb, L., 2015. Why ISIS is on the march in Sunni Iraq. *The Huffington Post*, 20 May.

Amnesty International, 1997. *Amnesty International Report 1997 – Philippines*, http://www.refworld.org/docid/3ae6a9f834.html

Amnesty International, 2013a. *Bangladesh: Indigenous Peoples Engulfed in Chittagong Hill Tracts Land Conflict*, https://www.amnesty.org/en/latest/news/2013/06/bangladesh-indigenous-peoples-engulfed-chittagong-hill-tracts-land-conflict/

Amnesty International, 2013b. *Indonesia: Victims of the Aceh Conflict Still Waiting for Truth, Justice and Reparation*, https://www.amnesty.org/en/latest/news/2013/04/indonesia-victims-aceh-conflict-still-waiting-truth-justice-and-reparation/

Anderson, L., 2013. Power sharing in Kirkuk: the need for compromise. In: J. McEvoy & B. O'Leary, eds. *Power Sharing in Deeply Divided Places.* Philadelphia: University of Pennsylvania Press, pp. 364–85.

Annan, K., 2004. *The Rule of Law and Transitional Justice in Conflict and Post-Conflict Societies, Report of the Secretary General.* New York: United Nations Security Council.

Anonymous, 1996. Human rights in peace negotiations. *Human Rights Quarterly*, 18(2), pp. 249–58.

Arjona, A., Kasfir, N. & Mampilly, Z., 2015. *Rebel Governance in Civil War.* New York: Cambridge University Press.

Armstrong, T., 1993. *Rapprochement Between East and West Germany, the United States and China, and Israel and Egypt.* Washington, DC: United States Institute of Peace.

Aspinall, E., 2008. Elections: consolidating peace. In: Aguswandi & J. Large, eds. *Reconfiguring Politics: The Indonesia–Aceh Peace Process.* London: Conciliation Resources, pp. 46–50.

Australia Associated Press, 2014. PNG leader apologises to Bougainville for bloody 1990s civil war. *The Guardian*, 29 January.

Awaluddin, H., 2008. Why is peace in Aceh successful. In: Aguswandi & J. Large, eds. *Reconfiguring Politics: The Indonesia-Aceh Peace Process.* London: Conciliation Resources, pp. 25–7.

Bakke, K. M., 2015. *Decentralization and Intrastate Struggles: Chechnya, Punjab, and Québec.* Cambridge: Cambridge University Press.

Bakke, K. M., Cunningham, K. G. & Seymour, L. J. M., 2012. A plague of initials: fragmentation, cohesion, and infighting in civil wars. *Perspectives on Politics*, 10(2), pp. 265–84.

Barnett, M., Fang, S. & Zurcher, C., 2014. Compromised peacebuilding. *International Studies Quarterly*, 58(3), pp. 608–20.

Bartelson, J., 2001. *The Critique of the State.* Cambridge: Cambridge University Press.

Barter, S. J., 2015. The rebel state in society: governance and accommodation in Aceh, Indonesia. In: A. Arjona, N. Kasfir & Z. Mampilly, eds. *Rebel Governance in Civil War.* New York: Cambridge University Press, pp. 226–45.

BBC News, 2007. Sudan to have shuttle government. 13 December, http://news.bbc.co.uk/1/hi/world/africa/7139757.stm

BBC News, 2010. Yassir Arman quits Sudan presidential poll. 31 March, http://news.bbc.co.uk/1/hi/world/africa/8597996.stm

BBC News, 2015a. OTR letters: Tony Blair says NI peace process could have collapsed without scheme. 13 January, http://www.bbc.co.uk/news/uk-northern-ireland-30776891

BBC News, 2015b. India signs peace accord with Naga rebels. 3 August, http://www.bbc.co.uk/news/world-asia-india-33762445

BBC News, 2015c. IRA 'army council' still exists but has 'wholly political focus'. 20 October, http://www.bbc.co.uk/news/uk-northern-ireland-34584424

Bell, C., 2000. *Peace Agreements and Human Rights.* Oxford: Oxford University Press.

Bell, C., 2008. *On the Law of Peace: Peace Agreements and the Lex Pacificatoria.* Oxford: Oxford University Press.

Bellamy, A. J. & Williams, P. D., 2010. *Understanding Peacekeeping.* Cambridge: Polity.

Belloni, R., 2004. Peacebuilding and consociational electoral engineering in Bosnia and Herzegovina. *International Peacekeeping,* 11(2), pp. 334–53.

Belloni, R., 2007. *State-Building and International Intervention in Bosnia.* London: Routledge.

Berdal, M., 2003. How 'new' are 'new wars'? *Global Governance,* 9(4), pp. 477–502.

Better World Campaign, 2014. UN Interim Security Force in Abyei (UNISFA), http://www.betterworldcampaign.org/un-peacekeeping/missions/abyei.html

Bieber, F., 2005. Partial implementation, partial success: the case of Macedonia. In: I. O'Flynn & D. Russell, eds. *Power Sharing: New Challenges for Divided Societies.* London: Pluto Press, pp. 107–22.

Bieber, F., 2006a. After Dayton, Dayton? The evolution of an unpopular peace. *Ethnopolitics,* 5(1), pp. 15–31.

Bieber, F., 2006b. *Post-War Bosnia: Ethnicity, Inequality and Public Sector Governance.* London: Palgrave.

Bieber, F., 2013. The Balkans: the promotion of power sharing by outsiders. In: J. McEvoy & B. O'Leary, eds. *Power Sharing in Deeply Divided Places.* Philadelphia: University of Pennsylvania Press, pp. 312–26.

Bieber, F. & Keil, S., 2009. Power-sharing revisited: lessons learned in the Balkans. *Review of Central and East European Law,* 34(4), pp. 337–60.

Bolton, O., 2014. Martin McGuinness fights back tears during Dr Ian Paisley tribute. *The Telegraph,* 12 September.

Braithwaite, J., Charlesworth, H., Reddy, P. & Dunn, L., 2010. *Reconciliation and Architectures of Commitment: Sequencing Peace in Bougainville.* Canberra: ANU Press.

Brass, P., 1991. *Ethnicity and Nationalism: Theory and Comparison.* London: Sage.

Brosché, J., 2008. CPA: new Sudan, old Sudan or two Sudans? In: U. J. Dahre, ed. *Post-Conflict Peace-Building in the Horn of Africa.* Lund: Department of Social Anthropology and Department of Political Science, Lund University, pp. 231–51.

Brown, G. K., 2009. Federalism, regional autonomy and conflict: introduction and overview. *Ethnopolitcs,* 8(1), pp. 1–4.

Caspersen, N., 2004. Good fences make good neighbours? A comparison of conflict-regulation strategies in postwar Bosnia. *Journal of Peace Research,* 41(5), pp. 569–88.

Caspersen, N., 2006. Contingent nationalist dominance: intra-Serb challenges to the Serb Democratic Party. *Nationalities Papers*, 34(1), pp. 51–69.

Caspersen, N., 2008a. Intra-group divisions in ethnic conflicts: from popular grievances to power struggles. *Nationalism and Ethnic Politics*, 14(2), pp. 239–65.

Caspersen, N., 2008b. Between puppets and independent actors: kin–state involvement in the conflicts in Bosnia, Croatia and Nagorno Karabakh. *Ethnopolitics*, 7(4), pp. 357–72.

Caspersen, N., 2010. *Contested Nationalism: Serb Elite Rivalry in Croatia and Bosnia in the 1990s*. Oxford: Berghahn Books.

Caspersen, N., 2012. *Unrecognized States: The Struggle for Sovereignty in the Modern International System*. Cambridge: Polity.

Cassese, A., 1993. The Israel–PLO agreement and self-determination. *European Journal of International Law*, 4(1), pp. 564–71.

Cederman, L.-E., Hug, S., Schadel, A. & Wucherpfennig, J., 2015. Territorial autonomy in the shadow of conflict: too little, too late? *American Political Science Review*, 109(2), pp. 354–70.

Checkel, J., 2013. *Transnational Dynamics of Civil War*. Cambridge: Cambridge University Press.

Civic, M. A. & Miklaucic, M., 2011. Introduction. In: M. A. Civic & M. Miklaucic, eds. *Monopoly of Force: The Nexus of DDR and SSR*. Washington, DC: National Defense University Press, pp. xv–xxv.

CNN, 1996. Netanyahu wins. 31 May, http://edition.cnn.com/WORLD/9605/31/netanyahu.wins/

Collier, P., 1994. Demobilisation and insecurity: a study in the economics of transition from war to peace. *Journal of International Development*, 6(3), pp. 343–51.

Conciliation Resources, 2011. *Individual Rights, Societal Choices: Confronting Legacies of Displacement in the Nagorny Karabakh Conflict*. London.

Conciliation Resources, 2012. *Innovation in Mediation Support: The International Contact Group in Mindanao*. London.

Cooper, N., Turner, M. & Pugh, M., 2011. The end of history and the last liberal peacebuilder: a reply to Roland Paris. *Review of International Studies*, 37(4), pp. 1995–2007.

Corbin, J., 1994. *Gaza First*. London: Bloomsbury.

Cordell, K. & Wolff, S., 2009. *Ethnic Conflict: Causes, Consequences, and Responses*. Cambridge: Polity.

Cornell, S. E. & Starr, S. F., 2009. *The Guns of August 2008: Russia's War in Georgia*. Armonk: M. E. Sharpe.

Dalsheim, J., 2014. *Producing Spoilers: Peacemaking and the Production of Enmity in a Secular Age*. New York: Oxford University Press.

Darby, J. & Mac Ginty, R., 2000. *The Management of Peace Processes*. Basingstoke: Palgrave.

De Waal, A., 2009. Mission without end? Peacekeeping in the African political marketplace. *International Affairs*, 85(1), pp. 99–113.

De Waal, T., 2010. Remaking the Nagorno-Karabakh peace process. *Survival*, 52(4), pp. 159–76.

Doyle, M. W. & Sambanis, N., 2000. International peacebuilding: a theoretical and quantitative analysis. *The American Political Science Review*, 94(4), pp. 779–801.

Džankić, J., 2015. The politics of inclusion and exclusion: citizenship and voting rights in Bosnia and Herzegovina. *International Peacekeeping*, 22(5), pp.526–44.

Elgindy, K., 2014. Opinion: When ambiguity is destructive. *Cairo Review of Global Affairs*, 22 January.

Erk, J. & Anderson, L., 2009. The paradox of federalism: does self-rule accommodate or exacerbate ethnic divisions? *Regional and Federal Studies*, 19(2), pp. 191–202.

Fabry, M., 2010. *Recognizing States: International Society and the Establishment of New States Since 1776*. Oxford: Oxford University Press.

Fall, A., 2010. *Understanding the Casamance Conflict: A Background*, KAIPTC Monograph No. 7.

Fearon, J. D., 2004. Separatist wars, partition and world order. *Security Studies*, 13(4), pp. 394–415.

Fearon, J. D. & Laitin, D. D., 2003. Ethnicity, insurgency, and civil war. *American Political Science Review*, 97(1), pp. 75–90.

Fearon, K., 2013. Northern Ireland's Women's Coalition: institutionalising a political voice and ensuring representation. In: Z. Yousuf, ed. *Accord: Women Building Peace*. London: Conciliation Resources, pp. 31–3.

Foley, M. W., 2010. Cautionary tales: soft intervention and civil society. In: M. Hoddie & C. Hartzell, eds. *Strengthening Peace in Post-Civil War States: Transforming Spoilers into Stakeholders*. Chicago: The University of Chicago Press, pp. 163–88.

Fortna, V. P., 2008. *Does Peacekeeping Work? Shaping Belligerents' Choices after Civil War*. Princeton, NJ: Princeton University Press.

Francis, C., 2011. *Conflict Resolution and Status: The Case of Georgia and Abkhazia (1989–2008)*. Brussels: VUB Press.

Gallagher, T., 2003. Identity in flux, destination uncertain: Montenegro during and after the Yugoslav wars. *International Journal of Politics, Culture and Society*, 17(1), pp. 53–71.

201

Gardner, J. & El-Bushra, J., 2013. From the forefront of peace and reconciliation: testimonies from women building peace. In: Z. Yousuf, ed. *Accord: Women Building Peace.* London: Conciliation Resources, pp. 9–18.

George, S. J., 1994. The Bodo movement in Assam: unrest to accord. *Asian Survey*, 34(10), pp. 878–92.

Ghai, Y., 2000. Ethnicity and autonomy: a framework for analysis. In: Y. Ghai, ed. *Autonomy and Ethnicity: Negotiating Competing Claims in Multi-Ethnic States.* Cambridge: Cambridge University Press, pp. 1–26.

Ghai, Y., 2008. Territorial options. In: J. Draby & R. Mac Ginty, eds. *Contemporary Peacemaking: Conflict, Peace Processes and Post-War Reconstruction.* Basingstoke: Palgrave, pp. 242–53.

Ghai, Y. & Regan, A. J., 2006. Unitary state, devolution, autonomy, secession: state building and nation building in Bougainville, Papua New Guinea. *The Round Table*, 95(386), pp. 589–608.

Goncharenko, R., 2014. Putin's plan 'F' for Ukraine. *DW*, 15 April, http://www.dw.com/en/putins-plan-f-for-ukraine/a-17571704

Greenhill, K. M. & Major, S., 2007. The perils of profiling: civil war spoilers and the collapse of intrastate peace accords. *International Security*, 31(3), pp. 7–40.

Grono, N., 2006. *The Role of the International Court in Peace Processes: Mutually Reinforcing or Mutually Exclusive?*, IPPR briefing paper.

Gutteri, K. & Piombo, J., 2007. Issues and debates in transitional rule. In: K. Gutteri & J. Piombo, eds. *Interim Governments: Institutional Bridges to Peace and Democracy.* Washington, DC: United States Institute of Peace Press, pp. 3–34.

Haas, R., 1988. Ripeness and the settlement of international disputes. *Survival*, 30(3), pp. 232–51.

Hadi, F., 2008. Human rights and injustice in Aceh: the long and winding road. In: Aguswandi & J. Large, eds. *Reconfiguring Politics: The Indonesia–Aceh Peace Process.* London: Conciliation Resources, pp. 66–9.

Hampson, F., 1996. *Nurturing Peace: Why Peace Settlements Succeed or Fail.* Washington, DC: United States Institute of Peace Press.

Hannum, H., 1998. The specter of secession: responding to claims for ethnic self-determination. *Foreign Affairs*, 77(2), pp. 13–18.

Hannum, H., 2004. Territorial autonomy: permanent solution to step toward secession. In: A. Wimmer et al., eds. *Facing Ethnic Conflicts: Towards a New Realism.* Lanham, MD: Rowman & Littlefield, pp. 274–82.

Harris, P. & Reilly, B., 1998. *Democracy and Deep-Rooted Conflict: Options for Negotiators*. Stockholm: International Institute for Democracy and Electoral Assistance.

Hartzell, C. A. & Hoddie, M., 2007. *Crafting Peace: Power-Sharing Institutions and the Negotiated Settlement of Civil Wars*. Philadelphia: The Pennsylvania State University Press.

Hayden, R., 2005. 'Democracy' without a demos? The Bosnian constitutional experiment and the international construction of nonfunctioning states. *East European Politics and Societies*, 19(2), pp. 226–59.

Hedl, D., 1997. Svi smo mi izašli iz rovova. *Feral Tribune*, 3 March, pp. 18–19.

Heraclides, A., 1991. *The Self-Determination of Minorities in International Politics*. London: Routledge.

Heraclides, A., 1997. The ending of unending wars: separatist wars. *Millennium*, 26(3), pp. 679–707.

Herszenhorn, D. M., 2015. Ukrainian leader is open to a vote on regional power. *The New York Times*, 6 April.

Hoddie, M. & Hartzell, C. A., 2010. *Strengthening Peace in Post-Civil War States: Transforming Spoilers into Stateholders*. Chicago: University of Chicago Press.

Hoffman, E. & Bercovitch, J., 2011. Examining structural components of peace agreements and their durability. *Conflict Resolution Quarterly*, 28(4), pp. 399–426.

Holbrooke, R., 1999. *To End a War*. New York: The Modern Library.

Holleran, M., 2014. Show us your country: Macedonia's capital transformed. *Dissent*, 61(3), pp. 20–4.

Hopmann, P. T. & Zartman, I. W., 2010. Overcoming the Nagorno-Karabakh stalemate. *International Negotiation*, 15(1), pp. 1–6.

Horowitz, D., 1985. *Ethnic Groups in Conflict*. Berkeley: University of California Press.

Horowitz, D., 1991. *A Democratic South Africa? Constitutional Engineering in a Divided Society*. Berkeley: University of California Press.

Horowitz, D., 2002. Constitutional design: proposals versus processes. In: A. Reynolds, ed. *The Architecture of Democracy*. Oxford: Oxford University Press, pp. 15–36.

Hovdenak, A., 2008. Trading refugees for land and symbols: the Palestinian negotiation strategy in the Oslo Process. *Journal of Refugee Studies*, 1(22), pp. 30–50.

Hughes, J., 2001. Chechnya: the causes of protracted post-Soviet conflict. *Civil Wars*, 4(4), pp. 11–48.

Hughes, J., 2007. *Chechnya: From Nationalism to Jihad*. Philadelphia: University of Pennsylvania Press.

Hultman, L., 2010. Keeping peace or spurring violence? Unintended effects of peace operations on violence against civilians. *Civil Wars*, 12(1–2), pp. 29–46.

Huseynov, T., 2010. Mountainous Karabakh: new paradigms for peace and development in the 21st century. *International Negotiation*, 15(1), pp. 7–31.

Institute of Peace and Conflict Studies, 2012. *Conflict Alert: Ethnic Fault Lines in Assam (seminar report)*. New Delhi.

International Crisis Group, 1998. *Whither Bosnia*, Balkans Report N°43.

International Crisis Group, 2000. *War Criminals in Bosnia's Republika Srpska*, Europe Report N°103.

International Crisis Group, 2005a. *The Cyprus Stalemate: What Next?* Europe Report N°171.

International Crisis Group, 2005b. *Montenegro's Independence Drive*, Europe Report N°169.

International Crisis Group, 2005c. *Nagorno Karabakh: A Plan for Peace*, Europe Report N°167.

International Crisis Group, 2006. *Aceh: Now for the Hard Part*, Asia Briefing N°48.

International Crisis Group, 2011. *Macedonia: Ten Years After the Conflict*, Europe Report N°212.

International Crisis Group, 2013a. *The Philippines: Dismantling Rebel Groups*, Asia Report N°248.

International Crisis Group, 2013b. *Indonesia: Tensions over Aceh's Flag*, Asia Briefing N°139.

Irwin, C., 2013. Public opinion and power sharing in deeply divided places. In: J. McEvoy & B. O'Leary, eds. *Power Sharing in Deeply Divided Places*. Philadelphia: University of Pennsylvania Press, pp. 295–311.

Jakobsen, P. V., 2000. The emerging consensus on grey area peace operations doctrine: will it last and enhance operational effectiveness. *International Peacekeeping*, 7(3), pp. 36–56.

Jarstad, A. K., 2008a. Power sharing: former enemies in joint government. In: A. K. Jarstad & T. D. Sisk, eds. *From War to Democracy*. Cambridge: Cambridge University Press, pp. 105–33.

Jarstad, A., 2008b. Dilemmas of war-to-peace transitions. In: A. K. Jarstad & T. D. Sisk, eds. *From War to Democracy*. Cambridge: Cambridge University Press, pp. 17–36.

Jeffery, S., 2006. Hamas celebrates election victory. *The Guardian*, 26 January.

Jeffrey, A., 2006. Building state capacity in post-conflict Bosnia and Herzegovina: the case of Brcko District. *Political Geography*, 25(2), pp. 203–27.

Jellow, S., 2013. *Securing the Sahel: From Mali to Niger*, Security Sector Reform Resource Centre.

Kaldor, M., 2007a. *New and Old Wars: Organized Violence in a Global Era*. Stanford, CA: Stanford University Press.

Kaldor, M., 2007b. *Human Security: Reflections of Globalization and Intervention*. Cambridge: Polity.

Kasapović, M., 2005. Bosnia and Herzegovina: consociational or liberal democracy. *Politička misao*, 42(5), pp. 3–30.

Kaufmann, C., 1996. Possible and impossible solutions to ethnic civil wars. *International Security*, 20(4), pp. 136–75.

Keil, S., 2013. *Multinational Federalism in Bosnia and Herzegovina*. Farnham: Ashgate.

Keita, K., 1998. *Conflict and Conflict Resolution in the Sahel: The Tuareg Insurgency in Mali*, Strategic Studies Institute.

Kim, J., 2005. *Serbia and Montenegro Union: Prospects and Policy Implications*. Washington, DC: CRS Report for Congress.

King, C., 2001. The benefits of ethnic war: understanding Eurasia's unrecognized states. *World Politics*, 53(July), pp. 524–52.

Kleiboer, M., 1994. Ripeness of conflict: a fruitful notion? *Journal of Peace Research*, 31(1), pp. 109–16.

Knight, M. & Özerdem, A., 2004. Guns, camps and cash: disarmament, demobilization and reinsertion of former combatants in transition from war to peace. *Journal of Peace Research*, 41(4), pp. 499–516.

Krasner, S. D., 2004. Sharing sovereignty: new institutions for collapsed and failing states. *International Security*, 29(2), pp. 85–120.

Kuperman, A. J., 2000. Rwanda in retrospect. *Foreign Affairs*, 79(1), pp. 94–118.

Kydd, A. & Walter, B., 2002. Sabotaging the peace: the politics of extremist violence. *International Organization*, 56(2), pp. 263–96.

Lake, D. A., 2010. Building legitimate states after civil wars. In: M. Hoddie & C. A. Hartzell, eds. *Strengthening Peace and Post-Civil War States*. Chicago: University of Chicago Press, pp. 29–51.

Lake, D. A. & Rothchild, D., 2005. Territorial decentralization and civil war settlements. In: P. G. Roeder & D. Rothchild, eds. *Sustainable Peace: Power and Democracy after Civil Wars*. Ithaca, NY: Cornell University Press, pp. 109–32.

Lapidoth, R., 1996. *Autonomy: Flexible Solutions to Ethnic Conflicts*. Washington, DC: United States Institute of Peace Press.

Lara, F. J. Jr & Champain, P., 2009. *Inclusive Peace in Muslim Mindanao: Revisiting the Dynamics of Conflict and Exclusion.* London: International Alert.

Lasslett, K., 2015. Australia's interest in Bougainville's independence is far from locals' wishes. *The Guardian*, 20 May.

Libaridian, G. J., 2005. The elusive 'right formula' and the 'right time': a historical analysis of the official peace process. In: L. Broers, ed. *The Limits of Leadership.* London: Conciliation Resources, pp. 34–7.

Lieberfeld, D., 1999. Conflict 'ripeness' revisited: the South African and Israeli/Palestinian cases. *Negotiation Journal*, 15(1), pp. 63–82.

Lijphart, A., 1977. *Democracy in Plural Societies.* New Haven, CT: Yale University Press.

Lijphart, A., 1995. Self-determination versus pre-determination of ethnic minorities in power-sharing systems. In: W. Kymlicka, ed. *The Rights of Minority Cultures.* Oxford: Oxford University Press, pp. 275–87.

Lijphart, A., 2002. The wave of power-sharing democracy. In: A. Reynolds, ed. *The Architecture of Democracy.* Oxford: Oxford University Press, pp. 37–54.

Lijphart, A., 2004. Constitutional design for divided societies. *Journal of Democracy*, 15(2), pp. 96–109.

Lode, K., 2002. Mali feature study. In: C. Barnes, ed. *Owning the Process: Public Participation in Peacemaking.* London: Conciliation Resources, pp. 56–73.

Lustick, I., 1979. Stability in divided societies: consociationalism v. control. *World Politics*, 31(3), pp. 325–44.

Lyon, J., 2015. Is war about to break out in the Balkans? *Foreign Policy*, 26 October.

Lyons, T., 2010. Soft intervention and the transformation of militias into political parties. In: M. Hoddie & C. A. Hartzell, eds. *Strengthening Peace in Post-Civil War States.* Chicago: University of Chicago Press, pp. 145–62.

Mac Ginty, R. & Richmond, O. P., 2013. The local turn in peace building: a critical agenda for peace. *Third World Quarterly*, 34(5), pp. 763–83.

Mampilly, Z. C., 2011. *Rebel Rulers: Insurgent Governance and Civilian Life During War.* Ithaca, NY: Cornell University Press.

Manning, C., 2007. Interim governments and the construction of political elites. In: K. Guttieri & J. Piombo, eds. *Interim Governments: Institutional Bridges to Peace and Democracy.* Washington, DC: United States Institute of Peace Press, pp. 53–72.

Martin, G. E., 2011. Managing DDR and SSR programs in the Philippines. In: M. A. Civic & M. Miklaucic, eds. *Monopoly of Force: The Nexus of DDR and SSR*. Washington, DC: National Defense University Press, pp. 183–92.

McCann, E., 2015. The troubles are back. *The New York Times*, 5 October.

McCartney, C., 2005. From armed struggle to political negotiations: Why? When? How? In: R. Ricigliano, ed. *Choosing to Engage: Armed Groups and Peace Processes*. London: Conciliation Resources, pp. 30–5.

McCulloch, A., 2013. The track record of centripetalism in deeply divided societies. In: *Power Sharing in Deeply Divided Places*. Philadelphia: University of Pennsylvania Press, pp. 94–111.

McDonald, H., 2015a. IRA still exists but in 'much reduced form', says official report. *The Guardian*, 20 October.

McDonald, H., 2015b. Northern Ireland power sharing edges closer to collapse. *The Guardian*, 10 September.

McEvoy, J., 2013. We forbid! The mutual veto and power-sharing. In: J. McEvoy & B. O'Leary, eds. *Power Sharing in Deeply Divided Places*. Philadelphia: University of Pennsylvania Press, pp. 253–77.

McFate, S., 2011. There's a new sheriff in town: DDR-SSR and the monopoly of force. In: M. A. Civic & M. Miklaucic, eds. *Monopoly of Force: The Nexus of DDR and SSR*. Washington, DC: National Defense University Press, pp. 213–31.

McGarry, J. & O'Leary, B., 2006a. Consociational theory, Northern Ireland's conflict and its agreement. Part 1: What consociationalists can learn from Northern Ireland. *Government and Opposition*, 41(1), pp. 43–63.

McGarry, J. & O'Leary, B., 2006b. Consociational theory, Northern Ireland's conflict, and its agreements 2. What critics of consociation can learn from Northern Ireland. *Government and Opposition*, 41(2), pp. 249–77.

McGarry, J. & O'Leary, B., 2008. Consociation and its critics: Northern Ireland after the Belfast Agreement. In: S. Choudhry, ed. *Constitutional Design for Divided Societies: Integration or Accommodation*. Oxford: Oxford University Press, pp. 369–408.

McGarry, J. & O'Leary, B., 2009. Must pluri-national federations fail? *Ethnopolitics*, 8(1), pp. 5–25.

McGarry, J., O'Leary, B. & Simeon, R., 2008. Integration or accommodation? The enduring debate in conflict regulation. In: S. Choudhry, ed. *Constitutional Design for Divided Societies:*

Integration or Accommodation?. Oxford: Oxford University Press, pp. 41–88.

Merikallio, K. & Ruokanen, T., 2015. *The Mediator: A Biography of Martti Ahtisaari*. London: Hurst.

Mikkelsen, C., 2009. *The Indigenous World 2009*. Copenhagen: International Work Group for Indigenous Affairs.

Mikkelsen, C., 2015. *The Indigenous World 2015*. Copenhagen: International Work Group for Indigenous Affairs.

Minorities at Risk Project, 2009. *Minorities at Risk Dataset*. College Park, MD: Center for International Development and Conflict Management, http://www.cidcm.umd.edu/mar/

Minzarari, D., 2014. The Gaugaz referendum in Moldova: a Russian political weapon. *Eurasia Daily Monitor*, 5 February.

Mohsin, A., 2003. *The Chittagong Hill Tracts Bangladesh: On the Difficult Road to Peace*. Boulder, CO: Lynne Rienner.

Mowlam, M., 2005. Assessing group and opportunities: a former government minister's perspective. In: R. Ricigliano, ed. *Choosing to Engage: Armed Groups and Peace Processes*. London: Conciliation Resources, pp. 18–21.

Natella, A., 2011. An overview of the parties' positions. In: N. A. a. I. Khintba, ed. *Transformation of the Georgian–Abkhaz Conflict: Rethinking the Paradigm*. London: Conciliation Resources, pp. 12–19.

Navasardian, B., 2006. A battlefield of confrontation or a common problem? In: E. Poghosbekian & A. Simonian, eds. *The Karabakh Conflict: To Understand Each Other*. Yerevan, Armenia: Yerevan Press Club, pp. 101–45.

Newman, D., 1995–6. Territorial discontinuity and Palestinian autonomy: implementing the Oslo II Agreement. *IBRU Boundary and Security Bulletin*, Winter, pp. 75–85.

Newman, E. & Richmond, O., 2006. Obstacles to peace processes: understanding spoiling. In: E. Newman & O. Richmond, eds. *Challenges to Peacebuilding: Managing Spoilers during Conflict Resolution*. Tokyo: United Nations University Press, pp. 1–19.

Nilsson, D., 2008. Partial peace: rebel groups inside and outside of civil war settlements. *Journal of Peace Research*, 45(4), pp. 479–95.

Nordlinger, E., 1972. *Conflict Regulation in Divided Societies*. Cambridge, MA: Harvard University Centre for International Affairs.

Norris, P., 2005. *Stable Democracy and Good Governance in Divided Societies: Do Power-Sharing Institutions Work?* Cambridge, MA: John F. Kennedy School of Government, Harvard University, http://

www.hks.harvard.edu/fs/pnorris/Acrobat/Powersharing%20solutions.pdf

O Tuathail, G. & Dahlman, C., 2004. The efforts to reverse ethnic cleansing in Bosnia and Herzegovina: the limits of returns. *Eurasian Geography and Economics*, 45(6), pp. 439–64.

Oberschall, A., 2007. *Conflict and Peace Building in Divided Societies: Responses to Ethnic Violence*. London: Routledge.

Oberschall, A. & Palmer, L. K., 2005. The failure of moderate politics: the case of Northern Ireland. In: I. O'Flynn & D. Russell, eds. *Power Sharing: New Challenges for Divided Societies*. London: Pluto Press, pp. 77–91.

O'Flynn, I. & Russell, D., 2005. Introduction: new challenges for power sharing. In: I. O'Flynn & D. Russell, eds. *Power Sharing: New Challenges for Divided Societies*. London: Pluto Press, pp. 1–11.

O'Leary, B., 2013a. An advocate's introduction. In: J. McEvoy & B. O'Leary, eds. *Power Sharing in Deeply Divided Places*. Philadelphia: University of Pennsylvania Press, pp. 1–64.

O'Leary, B., 2013b. Power sharing: an advocate's conclusion. In: J. McEvoy & B. O'Leary, eds. *Power Sharing in Deeply Divided Places*. Philadelphia: University of Pennsylvania Press, pp. 386–422.

Owen, D., 1995. *Balkan Odyssey*. New York: Harcourt Brace.

Özkan, B., 2008. Who gains from the 'no war no peace' situation? A critical analysis of the Nagorno-Karabakh conflict. *Geopolitics*, 13(3), pp. 572–99.

Paris, R., 2004. *At War's End: Building Peace After Civil Conflict*. Cambridge: Cambridge University Press.

Pearlman, W., 2009. Spoiling inside and out: internal political contestation and the Middle East peace process. *International Security*, 33(3), pp. 79–109.

Perlmutter, A., 1995. The Israel–PLO Accord is dead. *Foreign Affairs*, 74(3), pp. 59–68.

Philipson, L., 2005. Engaging armed groups: the challenge of asymmetries. In: R. Ricigliano, ed. *Choosing to Engage: Armed Groups and Peace Processes*. London: Conciliation Resources, pp. 68–71.

Podder, S., 2014. Mainstreaming the non-state in bottom-up statebuilding: linkages between rebel governance and post-conflict legitimacy. *Conflict, Security and Development*, 14(2), pp. 213–43.

Polman, L., 2004. *We Did Nothing: Why the Truth Doesn't Always Come Out When the UN Goes in*. New York: Penguin.

Popetrevski, V. & Latifi, V., 2004. The Ohrid Framework Agreement negotiations. In: J. Pettifer, ed. *The 2001 Conflict in FYROM*. Swindon: Defence Academy of the United Kingdom, pp. 29–36.

Powell, J., 2008. *Great Hatred, Little Room: Making Peace in Northern Ireland.* London: Vintage Books.

Powell, J., 2015. Negotiate with ISIS. *The Atlantic*, 7 December.

Putnam, T. L., 2002. Human rights and sustainable peace. In: S. J. Stedman, D. Rothchild & E. M. Cousens, eds. *Ending Civil Wars: The Implementation of Peace Agreements.* Boulder, CO: Lynne Rienner, pp. 237–61.

Reddy, P., 2008. Reconciliation in Bougainville: civil war, peacekeeping and restorative justice. *Contemporary Justice Review*, 11(2), pp. 117–30.

Regan, P. M., 2002. Third-party interventions and the duration of intrastate conflicts. *Journal of Conflict Resolution*, 46(1), pp. 55–73.

Reilly, B., 2001. *Democracy in Divided Societies: Electoral Engineering for Conflict Management.* Cambridge: Cambridge University Press.

Reuters, 2016. Russia says federal model is possible for Syria in future. 29 February.

Reynolds, A., 2000. Majoritarian or power-sharing government. In: M. M. Crepaz, T. A. Koeble & D. Wilsford, eds. *Democracy and Institutions: The Life Work of Arend Lijphart.* Ann Arbor: University of Michigan Press, pp. 155–96.

Richmond, O. P., 2009. A post-liberal peace: Eirenism and the everyday. *Review of International Studies*, 35(3), pp. 557–80.

Roeder, P. G., 2005. Power dividing as an alternative to ethnic power sharing. In: P. G. Roeder & D. Rothchild, eds. *Sustainable Peace: Power and Democracy after Civil Wars.* Ithaca, NY: Cornell University Press, pp. 51–82.

Roeder, P. G., 2007. *Where Nation-States Come From: Institutional Change in the Age of Nationalism.* Princeton, NJ: Princeton University Press.

Roeder, P. G., 2009. Ethnofederalism and the mismanagement of conflicting nationalisms. *Regional and Federal Studies*, 19(2), pp. 203–19.

Roeder, P. G., 2010. States and civil societies following civil wars. In: M. Hoddie & C. A. Hartzell, eds. *Strengthening Peace in Post-Civil War States.* Chicago: University of Chicago Press, pp. 53–78.

Roeder, P. G. & Rothchild, D., eds, 2005. *Sustainable Peace: Power and Democracy after Civil Wars.* Ithaca, NY: Cornell University Press.

Rogers, S., 2004. Beyond the Abu Sayyaf: the lessons of failure in the Philippines. *Foreign Affairs*, 83(1), pp. 15–20.

Rolandsen, O. H., 2011. A quick fix? A retrospective analysis of the Sudan Comprehensive Peace Agreement. *Review of African Political Economy*, 130(38), pp. 551–64.

Rothchild, D. & Emmanuel, N., 2010. Soft intervention in Africa: US efforts to generate support for peace. In: M. Hoddie & C. A. Hartzell, eds. *Strengthening Peace in Post-Civil War States: Transforming Spoilers into Stakeholders*. Chicago: University of Chicago Press, pp. 123–43.

Rothchild, D. & Roeder, P., 2005. Dilemmas of state-building in divided societies. In: D. Rothchild & P. Roeder, eds. *Sustainable Peace, Power and Democracy after Civil War*. Ithaca, NY: Cornell University Press, pp. 1–25.

Roy, S., 2002. Why peace failed: an Oslo autopsy. *Current History*, 100(651), pp. 8–16.

Samrat, 2012. Violence in Assam has deep roots. *The New York Times*, 26 July.

Sasse, G., 2002. Conflict prevention in a transition state: the Crimean issue in post-Soviet Ukraine. *Nationalism and Ethnic Politics*, 8(2), pp. 1–26.

Sasse, G., 2014. Crimean autonomy: a viable alternative to war? *The Washington Post*, 3 March.

Sasse, G., 2016. To be or not to be? Ukraine's Minsk process. *Carnegie Europe*, 2 March, http://carnegieeurope.eu/strategiceurope/?fa=62939

Scharf, M. P., 1999. The Amnesty exception to the jurisdiction of the International Criminal Court. *Cornell International Law Journal*, 32(3), pp. 507–27.

Schmitz, H. P., 2013. Transnational diffusion and the Lord's Resistance Army. In: J. T. Checkel, ed. *Transnational Dynamics of Civil Wars*. Cambridge: Cambridge University Press, pp. 120–48.

Schneckener, U., 2002. Making power-sharing work: lessons from successes and failures in ethnic conflict regulation. *Journal of Peace Research*, 39(2), pp. 203–28.

Schulze, K. E., 2008. A sensitive mission. In: Aguswandi & J. Large, eds. *Reconfiguring Politics: The Indonesia–Aceh Peace Process*. London: Conciliation Resources, pp. 36–9.

Selby, J., 2013. The myth of liberal peace-building. *Conflict, Security and Development*, 13(1), pp. 57–86.

Sell, L., 2002. *Milosevic and the Destruction of Yugoslavia*. Durham, NC: Duke University Press.

Simcox, R. & Pregent, M., 2015. Wanted: reliable Sunnis to fight the Islamic State. *Foreign Policy*, 29 May.

Sisk, T., 1996. *Power Sharing and International Mediation in*

Ethnic Conflicts. Washington, DC: United States Institute for Peace Press.

Sisk, T. & Stefes, C., 2005. Power sharing as an interim step in peace building: lessons from South Africa. In: P. G. Roeder & D. Rothchild, eds. *Sustainable Peace: Power and Democracy after Civil War*. Ithaca, NY: Cornell University Press, pp. 293–317.

Small Arms Survey, 2008. *Neither Joint nor Integrated: The Joint Integrated Units and the Future of the CPA*. Geneva: The Sudan Human Security Baseline Assessment.

Smith, D., 2014. Central African Republic's Seleka rebels call for secession amid sectarian war. *The Guardian*, 15 April.

Smith, S. S., 2002. The role of the United Nations Observer Mission. In: A. Carl & L. Garasu, eds. *Weaving Consensus: The Papua New Guinea – Bougainville Peace Process*. London: Conciliation Resources, pp. 12–13.

Snyder, J., 2000. *From Voting to Violence: Democratization and Nationalist Violence*. New York: Norton.

Sørensen, G., 1999. Sovereignty: change and continuity in a fundamental institution. *Political Studies*, 47(3), pp. 590–604.

Spear, J., 2002. Disarmament and demobilization. In: S. J. Stedman, D. Rothchild & E. M. Cousens, eds. *Ending Civil Wars: The Implementation of Peace Agreements*. Boulder, CO: Lynne Rienner, pp. 141–82.

Spears, I. S., 2002. Africa: the limits of power-sharing. *Journal of Democracy*, 13(3), pp. 123–36.

Spears, I. S., 2014. Evaluating 'two-state condominialism': a new approach to resolving the Israeli–Palestinian conflict. *Global Change, Peace and Security*, 26(2), pp. 195–210.

Sriram, C. L., 2007. Justice as peace? Liberal peacebuilding and strategies of transitional justice. *Global Society*, 21(4), pp. 579–91.

Sriram, C. L., 2008. *Peace as Governance: Power-Sharing, Armed Groups and Contemporary Peace Negotiations*. Basingstoke: Palgrave Macmillan.

Sriram, C. L., Martin-Ortega, O. & Herman, J., 2014. *War, Conflict and Human Rights*. London: Routledge.

Stankovitch, M. & Carl, A., 1999. One step towards peace. In: *Compromising on Autonomy: Mindanao in Transition*. London: Conciliation Resources, pp. 5–8.

Stedman, S., 1991. *Peacemaking in Civil War*. Boulder, CO: Lynne Rienner.

Stedman, S. J., 1997. Spoiler problems in peace processes. *International Security*, 22(2), pp. 5–53.

Stedman, S. J., 2002. Policy implications. In: S. J. Stedman, D. Rothchild & E. M. Cousens, eds. *Ending Civil Wars: The Implementation of Peace Agreements.* Boulder, CO: Lynne Rienner, pp. 663–71.

Stepan, A., 2013. A revised theory of federacy and a case study of civil war termination in Aceh, Indonesia. In: J. McEvoy & B. O'Leary, eds. *Power Sharing in Deeply Divided Places.* Philadelphia: University of Pennsylvania Press, pp. 231–52.

Svensson, I., 2009. Who brings which peace? Neutral versus biased mediation and institutional peace arrangements in civil wars. *The Journal of Conflict Resolution,* 53(3), pp. 446–69.

Szasz, P., 1996. The protection of human rights through the Dayton/ Paris Peace Agreement on Bosnia. *The American Journal of International Law,* 90(2), pp. 301–16.

Tavitian, N., 2000. *An Irresistible Force Meets an Immovable Object: The Minsk Group Negotiations on the Status of Nagorno Karabakh,* Woodrow Wilson School of Public and International Affairs, Case Study 1/00.

Taylor, R., 1992. South Africa: a consociational path to peace? *Transformation,* 17(1), pp. 1–11.

Tendai, M., 2011. Sudan: mission impossible or mission failure? *Al-Jazeera,* 5 July, http://www.aljazeera.com/indepth/opinion/2011 /07/201173141456895954.html

The Sudan Tribune, 2009. SPLM, opposition parties may nominate Sudan ex-PM as presidential candidate. 3 December.

Themner, A. & Ohlson, T., 2014. Legitimate peace in post-civil war states: towards attaining the unattainable. *Conflict, Security and Development,* 14(1), pp. 61–87.

Toal, G. & O'Loughlin, J., 2013. Land for peace in Nagorny Karabakh? Political geographies and public attitudes inside a contested de facto state. *Territory, Politics, Governance,* 1(2), pp. 158–82.

Toft, M. D., 2003. *The Geography of Ethnic Violence: Identity, Interests and the Indivisibility of Territory.* Princeton, NJ: Princeton University Press.

Toft, M. D., 2009. *Securing the Peace: The Durable Settlement of Civil Wars.* Princeton, NJ: Princeton University Press.

Tonge, J., 2014. *Comparative Peace Processes.* Cambridge: Polity.

Touval, S., 1996. Coercive mediation on the road to Dayton. *International Negotiation,* 1(3), pp. 547–70.

Trend Agency, 2011. Azerbaijani presidential administration: recognition of illegal 1991 'referendum' in Nagorno-Karabakh is impossible. 27 January, http://en.trend.az/azerbaijan/kara-bakh/1818873.html

213

Tuminez, A. S., 2007. This land is our land: Moro ancestral domain and its implications for peace and development in the Southern Philippines. *SAIS Review*, 27(2), pp. 77–91.

UCDP/PRIO, 2013. *Armed Conflict Dataset Codebook*. Oslo: International Peace Research Institute, (PRIO), Centre for the Study of Civil Wars.

Usher, G., 1999. *Dispatches from Palestine: The Rise and Fall of the Oslo Peace Process*. London: Pluto Press.

Van Meurs, W., 2003. The Belgrade Agreement: robust mediation between Serbia and Montenegro. In: F. Bieber, ed. *Montenegro in Transition: Problems of Identity and Statehood*. Baden-Baden: Nomos, pp. 63–82.

Vandekerckhove, N. & Suykens, B., 2008. The liberation of Bodoland: tea, forestry and tribal entrapment in western Assam. *Journal of South Asia Studies*, 31(3), pp. 450–71.

Verheul, A., 2011. Managing DDR risks in Sudan: a field perspective. In: M. A. Civic & M. Miklaucic, eds. *Monopoly of Force: The Nexus of DDR and SSR*. Washington, DC: National Defence University Press, pp. 193–209.

Voice of America, 2010. Clinton presses Armenia, Azerbaijan for Nagorno-Karabakh settlement. 3 July, http://m.voanews.com/a/clinton-meets-with-azerbaijani-president-97761024/121050.html

Waage, H. H., 2007–8. Postscript to Oslo: the mystery of Norway's missing files. *Journal of Palestine Studies*, 38(1), pp. 34–65.

Walker, S., 2014. East Ukraine goes to the polls for independence referendum. *The Observer*, 11 May.

Walter, B. F., 2002. *Committing to Peace: The Successful Settlement of Civil Wars*. Princeton, NJ: Princeton University Press.

Weiner, M., 1998. The clash of norms: dilemmas in refugee policies. *Journal of Refugee Studies*, 11(4), pp. 433–53.

Weller, M., 2005a. Self-governance in interim settlements: the case of Sudan. In: M. Weller & S. Wolff, eds. *Autonomy, Self-Governance and Conflict Resolution*. London: Routledge, pp. 158–79.

Weller, M., 2005b. Enforced autonomy and self-governance. In: M. Weller & S. Wolff, eds. *Autonomy, Self-Governance and Conflict Resolution*. London: Routledge, pp. 49–74.

Weller, M., 2008. *Escaping the Self-Determination Trap*. Leiden: Martinus Nijhoff.

Wolff, S., 2005. Electoral-systems design and power sharing regimes. In: I. O'Flynn & D. Russell, eds. *Power Sharing: New Challenges for Divided Societies*. London: Pluto Press, pp. 59–74.

Wolff, S., 2008. *Overcoming Political Deadlock in Gagauzia: Options for EUSR Mediation Team,* Centre for International Crisis Management and Conflict Resolution, University of Nottingham.

Wolff, S., 2009. Complex power-sharing and the centrality of territorial self-governance in contemporary conflict settlements. *Ethnopolitics,* 8(1), pp. 27–45.

Wolff, S., 2010. Building democratic states after conflict: institutional design revisited. *International Studies Review,* 12(1), pp. 128–41.

Wolff, S., 2011. Managing ethno-national conflict: towards an analytical framework. *Commonwealth and Comparative Politics,* 49(2), pp. 162–95.

Wolff, S., 2013. Little cause for celebration on South Sudan's birthday. *The Conversation,* 9 July.

Woodbury, J., 2015. *The Bougainville Independence Referendum: Assessing the Risks and Challenges Before, During and After the Referendum,* Indo-Pacific Strategic Papers, Australian Defence College.

Young, J., 2013. *The Fate of Sudan: The Origins and Consequences of a Flawed Peace Process.* London: Zed Books.

Zahar, M.-J., 2005. The dichotomy of international mediation and leader intransigence: the case of Bosnia and Herzegovina. In: I. O'Flynn & D. Russell, eds. *Power Sharing: New Challenges for Divided Societies.* London: Pluto Press, pp. 123–37.

Zaman, A., 2009. *Conflicts and People of Chittagong Hill Tracts (CHT) of Bangladesh,* https://southasiaspeaks.wordpress.com/2009/09/19/conflicts-people-of-chittagong-hill-tracts-cht-of-bangladesh/

Zamejc, A., 2013. Seeking peace: what needs to be done for the Nagorno-Karabakh conflict. *Caucasus Edition,* 15 July.

Zartman, I. W., 1995a. *Collapsed States: The Disintegration and Restoration of Legitimate Authority.* Boulder, CO: Lynne Rienner.

Zartman, I. W., 1995b. Dynamics and constraints in negotiations in internal conflicts. In: I. W. Zartman, ed. *Elusive Peace: Negotiating and End to Civil Wars.* Washington, DC: The Brookings Institution, pp. 3–29.

Zartman, I. W., 1997. Explaining Oslo. *International Negotiation,* 2(2), pp. 195–215.

Zartman, I. W., 2001a. Ripeness: the hurting stalemate and beyond. In: P. C. Stern & D. Druckman, eds. *International Conflict Resolution after the Cold War.* Washington, DC: National Academy Press, pp. 225–50.

Zartman, I. W., 2001b. The timing of peace initiatives: hurting stalemates and ripe moments. *Ethnopolitics,* 1(1), pp. 8–18.

Zartman, I. W., 2004. Sources and settlements of ethnic conflicts. In: A. Wimmer, ed. *Facing Ethnic Conflicts: Toward a New Realism.* Lanham, MD: Rowman and Littlefield, pp. 141–59.

Zartman, I. W., 2005. *Cowardly Lions: Missed Opportunities to Prevent Deadly Conflict and State Collapse.* Boulder, CO: Lynne Rienner.

Ziyadov, T., 2010. Nagorno Karabakh negotiations: through the prism of a multi-issue bargaining model. *International Negotiation,* 15(1), pp. 107–31.

INDEX

Note: Abbreviations used in the index are explained on pp.vii-viii